Shadow of the Valley

A FATHER'S WAR, A SON'S QUEST, AND COMBAT IN THE QUE SON VALLEY

VIETNAM

CODY BURLESON

ROCK MOUNTAIN PRESS

Shadow of the Valley: A Father's War, a Son's Quest, and Combat in the Que Son Valley, Vietnam

Published by Rock Mountain Press
Manitou Springs, Colorado

Copyright © 2024 by Cody Burleson

All rights reserved. No part of this book may be reproduced in any form or by any mechanical means, including information storage and retrieval systems, without written permission from the publisher/author, except by a reviewer who may quote passages in a review.

All images, logos, quotes, and trademarks included in this book are subject to use according to trademark and copyright laws of the United States of America.

This book is a true story told from the first-person accounts of veteran Marines who served in Vietnam in 1966-68. To the best of the author's knowledge, the events shared in this book are as they occurred and the author has done his best to check and cross-reference information with other veterans and with historical records. More than fifty years after the war, however, memories have faded and are sometimes contradictory. All of the people named in this book are real people and no names have been changed. Concerns with privacy or historical accuracy may be addressed through the Contact form on the author's website at: https://codyburleson.com

Publisher's Cataloging-in-Publication Data

Names: Burleson, Cody, author.
Title: Shadow of the valley: a father's war, a son's quest, and combat in the Que Son Valley, Vietnam / Cody Burleson
Description: Manitou Springs, Colorado: Rock Mountain Press, 2024
Identifiers: ISBN: 979-8-9897451-0-4 (softcover)
Subjects: LCSH Burleson, Cody | Vietnam War, 1961-1975—Personal narrative, American. | BISAC HISTORY / Wars & Conflicts / Vietnam War (HIS027070) | BIOGRAPHY & AUTOBIOGRAPHY / Military (BIO008000) | BIOGRAPHY & AUTOBIOGRAPHY / Historical (BIO006000)

Story advisor
Alexandra O'Connell, www.alexoconnell.com.

*To all the valiant service members of the
United States Armed Forces
who sacrifice all they have to uphold
and protect our liberty, who continually
pay the debt of freedom, and who bear
the heavy burden of war so the rest of us
may live our lives in peace.*

*And to Sidney,
may you find inspiration and pride in
these pages and the legacy of your
grandfather's courage.*

1st Battalion, 3rd Marines (the Battalion Landing Team
of Special Landing Force Alpha), Vietnam 1967

Photo by Bruce Axelrod

CONTENTS

Foreword	x
Chapter 1	
DAWN	1
Chapter 2	
A HOLLYWOOD EDUCATION	4
Chapter 3	
MIXED FEELINGS	10
Chapter 4	
DOWN IN A HOLE	13
Chapter 5	
MADIERA BEACH	18
Chapter 6	
MY FATHER'S WAR	24
Chapter 7	
SHIPP	28
Chapter 8	
A DARK PRELUDE	32
Chapter 9	
RED BEACH	38
Chapter 10	
THE CAGE	47
Chapter 11	
WATER RUN	50
Chapter 12	
LOST BROTHERS	55

Chapter 13
    NOT SO LITTLE BOYS   59

Chapter 14
    THE LAST EMBERS   65

Chapter 15
    CAVAZOS   71

Chapter 16
    SWEEP   74

Chapter 17
    AMBUSH   81

Chapter 18
    BERKHEISER   84

Chapter 19
    FRIENDLY FIRE   90

Chapter 20
    DEPOPE   92

Chapter 21
    WOUNDED IN ACTION   95

Chapter 22
    HITTSON ENLISTS   98

Chapter 23
    HITTSON MAKES A RUN   101

Chapter 24
    BIRD ON FIRE   106

Chapter 25
    GOMEZ   115

Chapter 26
    ROCKET MAN   118

Chapter 27
    CLOSE AIR SUPPORT   124

Chapter 28
    PURE ADRENALINE   130
Chapter 29
    PONCHOS   133
Chapter 30
    GHOSTS   145
Chapter 31
    WOUNDS OF THE HEART   151
Chapter 32
    SANCTUARY   161
Chapter 33
    INTO THE QUE SON   167
Chapter 34
    SEBASTIAN, TEXAS   181
Chapter 35
    UNION   185
Chapter 36
    HILL 110   190
Chapter 37
    IN MEMORIAM   213
Acknowledgements   357
Connect with the Author   362

FOREWORD

I met Cody Burleson at my Marine Corps Reunion about eight years ago. We gravitated to each other at a gathering of combat-hardened Marines who fought at the height of the Vietnam War—First Battalion, Third Marines. Our mutual interest in writing was discovered and profoundly shared.

I had just finished the manuscript for my book, ON FULL AUTOMATIC: SURVIVING 13 MONTHS IN VIETNAM. Cody read my manuscript, and that began a true friendship. He had been interviewing Marines from his father's unit and writing this incredible book honoring his father's combat service. Cody paused his writing project to help me finish mine. I immediately realized that Cody has a tremendous knowledge of the writing craft. He began sharing many ideas on creating an authentic piece of good literature. We worked countless days and nights editing and rewriting numerous stories for my book. His shared brilliance came out in my best-selling and award-winning memoir. I will always be deeply grateful for his assistance.

It's now my pleasure to introduce this book of his. As a combat veteran who has been awarded three Purple Hearts and who has fought in many of the same battles as his father, Cody's writing is so authentic that it made me feel like I was back in Vietnam. His descriptions were so explicit, you would have thought Cody had been there himself.

My book covers the major engagements I participated in, while Cody's delves deep into a few of the same battles. This focus allowed him to create a narrative that is visceral and intense. His writing brings back the same memories of insanity and the relentless combat operations we experienced. His descriptions are so accurate and, at times, terrifying that they give the reader a genuine sense of what it was like to be on the front lines of the Vietnam War in 1967.

I am proud to wholeheartedly endorse Cody's book. It's not just a terrific portrayal of events that actually happened but a testament to the courage and resilience of those who served. It was written in a way that expresses the raw and unfiltered feelings about our actual combat experiences.

William V. Taylor Jr.
US Marine and Author,
On Full Automatic: Surviving 13 Months in Vietnam

SHADOW OF THE VALLEY

CHAPTER 1

Dawn

"GUESS WHAT?" MY SISTER SAID, "I FOUND HIM."

She paused to chew on what sounded like a potato chip on the other end of the line. Air blew like heavy wind from her nostrils into the phone. It was as if she'd just raced up a flight of stairs, although I knew she had not. The labored breathing was a symptom of her obesity.

Relishing in the power of her news, she waited for it to sink in—for me to adjust to the gravity of what she had just said.

Had she just solved the mystery of our lives? We had talked and wondered about him for so many years, and she'd always said that she wanted to find him, but I never thought she really meant it. I'd always assumed that for my sister, Dawn, our real father was a hopeful ideal she carried like a talisman or a string of worry beads. It was often in the tougher times that she would conjure the thought of him—like after a raging fight with our stepdad, Bill.

One time, I watched in frozen astonishment as she dared him to hit her. She would have been a junior in high school if she hadn't dropped out already. I was a freshman, two years younger. Bill had her backed up against the kitchen counter with his nose close to hers. His face was red with fury, and spittle flung from his lips as he cussed at her. Seeing his arms stiffen and his veins bulge as he struggled to hold his fists down, I begged, in my mind, for Dawn to keep her damned mouth shut.

"Do it," she dared him, looking straight into his eyes. "You know you want to, so just do it!"

He slapped her so good and hard that when she got her head back in line, her hair was matted sideways—stuck like a blindfold in the tears around her eyes.

"Is that what you want?" he yelled.

"No, but that's what you do, isn't it? So, go ahead, do it again!"

He slapped her with his other hand and spun her head the other way. Again, she pulled wet strands of hair from her eyes and egged him on defiantly. Back and forth, it went that way, her face being thrown one way and the other, until he finally turned to see that I had been watching in horror. I saw a faint glimmer of shame in his eyes, and then he sent the both of us to our rooms.

After some minutes, I snuck into Dawn's room and sat beside her on the bed.

She stared at the ceiling for a while, sniffling as Bill's red handprints faded from her cheeks, and then she took a deep and determined breath through her nose and released it all at once from her mouth.

"You know what I'm going to do when I get out of here?" she said. "I'm going to find our real dad. Wherever he is, I'm going to find him."

"If he's still alive," I said.

"Oh, he's alive," she said. "He is, I know it."

She turned to her side and propped her head up on an elbow—suddenly and almost entirely transformed by the thought of him.

"I mean, don't you want to meet him?"

I shrugged my shoulders and shook my head. It seemed too late for that. By then, all I wanted was to finish high school, get my diploma, and get on with my own life—independent, free, and as far from home as possible. I wasn't sure how I felt about the man or whether I'd want to meet him. The idea just seemed unlikely to me—my sister's fantasy. I never thought she'd ever really go looking for him.

A couple of years later, when she had left the house, and I was still in, she called me with a mouthful of potato chips and the news.

"Yep, I found him," she was saying. "He lives in Mineral Wells."

I had passed through that town several times to go fishing.

"That's only two hours from here," I said.

"And guess what?" She said, crunching on another chip.

I pulled the earpiece a bit further away.

"What?"

"Well, guess," she said.

I sighed, annoyed. Dawn was always overly dramatic about everything.

"You're going to try to meet him?" I guessed.

She stopped crunching on her chip and paused for dramatic effect, to swallow it, or both, and told me.

"I already did," she said. "I met him."

CHAPTER 2

A Hollywood Education

HIS NAME WAS ALAN, and he had been in combat during the Vietnam War. For reasons of her own, Mom never told us anything more. I seem to recall her saying that he had nightmares about the war—tossing, turning, hollering, and jumping out of bed in a cold sweat. It's a bit cliché, I know, so I do wonder if I colored that part long ago with my boyish imagination. I'm very sure, however, that I questioned whether he'd ever told her about his experiences in the war.

"I asked him about it sometimes," she told me. "He always just said that he didn't want to talk about it. I think whatever happened to him over there was pretty rough."

Then, whenever I pressed for more, she would end the discussion abruptly, saying, "He was an asshole. He abandoned us when you were just two. That's all there is to it. There's nothing more to know."

Though I'm not sure my sister Dawn ever accepted that, I personally found it quite convenient. He was an ass, and that was all we needed to know.

Bill was our "dad" for as far back as we could remember, anyway. We even called him Dad—not "Daddy," like his own daughters called him, but still. He had serious anger management issues, sure, but he'd at least been there. He was the one who showed up.

It was Dawn who always talked about our real father.

"Would you want to meet him if you could?" she would ask.

"I don't know."

"I wonder what he looks like. Do you think we look like him?"

"I don't know."

"What if he had other kids too? Do you think, maybe, we have other brothers and sisters, and we don't even know about it?"

"I don't know."

I tried not to think about him; sometimes, I would even try to hate him as I thought Mom did. For example, Bill would so often direct his rage at me that I would actually grow tired of hating him, and I would direct my anger toward our real father for leaving us stuck with the pitiful man. Sometimes, it was convenient to think that everything that was wrong with our lives somehow stemmed from the moment when that "asshole" abandoned us.

Unlike the simple optimism my sister expressed, my thoughts about our estranged father were nuanced and confused, so I tried to avoid thinking of him altogether. But, truth be told, and as much as I pretended otherwise, I thought of him often. It seems I could not avoid a certain feeling of emptiness and self-doubt that was left in the absence of a father, or any male, for that matter, worth looking up to. Movies, more than anything, reminded me. As a child of the seventies and eighties, they heavily shaped and influenced my life.

When I was six years old in 1977, I became instantly enamored with Star Wars (A New Hope), a space adventure featuring a fatherless leading character, Luke Skywalker, who was on the path to becoming a Jedi. The Jedi were enlightened beings who had lightsabers and could move things with their minds.

Before the Jedi, I thought Ninjas were the most excellent kind of warrior. It was probably pretending to be a Ninja and jumping off dangerously high ledges that crushed my hip joint and landed me in leg braces for three years. It was fortuitous then that Jedi practice consisted of simply stretching my hand towards a distant flashlight and concentrating intensely on retrieving it through telekinesis.

Having a handicap at a time when most boys were uniting in sports necessitated a certain amount of isolation and amplified my self-doubt. Perhaps more than other boys my age, I identified with the young Luke Skywalker who, unsatisfied with being a farmer, dreamed of some greater destiny. There's an iconic scene where Luke gazes out upon the binary suns of planet Tatooine as they set on the horizon across the desert.

"Luke's just not a farmer," Aunt Beru tells Uncle Owen. "He has too much of his father in him."

At age six, presented with the idea that some essence of my father could be within me, I worried about my mother's assertion that he'd been an asshole. I chose instead to believe that I, too, had some greater destiny than the heavy metal braces on my legs and that the mystery of my real father was like that of Luke's—relating me to some greater story yet to be discovered.

I was nine when the second movie of the saga came out. The Empire Strikes Back featured a climactic lightsaber battle between Luke and the evil villain, Darth Vader, who supposedly killed Luke's father. Luke gets his hand sliced off by Vader's lightsaber and is then edged out over a precipice with no weapon and nowhere to go.

In his deep, James Earl Jones voice, Vader says to Luke, "Obi-Wan never told you what happened to your father."

"He told me enough," Luke cries, stepping out further over the precipice. "He told me you killed him."

Then, a mystery suddenly unraveled in a gut-punching twist, years in the build-up and emotionally cemented by a dark symphonic thrust from the film's brilliant composer, John Williams.

"No," Vader says to Luke. "I am your father."

"No," Luke screams. "No! That's not true!"

It's exactly what I was feeling inside.

My father is not really an asshole. That's impossible!

I would have to wait for the third film, Return of the Jedi, to learn there was still good in Vader after all, but by then, other films had taken root in my psyche. One featured Sylvester Stallone as John Rambo, a Vietnam War veteran.

After traveling on foot to meet an old comrade from the war, Rambo learns that his friend has died from exposure to Agent Orange. Shortly after, he's intercepted by a small-town Sheriff who considers him an unwanted nuisance and dumps him outside the town limits. Defiant, Rambo crosses the bridge back into town and then gets arrested on charges of vagrancy, resisting arrest, and possessing a concealed knife.

In the jailhouse, several officers pick on Rambo, which triggers flashbacks of the torture he endured as a POW in Vietnam. When the officers get a straight razor near his throat to shave him, Rambo fights them off, regains his knife, steals a motorcycle, and rides off into the forest. The officers give chase, eventually drawing "first blood" and forcing Rambo to use his combat skills to survive. At this point, John Rambo becomes a verifiable badass for which the officers are no match. He picks them off one by one with the stealth and craftiness of a Green Beret.

It was pure action-packed candy for an eleven-year-old boy, and after watching it, I proudly announced to my friends that my real father was in the Vietnam War. Of course, I couldn't say anything more about him. I had no idea. Up to that point, the whole of what I knew about the war had come from that movie. All the sensational action hero stuff in the woods won me over, but I had been especially attentive to all the parts relating to my father's war. While it was nice to think of my father as a possible badass, I also had to consider that, like John Rambo, he might be a troubled outcast who is tortured by horrible flashbacks of dead comrades and Asian attackers.

VHS home video stores and the satellite TV at my grandma's house provided endless movies. Even the R-rated ones I was not allowed to see in theaters became easy to access. Movies like Francis Ford Coppola's Apocalypse Now provided more images to stitch into my evolving vision of the Vietnam War. Pieces and parts of stories in the movies came together to help create ideas about my real father in place of all that I didn't know—a sort of Frankenstein surrogate forged in the mythos of Hollywood.

More than any other, however, the 1986 movie by Oliver Stone called Platoon most influenced my thoughts about Vietnam, war in general, and, by association, about my father. It was a blockbuster hit billed as the "first real movie about the Vietnam War." Some said it was the most realistic movie about war that had yet been made. Roger Ebert and Gene Siskel, famous movie critics at the time, both gave the film four out of four stars and two thumbs up. At fifteen years old, I walked two miles alone to the movie theater, bought a ticket to Crocodile Dundee, and slipped sideways into Platoon.

The opening score sets an immediately somber tone as the young grunt, Chris Taylor (played by Charlie Sheen), steps off the back of a C-130 cargo plane and onto a dusty airstrip in Vietnam. As he and a handful of other new guys deboard the plane, two soldiers begin loading filled body bags in their place. Chris appears distressed by the sight of a motley veteran who passes by and stares at him with starved, hollow, and frightening eyes—ghostlike and haunting.

"Well, I'll be dipped in shit—new meat!" the passing veterans say. "You dudes are gonna love the Nam, for-fucking-ever."

Cut to the jungle, and Chris, the FNG ("fucking new guy"), is cutting point with a machete, whacking out a path for the following platoon. They come upon the burnt body of a Vietnamese soldier lying against a tree as Staff Sergeant Barnes approaches from behind.

"Boy, what you waitin' for? Aint gonna bite you," he says. "That's a good gook. Good and dead."

Chris, suffering from heat exhaustion, the weight of his poorly packed rucksack, and the smell of the dead "gook", bellies over and barfs.

Thus begins a tour of duty that seems to cram all the worst of what happened in Vietnam into ninety minutes. Aside from jungle warfare and gore, the film featured drug use, rape, the murder of innocent civilians, village burning, and even GIs shooting other GIs (or "fragging" as it is sometimes called).

By the end of the movie, we are led to believe that Chris never finds something to be proud of as he had enlisted to do. Instead, he becomes a cold-blooded murderer who kills Sgt. Barnes, out of revenge and carries home a shame for the dehumanization he has endured.

For me, the movie created such an unsettling picture of war that I vowed to never get involved with the military. And for the first time, I felt a genuine sorrow for the stranger who was my father.

CHAPTER 3

Mixed Feelings

AFTER HAVING FOUND and met our "real dad," my sister urged me to meet him.

"He's actually very cool," she said. "You should call him. He said he wants to meet you."

If he really wanted to meet me, why should I be the one to make the call?

"Mmmmm, I don't know," I said.

"What do you mean you don't know? I'll give you his number. You have to call him."

I was on the brink of manhood. Another parent was the last thing I needed in my life. The parents I knew were contradictions—full of advice on how to live, yet rarely able to get through a single day without hurting themselves, each other, and anybody within yelling distance. At this point, what were we supposed to do with each other? Play a game of catch? Build a pinewood derby car? Amble through the zoo with ice cream cones?

"Why?" I asked, "Why do I have to? What difference does it make now?"

"Because he's your father, real flesh and blood, and he's really cool, and he said he wants to meet you if you want to meet him."

"If I want to meet him? I'm not so sure."

"Oh, don't be stupid. Just call him."

"And say what?"

"Say hi!" she said. "Hello, this is your son. How's it going?"

I could just imagine the two of us fumbling through painful pleasantries and the uncomfortable silence between awkward words.

"Fine," my father would say, "How are you?"

"Fine," I would lie.

I would not tell him that, according to my stepdad, I had grown to be a "good-for-nothing pig that will never amount to a goddamn thing." I wouldn't tell him that the woman he left was now chronically depressed—shut up in her bedroom with a tray full of pharmaceuticals. I wouldn't tell him that his daughter was shooting meth into her veins or that I'd been snorting it. Or that I'd been smoking pot since I was fifteen and had my first joint with Mom. Or that I liked to drink alcohol because it made the pain go away. We wouldn't talk about what that pain was, where it came from, why I had it, or what I was really supposed to do with it. I wouldn't ask him if he had any ideas about how I could find my own way in the world without any resources. And I certainly wouldn't tell him about my silly secret dreams of being a movie director or a special effects makeup artist.

"Fine," I would lie.

And then what? What if I lost control?

"Where the fuck were you all this time? How could you walk away from your own children, your own flesh and blood, and never look back? What kind of man doesn't love his own children?"

I dug one of Bill's cigarette butts out of an ashtray and lit it—another habit I wouldn't mention. The spent smoke smelled like shit, but it felt good burning my lungs and immediately lifted some of the weight of all that was spinning around in my head. I held the smoke down for as long as I could, working it like a joint to get the maximum high.

"We needed you. I needed you! God, I can't tell you how many times I needed you. I needed a father. But it wasn't you, either, was it? Why would I be stupid enough to think it could ever have been you? Mom was right about you. You're just an ass. You're a selfish fucking asshole."

I exhaled the smoke with an audible sigh and listened to Dawn smacking on the other end of the line. I could imagine no scenario where meeting our father could lead to any good, but I took his phone number anyway. At the least, it would allow me to end the phone call so that I could get Dawn's chip-crunching, lip-smacking, nostril-breathing nonsense out of my ear.

"You promise you'll call him?" she asked, excited that I'd accepted his phone number.

"Yeah," I said. "Sure. Whatever."

CHAPTER 4

Down in a Hole

AFTER BARELY GRADUATING high school, I found myself in the passenger seat of my friend Rocky Weber's truck heading south across Texas to San Marcos, where, by some inexplicable miracle, we thought we'd go to college. Our criteria were simple. We'd heard that San Marcos was a party town and that one could find plenty of beer kegs and girls around Texas State University. It also seemed like a good way to get out of my sister's roach-infested apartment, where I'd been sleeping since Bill had kicked me out of the house.

More than a year had passed since Dawn had given me Alan's phone number. I never called him, and Dawn, finally getting the hint that I had no intention to do so, had almost given up trying to make me. On my way out her door, she'd asked me casually if I still had his number, and I shook my head.

"Don't need it," I said. "Don't care."

And then Rocky and I hit the road.

Alternative rock boomed from the radio—acoustic guitars and

steel drums from a band named Jane's Addiction. Jane, a girl in one of their songs, wants to leave a boyfriend who treats her like a rag doll. She wants to leave him and then move away to Spain. But, she's strung out on drugs, so she sticks around—every day promising that she's going to kick tomorrow. It reminded me that I could've been Jane. It reminded me of the time I saw myself in the mirror after being up for three days straight on crystal meth.

"Dude," I'd said aloud to myself, "this ain't you."

And then I stopped driving for my sister's dealer and put that shit down for good.

My hand was wind-surfing across the many miles of crops and cow pastures in a state that seemed as big as the country of Australia. I could have been Jane, but I kicked and made it away. San Marcos was my Spain. I was sober and free.

I thought about Dawn, many miles behind us, and the promise we had once made to one another.

"We can never use a needle, no matter what. We'll never go that low."

I kept my promise, but she broke hers, I knew, because of the bruised punctures around the vein near the bend in her arm. I watched the lines on the highway shrink and fade away in the rearview mirror, and I wished her well.

"She's gonna kick tomorrow," said the song on the radio.

I sang along.

"She's gonna kick tomorrow."

What happened next was a blur. Indeed, there was a party in San Marcos that lasted for three months before Rocky finally forced us both to admit that we were finished and that neither of us was actually going to start classes at Texas State. I sat on the empty living room floor with my back against the bar, still reeling from his news.

"I can't pay my half of the rent," he'd told me just before he left. "I need it to get back home."

He had taken the little black-and-white television, which was really all we had, so the apartment was empty except for all the porch plants we'd stolen one crazed and irresponsible night. I had, in my bedroom, what had been there for all those months—a bed sheet on the carpet and a pillow. I had no vehicle outside. I didn't even own a bicycle.

Besides my feet, bedsheets, shoes, and the cheap telephone on the bar above my head, I had a half month's rent in my pocket. The moment I walked out the door with it all, I would be homeless. In a sudden panic, I stood and grabbed the phone from its base. Light flickered behind the translucent little rubber number keys. When I heard the dial tone, I put the phone back into its base, hanging up the line. The phone company had not yet cut the service, thank God. There was hope, but for what?

Surely, I could have gone back home. Even if Bill did not want me there, I thought that maybe I could convince Momma to put her foot down for me. But then the tension between Bill and me would increase, and I couldn't bear the satisfaction he would have gotten from seeing me fail. This is, I can say only now, probably not true of the man's intentions at all, but without the full extent of my prefrontal cortex, how could I have known that a seemingly brutal shove from the nest could be an act of love? He was never affectionate, that man.

"I figure since you've been staying out all the time anyway," he told me, "you ought to just go ahead and stay out."

"It sounds like you're asking if I want to leave home now?"

"No, that's not right," he said. "I'm not asking."

To go back would have meant defeat. It would mean that he had been right when he said I was "a goddamn pig that would amount to nothing." If I went back home, he would ride my ass every single day, as usual, but I imagined that it would all be vigorously amplified with the constant undertone of an insinuation that I was weak.

"Life's a bitch ain't it?"

It's something like he would say.

"I told you, didn't I? Whadda ya gonna do now, Mr. Smarty Pants?"

Right. What was I going to do?

My sister would take me in, but then I would be back with the cockroaches and the meth-heads. I'd go hungry again—living off the same pot of beans for an entire week. We would lie to the window attendant in the fast food drive-through and demand onions that were missing from a burger we never ordered. Then, we would take them home and add them to the pot of beans to keep them going. Next stop, tomatoes.

No.

Life with my sister and her clan of misfits was no life at all. I had already assured myself aloud in the mirror.

"Dude, this ain't you."

But if not that guy, then who? Who was I, really?

If I returned to that life, then I would be who I had always been—just a poor loser in a dysfunctional family. I'd be trapped in the gravity of my sister and the skitzers. As the days, months, and years passed, I would slowly fulfill Bill's prophecy for me. I would amount to nothing.

It was then, standing there in an empty apartment and leaning on my elbows over the phone that I thought about what might happen if I were to call Alan, my father. I remembered that Dawn had not only met him, but she had even gone to live with him in Texas, before he moved to Florida. She finished high school while in his care. She would know how to reach him in Florida. Perhaps, he would help me too, if I just reached out and asked.

I kneaded my face with both hands as if my head were clay. It felt good to press my fingers against both eyelids and rub firmly in little circles. It felt good to sigh aloud—to hear myself exhale and feel myself deflating ever so slightly.

What on earth would I even say?

"Hi. This is your son. How's it going? Uh… you don't know me, but I need your help."

You know what? Don't think about it. Just don't even think about it. Just pick up the phone.

I pick up the phone.

Again, light flickered through the keypad, and again, I heard the dial tone.

I hung up the phone and sighed again, adding an audible growl. It felt good to hear myself growl. If I were not in an apartment building, I could've screamed; how much nicer that would've felt.

I'll just get his number, for starters. That's not a commitment to actually call him. I'm just getting the number, just in case.

I picked up the phone and dialed my sister. Her baby was crying in the background when she answered, so I got straight to it.

"Hey," I said. "It's me. You got a phone number for our real dad in Florida?"

CHAPTER 5

Madiera Beach

AT THE END of our conversation, Alan said he would shelter me for a little while as long as I could travel the distance to Madiera Beach, where he lived. Whatever he had said before that part was gone by the time I returned from my out-of-body experience and hung up the phone.

Unfortunately for my landlord, my part of the month's rent was just enough to make the distance on a Greyhound bus, where, with my forehead against the window, I saw the border between Texas and Louisiana for the first time.

"Welcome to Louisiana," I read on a passing sign. "Bienvenue en Louisiane."

I had traveled almost half a day just to get to the border of my state, and there were almost a thousand miles to go. Even just the eastern part of Texas was foreign to me. Pine trees, as tall as any I'd ever seen, would pass for miles in dense forests that pushed up against the interstate on both sides. I had no idea at the time, but

I would later learn that this was the part of Texas where my father lived before shipping out to Vietnam. I would learn that he had been a logger here, to pay his way with a family he'd endeared himself to, and with a man he'd come to think of as his foster father. His real father was also rarely around, and when he was, he was abusive like my stepfather, Bill, had been. I would soon learn many things about Alan, but nothing yet of what I was most curious about, which was his war.

I was relieved to learn he was "cool," as my sister had asserted. He met me at the bus stop in flip-flops, shorts, a t-shirt, and a baseball cap—unassuming beach attire that fit with the palm trees and the warm salty air. The only visible indication that Mr. Tropical Tan was also Texan was the bill on his baseball cap bent down on each side, tight around the eyes the way we do it back home. When he spoke, however, it surely betrayed his origin. His accent and vocabulary sounded somehow more redneck than my own.

For three months, I stayed with him on the beach where he lived and worked with his girlfriend, running a set of rental condos. He gave me a private room and graced me with odd jobs to make me feel useful. Surely, he was nonjudgmental because, despite my lack of skills, he never so much as shook his head at me. At least not in front of me. He simply graded me down to the busy work he knew I could do, like watering a client's lawn down the beach.

There, I stood one morning with the water hose in my hand, watching the sun rise through orange, pink, and purple clouds on the placid surface of an inlet. Two bottlenose dolphins broke the mirror, sending ripples through the reflection of the sky up close near the end of the dock. They spit exhaust through their blowholes, and I kinked the water hose so that I could listen.

Magic moments in solitude are easily found around the beach. It's something I think now that my father had been aware of in the sort of secretly wise way of a sage. He asked little of me, but what was healthy for me. He made no hint or insinuation that I needed to get a job, advance, make a plan, or do anything other than what I was, which was mostly just thinking. I had a lot of mud and muck from the past swirling around in my head, and I just needed to be still long enough for it to settle.

One afternoon, a storm blew in from the west across the bay. The beach was quiet and empty, so I sat alone in the sand with three beers and a portable CD player. I listened to the long, instrumental rock songs of Pink Floyd as lightning flashed quietly behind the clouds across the horizon. For a poor Texas redneck, the moment was downright spiritual. The ocean was wider and went further than I had ever imagined, and the storm, so far away, must have stretched for miles.

Then, as the dusk fell to darkness, the sky around the flashing clouds became a portal into space, a thousand tiny sparkles of light, like pin-pricks in a dome between us and heaven. I felt swaddled, not swallowed, by the vastness of it all, and for the first time, probably ever, like everything would be okay. No matter what happened, my life was going to turn out good. It could be anything I made of it. There was nothing to be afraid of. The universe had my back.

Even to this day, I can say those were the best three beers I've ever had—given to me by my father, the redneck shaman who seemed to know that what I needed in that time of my life was rest and reflection—quiet hours to think about where I wanted to go and what I wanted to do with my life.

Three months passed with easy days. There were light chores to do in the mornings, but even Alan clocked out of his working days early.

"It's what you call a semi-retired lifestyle," he told me.

We would work until, at most, two o'clock in the afternoon, and then we would break for a beer at some breezy bar on the beach. I would hold a french fry in the air until one seagull in a growing flock would get the courage to dive down and snatch it. Alan would allow this until the place started to look like a scene from an Alfred Hitchcock movie, and then, after shooting an embarrassed look at the bartender, he would politely remind me that the fries were meant for me. We would talk and get to know each other better, but we never talked about Vietnam. I never felt quite right about bringing it up; if I did, he would give a short reply.

"It was such a long time ago," he would say. "I don't really remember that much."

I took this to mean he didn't want to discuss it. How could he not remember much about his war? In First Blood, John Rambo said, "I can't get it out of my head. I see it every day." In Platoon, Chris Taylor says at the end, "The war is over for me now, but it will always be there, the rest of my days." Ron Kovic, played by Tom Cruise in Born on the Fourth of July, is frozen by a flashback when the sound of a crying baby somewhere in the crowd takes him back unwillingly. If Alan was haunted by the war like I supposed most veterans were, he did a good job hiding it. Or, maybe, I also thought, his war could have been uneventful. Maybe he had been "in the rear with the gear" and never saw combat. What if he was embarrassed because he thought his war didn't measure up to my Hollywood expectations?

It never occurred to me then that my lack of maturity might have had something to do with what he was willing to share. It also did not occur to me that even more than twenty years after the war, he might still be wrestling with demons in his own private way—unresolved to speak of it yet to anyone at all, much less me. As if he would tell this dumb kid about what happened to him in Vietnam. As if I would understand. As if I even could understand!

As much as I struggle to understand even now, I'm glad he did not attempt to tell me then. Had I not been so clueless, I might have read some of the signs. He pointed out across the ocean, for example, and said that he had worked on an offshore oil drilling platform for months at a time—far enough out that you couldn't see land in any direction. The salty air eats on those rigs so much they must be repainted nonstop. He would hang several hundred feet above the water and paint until sundown, and then, when the rig had been repainted, he'd move back to the spot where he'd started and start all over again. Every so often, he'd go back on land with some of the men, blow money in the bars or whatnot, and then he'd return to the rig where it was quiet.

"I liked being out there away from everything after the war. Away from all the people," he told me. "I liked the solitude."

It would be several years later that I would learn how self-isolating could be a form of self-preservation, a way of avoiding triggers, and a way of avoiding potentially negative responses to feelings or any need to explain feelings or to be understood. Self-isolation, I would learn, is extremely common in those who've been in a war zone. Veterans will often push friends, family, and even their spouses away.

I sensed that Alan's current girlfriend had not been around for long, and I wondered how much longer she would be. Before this woman, he'd been in several relationships after my mom. My sister, Dawn, had told me as much. Fifteen or sixteen, it turns out, not counting the occasional one-night stand. Some had even been marriages.

But even knowing these things, I had no concept of how they might have related to Post Traumatic Stress Disorder. How could I have known when even he did not? It was to be another six years before he finally saw a therapist at the VA hospital and received a diagnosis and the formal name for his condition: PTSD.

After three months with my father, I left Florida with a different opinion of him. I had found my father and a good friend who was at least no more screwed up than I was. Had I really only reached out for his help, or had I reached out for him? Whichever it was, or both, he served graciously. For three months, he was fully present and helpful to me—asking hardly anything of me.

Whatever bitterness I had felt about the fact that he'd abandoned our family was gone. I returned to Texas with confidence in starting over and finding my own way in the world. We'd said, "I'll be seein' ya," and not "goodbye," and I was somehow stronger because I knew it to be true. A hole that I'd carried for years in my heart had been filled. Though I had not found my father's war or what happened to him in Vietnam, I had at least found him. And as did Luke of Vader in Return of the Jedi, I had found that there was still good in him.

CHAPTER 6

My Father's War

YEARS LATER, THE SILHOUETTE of my father, Alan, sat motionless at the end of my fishing dock, a stark contrast against the silver mirror of Possum Kingdom Lake. He had been there for hours—not fishing, not on his phone, just... sitting. A mesquite-carpeted hill across the lake looked like the jungle-covered hills in Vietnam that I'd seen passing under Huey helicopters in the movies. Did it remind him of the war? As the Texas sun set behind us, I wondered: Was he there on the lake, or was he somewhere in Khe Sanh, long ago, standing watch against the wire?

It struck me then that I had never asked him about Vietnam. Despite years of tip-toeing around his PTSD, despite the Hollywood-driven narratives I'd consumed, I had never sought the truth of his experiences. The realization hit me like a thunderbolt: I wanted—no, needed—to know his story before it was too late.

"I'll tell you what I can remember," he said when I finally asked, "but my memory of the war is poor. I've blocked a lot of it out."

The effects of his time in Vietnam were evident, even years after he'd received therapy and medication. Once, when meeting me at a bustling Orlando hotel when I was at a business conference, he found the single quietest bar in the entire resort complex. "I don't do well with big crowds," he confessed, visibly anxious. "It puts me on edge."

When I visited Alan's rural home in the Florida swamps, I found a veritable zoo of seemingly purposeless animals. Cage-free roosters and chickens strutted about in such numbers that navigating the yard became an impromptu game of poultry dodge. A sharp turn could send a small flock clucking through the air with a trail of feathers.

A motley crew of three or four dogs trotted alongside us, accompanied by a pig who seemed convinced it was one of the canine pack. Another pig, far too fat for such adventures, lay in a mud pit under some shade. As Alan introduced me, this pig lifted its head slightly and grunted with what I can only describe as pig-like satisfaction. The phrase "hog heaven" sprang to mind.

There were at least four horses that I could see. Ducks. A baby emu. A couple of peacocks. A noisy old parrot. A massive Brahman bull completed the barnyard tableau while in the pond—because why not?—a very real and uncaged alligator lurked beneath the water's surface.

Alan's justifications for this personal ark were as eclectic as its inhabitants. The cow, he explained, could make good beef, but slaughter was out of the question. The chickens supplied more eggs than his household could ever consume. He even had a prize pig he had no intention of turning into bacon. When I asked why on earth he wanted to care for so many animals, he simply shrugged and said, "They're my therapy animals. They take care of me!"

These glimpses into his character made me realize how little I knew about his war. What had the movies gotten right, and what had they gotten wrong? Why had my formal education glossed over this significant chapter of history? Had I been so complacent with my preconceptions that I'd failed to seek the truth?

"I started going to reunions and meeting up with some of the guys from my unit," my father continued. "Things started coming back to me, and I'll tell you what I can remember, but If you really want to know, I should hook you up with them. They'd be able to tell you much more than I can."

Little did I know that this conversation would be the beginning of a years-long journey. I would meet numerous veterans, each with their own piece of the puzzle that was my father's Vietnam experience. Their stories would prove more astounding than any fiction I could have imagined.

As I delved deeper, I became acutely aware of the urgency of my task. These aging veterans—some battling illnesses potentially linked to Agent Orange exposure—might be sharing their stories for the first and last time. "I'm just glad that somebody cares," one told me, a sentiment that echoed the bitterness many felt upon their return home.

They didn't come home to ticker-tape parades like the men of World War II. No warm welcome waited for them at the airport. They came home to a nation that had grown weary of the war, many believing the war was wrong, and many actively lashing out at the men who fought it—as if those men had done anything but what they thought was an honorable duty to their country.

As I got to know these men, their individual stories, and their collective unit story, I began to see and understand that, PTSD or not, they all bore a scar upon their hearts. This scar was not inflicted by the enemy but by their own country and the bitterness of their reception home. For American liberty and freedom, they offered their lives, and they watched in agony as it drained from their brothers on the battlefield. They gave their youth, innocence, and an irreparable piece of their souls seeing and doing things that no man should ever be called to see or do. Then, those who survived faced hostility or indifference back home—a wound that, for many, cut deeper than any physical scar.

Discovering the stories of my father's unit has been a profound gift. This book is my attempt to honor these men and preserve their experiences for future generations. It tells of things that have never been told, and I hope those things astound, fascinate, and inspire you as much as they have me. In reading this book, I hope you can come to appreciate its heroes as much as I have and that you will see, as I have, something about what it means to be a Marine—or "Semper Fidelis" as those Marines say, *Always Faithful*.

My father's incomplete recollections led me to seek out other veterans, unveiling this larger narrative. The most entire account, for example, was provided by retired Major Kenneth Hicks, a man of sharp memory whose account forms the backbone of this story, supplemented by many others. But while his story serves as an anchor and an example of my father's experience, this is ultimately about a brotherhood of Marines who have collaborated to share their collective experience.

This is the story of the 1st Battalion, 3rd Marines (1/3) in Vietnam, the Battalion Landing Team of Special Landing Force Alpha. It's an epic tale for the annals of history and the proud lore of the Marine Corps—a testament to men against whom I hold my own life cheap, who I now regard as dear friends, and who are all great Americans.

CHAPTER 7

Shipp

TWO DAYS BEFORE Memorial Day, in 1967, the newspaper where I live here in Colorado Springs published a letter that was sent home to a mother and father from a young Marine in Vietnam, Corporal James Clair Shipp (Jim). I have the letter here, on aged and yellowed paper—clipped from when it was published in the Gazette Telegraph. It begins:

"Dear Mom and Dad,

This is going to be a real tough letter for me to write, but since I know you're probably worried clear out of your mind, I've got to attempt."

The letter had been written aboard a ship in the South China Sea, just off the coast of Vietnam, so by the time it finally made it all the way here to a mailbox just 16 miles from where I live now, Mr.

and Mrs. Shipp probably already knew that something terrible had happened. I can imagine the letter trembling in Mrs. Shipp's hands as she read the words that, thankfully, were penned by her own boy.

"It is only through the great Great Grace of God that I'm still alive," her son had written.

Let us pause here for a minute because you know that Mrs. Shipp did. If you ever had a child, then surely you can imagine how it felt to hear her son's troubled voice echoing through the words of the letter. It's difficult to read when tears are welling up in your eyes and when you have to work to get a swallow past the lump in your throat, but she sat down anyway and read the letter slowly aloud to her husband, Byron, who consoled her, no doubt, with a soft touch and a patient ear.

When their boy, Jimmie, announced that he was joining the U.S. Marine Corps, they begged him not to do it. A war was going on, and if he joined, he'd end up there, they knew, far across the world in some country most folks had never even heard of. He had known it too, and at the time, that fact appealed to him. As hard as they tried, they couldn't talk him out of it.

It's worth mentioning, in case you didn't know that here in Colorado Springs, service to the country has always been a huge deal. We've got a big Army base here (Ft. Carson), an Air Force Base (Peterson), and the United States Air Force Academy. All the big aerospace and defense companies like Lockheed Martin and Northrop Grumman are here. And then, of course, we've got NORAD, which was tunneled into the granite of Cheyenne Mountain during the height of the Cold War. It became fully operational just three months before Jimmie wrote the letter home.

It's fitting, I think that this is also where Katharine Lee Bates found the inspiration to write the poem that became our patriotic song, "America the Beautiful." In 1895, she traveled to the summit of Pike's Peak, a grand mountain that is capped with snow, even in May, and that I'm graced to see every day just outside my office window. On her way back down the mountain, Katharine wrote the following in her diary:

> "...we stood at last on that Gate-of-Heaven summit...and gazed in wordless rapture over the far expanse of mountain ranges and the sea-like sweep of plain."

When she got back to her room down in town at the Antler Hotel, she remarked to friends that other countries such as England may have been "great," but they had not been "good" and that "unless we are willing to crown our greatness with goodness, and our bounty with brotherhood, our beloved America may go the same way."

Based on her experiences here, she later wrote a poem, originally entitled "Pikes Peak," that became the song "America the Beautiful."

Jimmie went to school here with that glorious mountain over his home on the western horizon and with the story of Katharine Lee Bates, who, by rendering the soul of "America's Mountain," helped forge the soul of a great nation.

Is it any wonder that he wanted to be a Marine?

In school, they once played black-and-white motion pictures with cartoons of turtles hiding in shells. Playful jingles taught the kids how to "duck and cover" if the communists dropped an atomic bomb. South Vietnam is just one of many dominoes, they told us. If we let the communists have it, then what's next? Country by country, the dominoes will fall, they said, until the communists have taken everything and have met us on our doorstep with their nuclear weapons.

Jimmie knew very well that if he joined the Marine Corps, he would have to go to war, but that was reason all the more, was it not?

Though still a patriot that Saturday on the ship, far and away from the Southern Front Range of the Colorado Rockies, he struggled to make sense of his first real combat experience.

From the noise and the madness still reeling in his head, he found it difficult to find sensible words—words tame enough to share with his mom and dad, but perhaps more so, to keep himself tethered to the world he thought he knew. His father, Byron, could sense it in the language on the page, though—his boy was not the same, and he was never going to be.

James (Jim) Shipp and my father, Alan Burleson, 1967.

CHAPTER 8

A Dark Prelude

"He (God) kept me alive for some reason, which I don't know yet, but whatever he has in mind for me, I will happily comply.

Now, I wouldn't be telling you all that I'm going to tell you, but I figure that newspapers have long since alarmed you, so here goes."

JIM SHIPP SERVED with the 1st Battalion, 3rd Marines (1/3) alongside my father in Delta Company. That's how I know about what happened to him and the other boys who survived the battle he wrote about in the letter to his parents. It's how I know about the parts he left out of the letter, so as not to worry his parents any more than he had to. I am sharing those parts of the story here now, the way that Jim, my father, and several other veterans of 1/3 shared them with me.

The young Marines of the battalion were part of a new kind of reaction force known as Special Landing Force Alpha (SLF Alpha). Deployed near the height of the Vietnam War, theirs was one of the most active Marine combat battalions of the entire conflict. Just off the coast of Vietnam, they cruised on Navy vessels around the northernmost tactical region known as I Corps (pronounced "eye core"), where South Vietnam meets North Vietnam at the DMZ. With a squadron of helicopters, and with amtracs for beach landings, they could be inserted flexibly to reinforce a troubled unit or close on enemy forces wherever they were spotted. After the first battle that Shipp wrote home about, their operational tempo shot through the roof and put them in a blur of back-to-back operations that lasted from May into the next year.

DMZ is an acronym for "demilitarized zone," which I've always thought is a perplexing use of words because "demilitarize" means "to rid a place of military characteristics or uses." As it turns out, the DMZ was one of the most highly contested and bloodiest regions in the whole damned country, and by damned, I mean it in the old way.

Another name sometimes used was the "Dead Marine Zone," though to be clear, more enemy combatants, the Viet Cong (VC) and North Vietnamese Army (NVA) were killed there than were Marines. The place was sprayed with the highly toxic herbicide Agent Orange and bombed with B52s. Trees had been mowed down, and the earth plowed over with tractors, leaving nothing for miles from the eastern sea to the jungle-carpeted mountains of the west but gnarled roots and an ever-present stench of death in the thick tropical air. By damned in the old way, I mean damned to all hell.

Of the DMZ, Ken Hicks said, "All I could think of was that painting of Dante's vision of hell."

Ken participated in the operation that Jim wrote home about, though that was further south in the Que Son Valley. Let's get back to that.

"On the 28th of April we made a beach landing somewhere

between Da Nang and Chu Lai. It was very, very hot as we were in a sandy desert-like area when we landed, and we lost several men due to heat exhaustion. This was all part of Operation Union, and it wasn't really bad as there were only snipers who couldn't hit crap. They were so bad that half the time, you couldn't tell that we were being shot at. Only once in a while did a round hit close."

The first of many haunting events that Shipp did not share in the letter was one that Ken shared with me—a dark prelude to their first operation, which occurred even before the company made their landing.

The operation was known as Beaver Cage, though veterans would later call it "Beaver Cage/Union" because it got intermixed with Union, an operation involving other Marine units that started around the same time and in the same area south of Da Nang.

To this day, I'm not sure why the operations were named as they were. Back then, most of the Marines didn't even know the names themselves, much less their meaning or strategic relevance. They were usually told only that they were going out and to be ready.

For Beaver Cage, Delta Company would make an amphibious landing on the beach while other companies of the SLF's Battalion Landing Team would be inserting further inland by helicopters. This meant that on the day before the operation, they first had to transfer from the USS Bayfield to the USS Point Defiance, a Landing Platform Dock (LPD) that carried amtracs.

Three at a time, the Marines crawled over the side of the Bayfield to climb down cargo nets into Mike boats. In addition to their field gear—packs, cartridge belts, canteens, weapons, bayonets, knives, C-rats, an E-tool, helmet, and a flak jacket, each man also wore a kapok life jacket. Ken carried the additional burden of a large radio, so climbing down into the Mike boat was a challenge—especially since it was ebbing with the ocean swells.

"As the Mike boat bounced around against the Bayfield," Ken

says, "the cargo net would go slack and then tighten up again and pull us away from the side of the ship. You had to time it just right to get off the net and into the Mike boat as opposed to being squashed between the Mike boat and the Bayfield or falling into the water with all that gear. We didn't believe the Kapok life vests would be enough to keep us afloat."

When they pulled alongside the Point Defiance, or the "Point D," as Ken calls it, they went up cargo nets to get aboard, set themselves down, and waited for the next morning. Ken found a spot near the Point D's flight deck on the aft of the ship and settled in with all his gear.

Sometime after it became dark, a helicopter landed, so Ken stood at the edge of the flight deck, which was raised to about chest level, and watched with interest. The chopper was a Sikorsky UH-34, not the more modern Huey helicopters that are typically featured in movies about the Vietnam War. This is a kind of chopper where the pilots sit high over the cargo hold and above a bulbous nose that makes the craft look sort of like a big green grasshopper.

The Marines, I'm told, always got the hand-me-downs—never anything new.

Ray Kelley, a Delta Company machine gunner the boys call "Machine Gun Kelley," shakes his head as he tells me about it.

"Those helicopters we were flying, the 34s, were from the Korean War. The Army didn't want them anymore, so we ended up with them. And we were supposed to be a premier fighting force?"

There was just enough subtle lighting around the flight deck for Ken to see a group of combat engineers from the company exit a hatch, run across the deck, and load gear and sea bags onto the chopper. The engine roared to full power, and the crew chief slid the hatch shut. The old chopper began to lift.

When a 34 is lifting off, it has the benefit of ground effect—it performs better when it's still close to the ship's deck. However, as soon as it moves away from the deck, the ground effect is gone, and a fully loaded chopper can drop towards the ocean. It must immediately tilt forward during this drop to catch wind in the blades and gain airspeed. Veterans have told me there were times before gaining airspeed that it seemed they could almost reach out and touch the water.

Ken watched the chopper slip to the left, over the flight deck, and downward out of view. He heard a splash and was sure the chopper had crashed because the noise from the engine silenced almost immediately. Klaxons sounded, and a powerful 24" searchlight above the flight deck came on. Marines rushed to the railing to peer overboard. The blades had already stopped spinning, and the chopper's body disappeared quickly. A red light on the nose went dim as it fell into the depths. By then, only the tail rotor was left to be seen following the fuselage down into the darkness.

On the surface, in the searchlight's glow, Ken could see the heads of two men bobbing in the water. He followed the searchlight, looking intently for the rest, whom he'd watched climb aboard, but they never appeared. Life rings were thrown out, and then the Marines backed away to ensure the Navy boys had room to do their jobs.

"The Marines on deck were in complete and total shock," Ken tells me.

"The aircraft sank fast," noted Marine veteran Michael Meeker. "Navy crew members of ship ran out with M-1 rifles to keep any sharks off survivors if they came. Saw only a few crew members swimming and no grunts. We were loaded down with full gear and ammo for the operation ahead."

According to the logbook entry of the Point Defiance, dated April 27, 1967, another chopper soon arrived to aid the search. The two Marines Ken had seen bobbing in the water were the pilot and the co-pilot. He'd always believed that only two survived, but many years after the war, he would learn that a 2nd Lieutenant, one of the combat engineers, was able to get out through a side window. By then, the 2nd Lieutenant had gone down so deep with the chopper he couldn't even see the searchlight's glow above, but he eventually broke the surface, gasping for air.

The logbook states that by 2120 (9:20 PM), an additional two men had been saved, but six Marines were declared lost, and their bodies were never recovered.

"It was not a good start," Ken says, almost in a whisper.

CHAPTER 9

Red Beach

A DULL SHUFFLING OF BOOTS echoed through the metal corridors as Marines filed into the mess deck. It was just past two in the morning, according to a clock that hung there. The memory of the lost men still lingered, knotting the hearts of those poised on the brink of the unknown. None of them talked much. Ken couldn't remember having gotten any sleep in the hours before. Maybe none of them had. Marines were already dead, and the rest of them had yet to embark on what, for most, was to be their very first operation—they had no idea what to expect when they reached the shore. Was it steak and eggs they served that morning? Ken thinks so, but he does not remember eating at all.

After breakfast, they climbed down ladders into the hot and humid well-deck of the ship to load onto the amtracs. A fog of diesel exhaust rested in dim red light on the air. The "tracs," as Ken had taken to calling them, had their engines running—a chorus of pistons rumbling like the guttural growls of angry beasts—like deep and resonant drums leading the beat of each man's heart to rise—a call to some ancient rite of war and blood and brotherhood.

"The smell of exhaust was nauseating," Ken says.

In the headquarters section, Ken, with his radio in tow, was part of a strategic dispersal. The Executive Officer, the Commanding Officer, the 1st Sergeant, the Company Gunny, and the fire support representatives were meticulously distributed among the tracs. This calculated arrangement was a safeguard, a measure taken to ensure that the loss of a single vehicle wouldn't cripple the company's leadership.

Every man bore a number, and to each trac, a number was given, chalked on the iron flank and on a sign held by a crew member. Ken found the number matching the one he carried and moved over the ramp into the craft. There he sat, and with the back of his hand, he wiped the salty sting of fuel-infused sweat from his eyes. Around him, each man was a mirror of his own state, their faces weary already and eyes shadowed with the weight of unspoken fears—a silent testament to the collective apprehension that clung to them as closely as their sweat-drenched uniforms.

Once everyone was inside, hydraulics engaged, and the ramp on the front and the overhead hatches were closed. Although the inside of the vibrating machine was painted white, it closed the men in total darkness.

"It seemed like forever," Ken says. "But then I heard a change in the pitch of the engine. As the amtrac started to move, we started moving in that herky-jerky way, and then our trac angled forward, down the ramp, and into the water of the flooded well deck. There's no seat belt; you're just sitting there holding on to your seat."

The ride smoothed out after they'd gone down the ramp, gunned the engine, and moved out into the open sea. From inside the trac, Ken could still not see much of anything—only the ocean water passing over two small glass vision blocks near the top. Ken felt cold sea water dripping through the rubber-sealed barn doors overhead.

The LSD had launched a control boat that each amtrac moved

PFC Kenneth (Ken) Hicks in his Kapok life vest.

Marines loading onto a Mike boat from the USS Bayfield. Photo from Marine veteran James Haight who said, "I always thought of 1st Battalion / 3rd Marines in Vietnam as the last of the old Corps because of going over the side, down the rope ladders."

toward. They circled, swelling the ocean all the more, waiting for the rest of the amtracs to come out. When all the tracs had joined the circle, they formed up into a line and, upon signal, headed for Red Beach.

"One hundred yards!" someone yelled.

A Marine belted over the rumble of the engine, "Lock and load!"

Ken pulled the charge handle back on his M16, locked the bolt to the rear, and ensured the rifle safety switch was on safe. He took a magazine out, banged it on his helmet to seat the rounds, snapped it in, and then tapped it once to ensure it was snug. He pushed the bolt release, which chambered a round, tapped the forward assist to make sure the bolt was fully seated, and then closed the dust cover on the side over the ejection port. He held the rifle between his legs and waited.

"Fifty yards!" came a yell, and then, just seconds later, Ken felt the tracks hit the sand of the beach. The trac shuttered briefly, crawled upward onto the beach, and stopped. The ramp came down, and sunlight flooded in. Marines were squinting as they rose to their feet.

"Move out! Get off the trac! Move! Move!"

Ken moved forward and started running when he reached the ramp, which was still going down. Stepping out, they were greeted not by gunfire but by the persistent whir of a camera, a South Vietnamese news crew documenting the moment with an eerie detachment. When the Marines saw the civilians working casually, the only shooting being done on 16mm film, they stopped running. The cameraman then cut, lowering his equipment with a nod, satisfied he'd captured the newsworthy action shot he wanted.

Shortly after, as Shipp mentioned in his letter, they heard a couple of pops from sniper rounds. Everybody hit the sand. Another pop, pop, and a pause. Nobody could tell where the sounds were coming from—just somewhere inland. There were a few more pops, and then it stopped.

"Charlie," the enemy, only one or perhaps a few, had slowed the

Marines down a little and then disappeared. Shipp had written to his mom and dad that the snipers couldn't hit crap.

"Half the time you couldn't tell that we were being shot at," he wrote. "Only once in a while did a round hit close."

As far as the beach landing goes, that may have been intentional. Bill Taylor, a veteran from the battalion's Charlie Company, tells me that sometimes the VC would engage only lightly and then fall back, engage lightly again, and then fall back again. An entire Marine company could be slowed down in this way while the VC gained valuable time.

"And sometimes," Bill tells me, "They were trying to draw us into a trap. Marines are trained, after all, to move toward fire, not away from it."

"Yes," Ken agrees, "And that is so ingrained that even to this day if I hear gunfire, I have the urge to move toward it and stop it."

Intentional or not, it was surely enough, at least on this day, to let the land and the climate swallow up the Marines. Heat and thirst were sometimes greater enemies than the NVA and the VC.

"We were pouring sweat, just pouring sweat," Ken says. "I was soaked in it. It looked like somebody sprayed a hose on me."

They waited in the sun for four gun tanks and one flame tank to arrive on LCMs (Landing Craft Mechanized), and then Ken got a call on the radio for First Lt. Huddelson, the company XO, the "Delta 5 Actual."

"Sir, they want you," Ken said. "They want the Actual."

Huddelson talked to his command for a bit, gave the radio handset back to Ken, and then got the company up and moving several hundred meters inland. They began to sweep in a direction that seemed to be parallel to the coast, though none could see the ocean anymore. The tanks were with them, and they walked slowly in deep, soft sand.

"In the sand, it felt like you took two steps forward and one backward," Ken says. "We're wearing flak jackets, which trap body

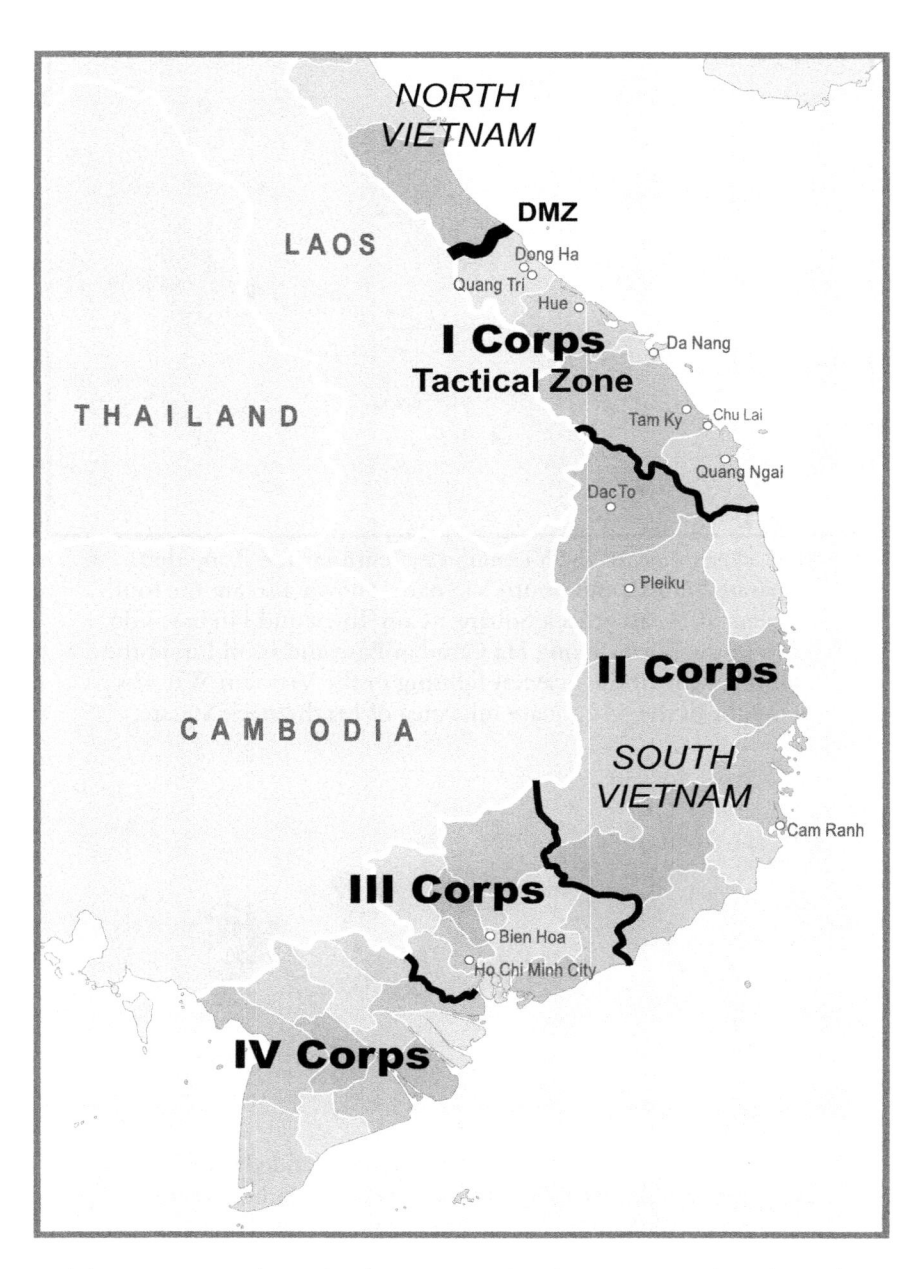

The DMZ was along the demarcation line between North and South Vietnam. Special Landing Force Alpha and its Battalion Landing Team of 1st Battalion, 3rd Marines operated there and in I Corps, the northernmost of the four South Vietnamese tactical zones.

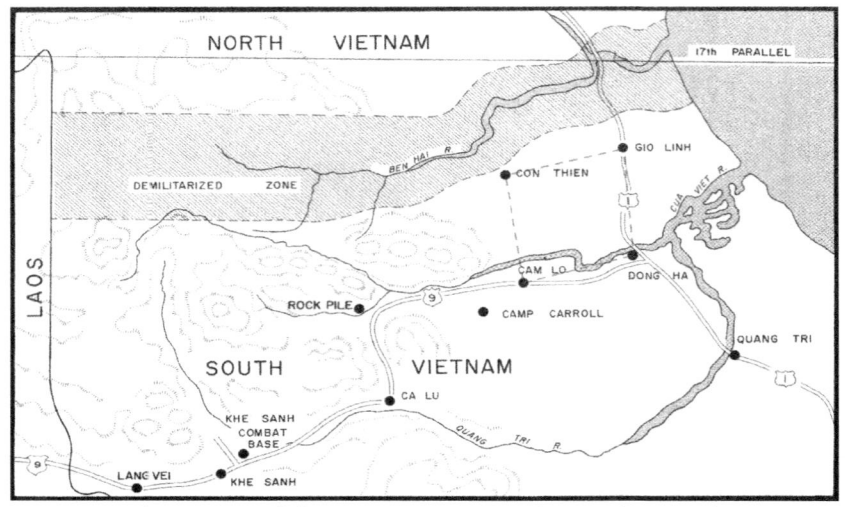

A closer view of the Vietnamese Demilitarized Zone that separated North and South Vietnam. Shown also are the four corners of "Leatherneck Square": Con Thien and Firebase Gio Linh in the north, Dong Ha Combat Base and Cam Lo, in the south. Some of the heaviest fighting of the Vietnam War was fought in the 54+ square mile area of Leatherneck Square.

The first Marine combat troops in Vietnam landed north of Da Nang on March 8, 1965. Two years later, my father's company commenced Operation Beaver Cage, south of Da Nang, on Red Beach—part of a troop build-up that would peak at over 540,000 in 1969. By the end of the war, over 58,200 US service members were dead—almost 20% of them all killed in 1967, the year my father was there. Of all branches of the US forces, the Marine Corps made up only 14%, but lost the highest percentage of its own men which accounted for 25.5% of all US casualties.

heat, and it's already hot and humid. We're drinking water from our canteens pretty quickly."

They had already sat in the amtracs aboard ship for over an hour in the heat, pouring out sweat. It didn't take long before those heat casualties that Shipp wrote home about began.

"We lost several men due to heat exhaustion" was all that he would write, which was a bit of an understatement if you'd been there to see it.

First, there was flushed red skin on some of the Marines—confused and disoriented faces on others.

"We all started out with two canteens," Ken says. "I think I scrounged up a third before we landed. You can go through four canteens in half an hour."

Some of the men bellied over with severe cramps.

"It's either heat stroke or heat exhaustion," says Richard Kuschel, a Corpsman from Alpha Company. "Most of them were heat exhaustion. That's where you get cold and clammy. It's like you're going into shock, but heat stroke is the opposite. You get really hot, and flushed, and dry."

Some vomited, and others fainted outright—eyes rolling back in their heads as they collapsed against the warm, white sand.

"One-hundred and twenty-one of them in the first day," says Donald F. Teal, M.D., who was the Navy Medical Officer in charge of medical care back out with the fleet on the USS Okinawa.

The declassified command chronology confirms this. The written summary for that first day, April 28, 1967, says that more than 100 personnel were medevaced.

"They couldn't function," Dr. Teal tells me. "They might as well have been shot, other than they recover faster, but they could not continue. In fact, these 121 guys were out of action until we got them hydrated. Many couldn't walk up the stairs from the hangar deck into the hospital—the emergency room area. We'd bring them in on stretchers, an equal number of Navy and Marines carrying each of the casualties until we could evaluate who was worse."

In support of Operation Union, the company continued sweeping for two more days along the coast until being choppered further inland, closer to the western mountains where other Marine units had been kicking the hornets' nest and pushing NVA down into the Que Son Valley. For Delta Company, those first few days had been relatively uneventful. There'd been sniper fire, Ken recalls—a little more accurate, in his recollection, than Shipp would share with his parents.

"The tanks we had with us drew a lot of sniper fire," he tells me. "I watched the tank commanders in their cupolas with their eyeballs sticking out of the hatches. They were not going to expose themselves. Every so often, you heard a shot and a ricochet off the side of the tank. They were bullet magnets."

There was also an incident with one of the platoons that rounded up some VC suspects in a ville. When one of the suspects made an attempt to run away, Marines opened fire, and a couple of children were hit and seriously wounded. This was not witnessed by Ken but overheard when an MP Sergeant attached to the company later described the incident.

It was eleven days before Shipp wrote the following words in the letter to his parents.

> *"After four days we were heli-lifted far inland to initiate, Operation Beaver Cage. I believe the date on that was May 2. On that date began 10 days of pure hell. If there was ever a worse thing invented than the Hell of war, I hope I'm spared of ever seeing it. Rest assured that I'll never see Satan's Hell because the Lord and I have never been closer."*

CHAPTER 10

The Cage

ACCORDING TO A declassified Command Chronology, on April 30, 1967, the third day after the company landed, they were choppered about ten miles further inland to LZ Buzzard for Operation Beaver Cage. Helicopter landing zones were identified by the names of birds. Battalion Command, Charlie, and Alpha companies had been put in at LZ Oriole, about ten miles inland from Red Beach. Two days later, Bravo Company heli-lifted into LZ Cardinal, also about ten miles inland. Movement throughout the operation would eventually cover at least ten additional LZs with names like Canary, Eagle, Finch, Magpie, and so forth.

The company was experiencing supply problems. Being a radio man at the time, Ken heard the CH-46 twin-rotor supply choppers had been grounded. Apparently, the 46s kept breaking apart under stress because of some kind of design flaw, so the Special Landing Force's fleet of 34s had to take up the slack. Those, however, were already busy moving troops in support of the operation. What little they could move in addition to men was barely enough—the Marines were out of C-rations and were receiving no fresh water from the ships. Along with the weight of his own gear, each man carried the personal burden of staying hydrated.

"It was kind of surprising to see cases of bottled water on the news footage of the Iraq and Afghanistan wars," Ken says. "In Vietnam, we had canteens to fill, and even two were not enough. We were taking canteens from the heat casualties that were being sent back. I ended up with four, which could hold about a gallon of water, but we could still go through all that in a single hour. You didn't sip from it—you just gulped it straight down. Water was always an issue. When we couldn't get it from a ship or somewhere safe, we had to use purification tablets, which made it taste like iodine."

After they'd landed further inland, Delta Company spent the next three days on Search and Destroy—humping through farm fields and villes. They found green pineapple and sugar cane, but neither was ripe for picking.

"Not too edible and not too sweet," Ken says. "They'd give you a quick burst of energy, but it burned out fast. Gave you the shits. We cut gourds and ate those. They were like eating wood. Also gave you the shits. I had a C-rat can of peanut butter, so I divided that into thirds and shared it with the squad."

The after-action report says the company got into a firefight on the first of May. On the second, they shot and wounded one VC and captured three found crawling out of a tunnel. On the third of May, after more Search and Destroy, they set up on a small hill, marked 65 on the map.

Because the hills in Vietnam were all marked by their height in meters, they would come to be named and known to the Marines, and sometimes to history, by those numbers—especially when significant events occurred there. Though this hill in the Que Son Valley, 65 meters in height, may not yet be known to history, it would never be forgotten by the men who dug in there when the sun rose that next morning on the 4th of May. The valley down below the hill, at least, would be remembered by some of the surviving Marines as the Valley of Tears. Shipp mentioned this in his letter home.

"On with the story," he wrote.

> *"We landed in a vast rice paddy covered valley surrounded by tall mountains. In the words of one of my buddies, and echoed by us all, this was truly to be the Valley of Tears. On the 3rd of May nothing much really happened. It was, of course, very hot (120 degrees) but not as hot as on the beach. We lost some more heat casualties, but that would only make it a normal day."*

When Shipp's buddy (actually Lance Cpl. Raymond Kelley) used the term "Valley of Tears," he was not just referring to the valley area just below Hill 65 but the entire Que Son Valley, which was to give the whole battalion hell throughout the operation.[1] Delta Company might've had one last quiet night up on Hill 65, but Charlie Company was already in a heavy fight, and a few miles to the south and west of the hill, 9 Marines in Alpha Company were about to be wounded in action. Fourteen more were going to die.

---

1   Charlie Company's Colonel Jerry Reczek (USMC ret.) tells me he has also heard of the Que Son Valley referred to as "Coffin Valley." "That valley," he says, "was to become one of the most contested areas of operations in all of I Corps, the U.S. Marines' area of operations."

CHAPTER 11

Water Run

AS OF THE MOMENT I publish this, it will have been 57 years since the infamous "water run"—plenty of time to obscure the memory of what happened. Before I tell the story, I want you to know why I use the term "infamous" to describe the event.

All veterans of 1/3 are familiar with the story. At Third Marine Division reunions, for example, they fill the bathtub in one of the hotel rooms full of ice and beer and leave the room generally open so the Marines can drop in at any time. They call this room "the bunker," and going there to have drinks and reminisce with other veterans is the only reason my father goes. He couldn't care less for the local attractions, the guided tours, or the dress-up dinners, so I sit in the bunker with him, a fly on the wall, nibbling on pretzels and just listening. Again, as it was last year and the year before, I hear something said about "the water run." I will make a mental note to learn more—to ask each Marine about it later in private interviews.

This event is "infamous" to me, not just because of the sad tragedy that it was, but because, in the accounts shared, there seems to have been some speculation and rumor—only what men on the shore party were hearing, for example, as the wounded and the dead were carried in. I found contradictions even in the stories of those who experienced the event. The story may be well known, but it is not necessarily well remembered after all these years.

One fact I know to be true is that of all the men who could say what happened during that water run, not many survived. From those who lived, we have a handful of unforgettable fragments—haunting mental pictures snapped in the fog of war that have hung unwillingly in the galleries of their minds. In a sense, I can even appreciate the minor discrepancies in the accounts of those Marines, each man now in his mid-seventies. It gives me some sense of what it must feel like to live with such memories—on the one hand, wanting to piece it all back together in some sensible way and yet, on the other, wanting to avoid certain images and the feelings that resurface when they come to mind.

In the early evening of May 3, 1967, after another long, hot day sweeping up toward the Que Son Valley, Alpha Company stopped to dig in. They chose their position knowing a creek they'd encountered earlier in the day was just a short hump away—cool, clear water for about two-hundred men who were exhausted, dirty, hungry, and already again, thirsty.

Alpha Company's plan was to send out killer teams and set up ambushes throughout the night, but their movement during the day had been far less than stealthy. Mark Kennedy, who'd been on the sweep, considered this as he and his squad dug in with their entrenching tools. The company had been on low ground throughout the day, with higher ground overlooking them. Mark knew that from under the canopy of the dense foliage carpeting the hills, the enemy could move without being seen and could have easily been watching them.

"And believe me," he says to me, "we made noise on a damn sweep.

It was like an elephant going through a cotton patch."

"Man, if they're out here," a nervous young Marine had said to him, "don't you think they'd hear us?"

"What are you shitting me?" Mark replied. "They're following us. They know exactly where we're at right now."

Though he was exhausted and the ground unforgiving, Kennedy continued to dig. As he was shoveling, a squad-sized work party was organized to head out on a patrol toward the creek. A couple of guys were picked from different squads to gather empty canteens from as many men as possible, hoisting them on web belts to carry them in bulk. Kennedy gave up his empty canteens and stayed behind as the nine to eleven men set out.

"You didn't really give a rat's ass which canteens you got back," he says. "You just got two canteens back. You gave them two; you got two back."

Up front, at the head of the departing column, was a twenty-year-old named James Iverson Balch. As a Corpsman, Balch may have been trained on the symptoms and dangers of dehydration, heat exhaustion, and the life-threatening criticality of heat stroke. If not, he had at least witnessed it all first-hand in the days since the company had started the operation. On each day, he had rendered aid to overexerted men—pouring his own water on their faces, stretching out the fingers of their clenched hands, and sometimes even having to keep them from biting their tongues. So, early that evening, when the group was organized to go out, I imagine Balch went enthusiastically.

Chris Valdez, a classmate who attended Hospital Corps School with Balch, wrote years later that "Jim" had a great laugh and was one of the kindest people he'd ever met. David Wood, a friend who worked with him at the Naval Hospital in Charleston, South Carolina, echoed the sentiment when he wrote, "I remember, especially his laugh and his sense of humor."

I can see it in a photo of Balch that I found online—a dimple-pushing grin on his face and a bright twinkle in his eyes. He looks like the kind of guy who, despite all circumstances, was pleasant to be around—the kind of Corpsman whose mere presence was medicine for weariness and melancholy.

It was rumored that some of the men on the patrol left their weapons behind to carry more canteens. In fact, Antonio Ramos, a shore party Marine, who happened to be in the field with the company that day, tells me that while he never heard an officer giving the order, he remembers hearing comments through the grapevine of the line.

"You don't have to bring a weapon," he remembers it being said. "The important thing is to bring canteens—to carry as many as possible."

If it really was suggested that Marines leave their weapon behind, Kennedy assured me that no one heeded the advice.

"No, they took weapons. I promise you, they took weapons," he says. "There ain't a Marine in that outfit that I knew who'd go anywhere outside of any lines without their weapon."

"I don't know why it ever got called a water run," says Richard Kuschel, another Corpsman in the column. "It was a patrol. When we got to that creek, we were looking for the NVA. That's what we were there for."

It was close to 1830 when the squad arrived near the creek. As the column followed steadily along the water's edge, Kuschel began to feel uncomfortable with the situation.

"There was a steep hill on one side and a sloped hill on the other," he recalls. "There was a pagoda up on the sloped hill. At the head of this, there was a rice paddy dike. There were rice paddies up above."

It was the big steep hill that worried him.

"They're known for being in spider holes and tunnels on the side of hills like that," he tells me.

Several other "older guys" who had been in country for a while shared his concerns.

"Some of them, it was their second time around," he says, implying that "old salt" Marines were advising against the squad leader's demands to keep the column moving forward. The air was suddenly thick with a sense of danger.

"This is where they're going to be," Kuschel whispered to the squad leader. "They're here. This is an ambush if I ever saw one."

The squad leader didn't listen. He made them go all the way up the creek, and when the front guys and the point guys got up to the rice paddy dikes, he told them all to halt and fill canteens.

"So, these guys stop," Kuschel says. "They take their packs off, set them down, lean their rifles up, and squat in the creek filling their canteens."

Kuschel stood on guard with the others and up on a rise near some rocks. As the minutes passed, he grew increasingly uneasy. He edged closer to the larger rocks that would provide the best cover.

"And that's when they opened up on us," he says.

CHAPTER 12

Lost Brothers

BACK WHERE 2ND PLATOON had filed into the company's line for the night, Kennedy and his squad were still digging. A focused rhythm had formed as they hacked away with their entrenching tools, but it abruptly stopped when the Marines heard the sound of machine gun fire nearby. It had been fifteen minutes since the patrol had set out toward the creek.

With his entrenching tool frozen in his hands, Kennedy listened to the northwest where the patrol had gone. He glanced quickly at the men around him, their anxious faces each confirming what he had heard—machine gun fire and then return fire from M16s. The sounds were unmistakable. Everyone in the squad dropped their entrenching tools and reached for their gear and rifles.

Just seconds later, a distressed radio call came into the CP from the squad leader down at the creek, and Kennedy's squad was immediately rounded up to head down and join the fight. His squad leader called for a machine gun attachment and for an FO to direct mortars and artillery. Then, with his PRC 25 ("prick 25") radio operator at his side, he led them quickly out.

When they arrived near the creek, they found most of the ambushed squad fighting from behind the rocks. Four Marines were seriously wounded, and Doc Kuschel's hands were bloody from the work. Over their agonized screams and the ongoing gunfire, Kennedy and his squad assessed the scene.

Over the rocks and across the creek, beyond a set of rice paddies, machine gun fire erupted from the shadows of a tree line.

"It was a bunker that was thick enough, made of logs and stuff, about maybe four feet above the ground," Kennedy says. "They were firing from that. Our M79 guy and the M60 guy neutralized that machine gun quickly. Then, he started suppressing the area with that M79. By the way, he's firing over the head of Spicer and Verbilla behind that rice paddy dike, you see?"

Two Marines, LCpl Eugene Spicer and PFC David Verbilla, had gone out to assault the gun position when the ambush started but were now lying behind the paddy dike about ten yards apart. Veteran accounts suggest that they had not been directed to go out but had set out bravely of their own accord.

"You'd have to know, Spicer and Verbilla," Kennedy says. "They were very close friends, like brothers, and one wasn't going to go without the other. It's just that simple."

While they were going out, the other guys behind the rocks were laying down a base of fire over into the tree line. Once Spicer and Verbilla got in closer, they would provide their own base of fire so that more Marines could come out of the cover of the rocks and move up. In this way, trading off the covering fire, they could eventually get everyone closer to take out the enemy outfit. But Spicer and Verbilla's covering fire never came.

Whether they were just keeping their heads down or dead, Kennedy and his squad couldn't tell, but they knew they had to get there quickly and find out for sure, so, under a base of their own covering fire, they made their way.

Once they'd gotten closer to Spicer and Verbilla, their own machine gunner started kicking back against the NVA—firing over the dike where Spicer and Verbilla lay. As the gunner fired, their M79 guy was able to walk his grenades to the bunker and take out the gun.

Even with the gun neutralized, enemy fire continued to erupt from the tree line. A reinforced squad, maybe more, was still out there. It was clear now why Spicer and Verbilla never gave their covering fire; they'd never had the chance. While focusing their attention on the gun in the bunker, they'd both been shot—most likely by one or more snipers on the flank.

"Cadre VC," Kennedy said. "Like a little militia. Because they had a machine gun and a couple of RPGs, I assume it was an outfit from a sapper unit. Their main task was probably to put out mines and stuff like that—booby traps, that's what they did."

Kennedy studied the ground in the shadows of the vegetation, looking for sources of fire while the FO from the platoon CP started calling in artillery and mortar fire.

"People, when they first got over to Vietnam," he tells me, "they always looked up in the trees, but the VC didn't shoot you from trees. They shot you from little spider holes."

By then, the platoon commander had gone down there, got a Huey Gunship on station, and had it strafe the whole area. It was an ideal time to make a dash for Spicer and Verbilla. When Mark's fire team was asked to do it, they quickly formulated a plan. Nobody had to direct them.

"We would let our machine gun cut down in the middle of where we were gonna have to go," he says. "Then, while he was doing that (him and his A-gunner), our squad would open the pathway and fire to the left and the right of us. Their fields of fire would cross to keep the people out there down while we were going out to get Spicer and Verbilla, and it worked. It worked very well, as a matter of fact."

When they were no longer receiving return fire, they ran out in pairs of two. A Marine from Philly named Ray Bencivengo went out with Kennedy to get Verbilla while two others went for Spicer. Verbilla didn't look good, but there was no time for taking vitals and it was no place to provide aid. Bencivengo handed his rifle to Mark, removed Verbilla's flak jacket to lighten the load, lifted him quickly over his shoulder, and started running back.

"I'm facing towards the tree line and going backward," Kennedy tells me. "I'm running backward as best I can and then sideways. We get about half the way back, and Bencivengo said, 'Man, we have to switch.' I stopped, and he stopped. I handed him both rifles, got right behind him and took Verbilla. We took off running again and he was facing the tree line in case we had to shoot, and we did shoot."

They only switched one time like that, halfway, he tells me. The other two guys were performing basically the same routine with Spicer. At one point during Kennedy's carry, he heard the unmistakably sickening sound of a bullet slapping into Verbilla's back and then felt it hammer against his own flak jacket. Alive or dead already, Verbilla had just been shot again, Kennedy was sure.

"When we got back behind the rocks into relative safety, we just collapsed there," he says. "...and then we realized that they were definitely both dead. As far as I know, Spicer and Verbilla were the first ones to be killed on that ambush."

Kennedy and Bencivengo both later recommended that Spicer and Verbilla should have been awarded, at least, Bronze Star Medals posthumously because of their initial reaction to the ambush.

CHAPTER 13

Not So Little Boys

DOC KUSCHEL HAD critically wounded men who were in desperate need of a medevac, so he'd been moving them further away from the hot zone—laying them down in the pagoda up on the hill, which itself was somewhat protected by rocks. From there, he figured he could get them over to the other side of the hill where medevac choppers might be able to reach them.

"It was a real confusing time—running around, dragging people out, and trying to bandage them up," Kuschel tells me.

Three additional squads trickled onto the scene in addition to Kennedy's squad, which bolstered the Marines' defensive capabilities but also heightened the overall tension and complexity of the situation.

A Native American boy was there in the pagoda who had gotten one of his testicles shot off—a Kiowa Indian, Kuschel thinks. He wrapped the boy's wound tight in A-B-D battle dressing and then kept the boy's mind from dwelling on his groin by directing him to help with the rest of the wounded.

"I had one guy who was shot three times to the chest," he says. "I had to wrap him up with Vaseline gauze to plug the bullet holes and then an ACE bandage to hold the gauze in place."

He turned the Marine on the side of his chest that was wounded, using the Marine's own body for compression.

"Somebody said that Joe Volendo, the other Corpsman, was down there and wounded, so I went for him. I had that American Indian keep an eye on the guy who was shot in the chest, and I told him to holler for me if he went into shock. The guy who was shot in the chest came back a couple of months later. He came back to the company. That's hardcore. He could have gone home, but when he got out of the hospital, he came back. I couldn't believe it."

Kuschel shakes his head, then takes a deep breath and lifts his eyebrows.

"In any case, the fight went on pretty much all night," he says. "They shot artillery and mortar rounds, and the fight went on all night."

Antonio Ramos had to go out with a couple of Marines to retrieve one of the wounded. The grunts, they were told, would be pulling the wounded Marine back out of the hot zone, and then Ramos and his team were to get him and carry him back inside the perimeter where there was space wide enough for a medevac to land.

On the way back, his group all stumbled into a mud hole, nearly waist deep, and struggled to get out while keeping their wounded Marine in the poncho on which they carried him.

"He wasn't that badly wounded, but he was wounded," Ramos says. "He said, 'You guys, let me get off this poncho. Just let me get off, and you get out.'"

As soon as they got him back to the perimeter and out on a chopper, they had to go back to the front for more wounded.

"Time moved very fast," Ramos says. "I remember running out there to pick up somebody, and the Gunship started firing right over my head. Man, my knees buckled, and I dropped when I heard that thing."

As a shore party man, Ramos normally flew into the field with the first wave, controlled the landing zone, and left with the last wave. Now, he was thrust into the field with a Corpsman and a group of three combat Marines, or "grunts" as he calls them, and out of his element. By the time they had made their third trip back into the combat zone, it was dark, and he was terrified.

The Marine they carried this time was severely wounded and moaning in pain. During the journey back to the perimeter, the group froze at the sound of footsteps nearby—so close they could not throw a grenade without putting themselves in danger. The wounded Marine's mouth was covered to mute his moaning.

"Spread out, spread out," one of them whispered, recognizing that a grenade might be thrown at them instead.

They waited at the ready, listening intently to the footsteps on the underbrush. It sounded like a small group of men—three to five, at least. After several minutes, the footsteps finally moved away from them, and they grouped back around the wounded Marine, whose moaning remained silenced, even without a hand over his mouth.

"This will always stay with me," Ramos tells me. "The Corpsman said, 'We can't bring him back. He won't make it.'"

"What?" he says.

"He won't make it, he won't make it."

"We had to leave that guy out there," he says. "That was very shocking to me because I'd been told that Marines never leave their buddies behind. I was very distraught about the whole experience—not knowing whether or not that guy was still alive."

"I ended up in a depression kind of a gully," says Doc Kuschel. "We had more guys there, badly wounded, and they were making all kinds of noise, but there was just no way for me to get them out of there."

Back in the lines, Antonio got word of the others still out there, wounded and dead, that could not be carried back.

"They say that we could not send units back out just to pick up the wounded because it was too risky," he says. "We were going to get more casualties, that's what would happen—or there was a possibility of getting more casualties. They had to be left out there. And that was really…it was a bad thing for me."

When they returned to the lines, they went to where they had set up an LZ to take the wounded out. Ramos had to stand out in the darkness, in the middle of a wide open area, with two flashlights to wave in the helicopter.

"You can imagine," he says, "I was shitting in my trousers because, at night, all they have to do is shoot in the middle of the flashlights."

"Now, all of the guys that got killed that night weren't on the water patrol," Kennedy continues. "We had guys that were killed from mortar rounds and artillery rounds and small arms fire because they tried to hit us later that night after we had gotten back and gotten people medevaced out. They hit our lines—the whole company. So, a bunch of these guys that are in Alpha Company, they weren't necessarily in my platoon or in any single platoon. They were hit all up and down the lines, but the water patrol that got ambushed was from our platoon, the initial water patrol that went out there."

After tearing up the tree line beyond the rice paddies with two Huey Gunships and artillery, Kennedy and others started to move back to the lines by fire teams. Four Marines at a time would take off and head back, and the next four would go back, then the next four. By doing that, they all got back inside the lines.

"And then, believe it or not, we had to finish digging foxholes, and we still hadn't had anything to eat," Kennedy says. "I ate cold ham and mothers."

"Mothers," in this context, is short for "ham and mother fuckers" which is Marine slang for ham and lima beans—on average, probably the least favored C-ration.

"I like ham and lima beans, but I liked it when I could heat it up. I didn't much care for it cold, but I ate it cold because I was hungry. I'll never forget that. That was the first time I ate cold ham and lima—ham and mothers."

Mark says that he remembers seeing Puff that night—a sight that all veteran Marines agree is an awesome thing to behold. By awesome, I mean in the classic sense, before my generation weakened the word with common use. Puff is short for "Puff the Magic Dragon," a song by Peter, Paul, and Mary that had been popular in 1963 when the Marines were in their early teens. The Douglas AC-47 Spooky was a fixed-wing gunship, an airplane with three 7.62 mm miniguns to provide close air support for ground troops. It earned the name of a dragon because its miniguns fired so rapidly that the red tracers from the rounds formed a solid red beam from the night sky to the earth, like a dragon's breath, decimating the landscape. Puff could orbit a target for hours, providing suppressing fire over a tight elliptical area (about 52 yards or 47.5 meters in diameter), placing a round every 2.4 yards during a three-second burst. The aircraft also carried flares it could drop to illuminate the battleground.

Consider those young men, still just boys on the brink of manhood, watching in awe as their pet dragon laid waste to the enemy—its chest-penetrating roars buzzing loudly in the night with each three-second burst of fire. While it struck them all with wonder and awe, it was also slightly horrifying, and some veterans tell me they couldn't help but feel a strange emotion mixing with their elation—a certain dreadful empathy for anything, animal or enemy, that was caught under the soaring beast. In the silence between each burst, a song echoed back from childhood in the minds of the young men. Light-spirited acoustic guitars and the sweet harmonic mix of Peter's tenor, Paul's baritone, and Mary's contralto. It's uncanny and an eerie fit for the scene, but for some, it couldn't be helped. And to think—the song's writers have always claimed it to be about the end of childhood innocence.

Puff, the magic dragon lived by the sea

SHADOW OF THE VALLEY

And frolicked in the autumn mist
in a land called Honahlee

A dragon lives forever but not so little boys

Painted wings and giant's rings make way for other toys

CHAPTER 14

The Last Embers

DOC KUSCHEL WAS still pitted in the gully with the wounded that he couldn't get out. The Marines with him were quiet; some were now heavily sedated with morphine. Those who were lucid were waiting for the enemy to come. Save for the sounds of distant gunfire, the moments in between were uncomfortably quiet. Under the stars in such a rural land, one would expect to hear the insects at least, but every living thing had been stunned mute. From that silence, not more than fifty yards away in the darkness, they heard the screams of what sounded like captured Marines, but it was hard to tell. Each voice was soon after silenced by a single respective shot until there were none left to scream.

The next morning, some of the grunts were rounded up to go back out, and Ramos went with them.

"We brought back three dead bodies," he says, "the guy that had been left the night before when I was out there and two other guys that were over at a dry rice paddy. One was a very big guy—very heavy."

They struggled to carry the heavy body in a poncho.

"Well," one said, "let's go to that bamboo grove, cut a bamboo, and carry him back inside a poncho with a pole."

"No way," Ramos said. "We're not going to go out there. Man, we're going to get ambushed again."

With only three guys with him to carry the bodies, they could only carry them for short distances before stopping to rest and readjust.

"Fuck it, man, let me do it," one of the Marines said, lifting the smallest of the dead Marines up and over his shoulder. Ramos walked behind them and watched the dead one's lifeless arms swing in the air beside the Marine that carried him. Blood drooled in intermittent streams from the mouth of his bobbing head.

Oh, my God. Ramos thought about the mothers and fathers of the dead Marines in front of him. *The family of these guys are probably back in the United States praying for God to keep their sons alive and don't even know it yet—they're already dead.*

When the Marines came in the morning, Kuschel went out with them, particularly intending to find his fellow Corpsman, James Balch. Joe Volendo, the other Corpsman, got shot in the leg, so he had been medevaced out.

"Then there was Conner," he says. "I think his name was Conner. He was a skinny blond guy—also a Corpsman. He was down on his knees, bandaging somebody up, and they shot him. And we got him medevaced out. I don't know whatever happened to him—if he lived or not. But Balch was still missing."

Then they found the men who Kuschel heard screaming in the night, each with an unexpectedly small hole in the forehead surrounded by a gray splash on the flesh from burnt cartridge discharge particles.

"They had caught them during the night, and they were torturing them," Kuschel says. "We could hear that. They put them all in a row, lined them up, and shot them in the forehead, all of them. It was probably half a dozen guys, all guys I knew. We were finding bodies all over the place."

Since Kuschel knew that Balch had been up at the head of the column when the ambush had first begun, he went with some of the men up to where the rice paddy was, above the hills, up at the head of the creek.

"We were going along that rice paddy, and then they opened up out of the same hill on us again," he says. "That morning, I was with a black guy. His name was Eugene Murry, and he was a big guy. He and I got behind a rice paddy dike, and I had a rifle that I picked up and had just finished emptying a magazine. I went down to reload, and he stuck his head up, and they shot him right through the neck. I caught him when he dropped. I stuck my thumb in there to try to stop the bleeding, but I could feel his spine was shot in half. He died right there."

Responding to the gunfire, more Marines moved up to Kuschel's position. They called the Huey Gunships again, and when it all died down, they finally got up to where the head of the column had been when the ambush started. There, they found Balch.

"That's where we found him," Kushcel says. "but he was dead. It was obvious that he'd been taking care of two Marines, but they died there with him."

That was pretty much the end of it.

"They blew up the side of the hill right after that," he says. "Called in air support. The last dead guys we found were Balch and the Marines that were with him. And then we got the hell out of there."

Years later, Doc Kuschel went looking for James Iverson Balch one last time and found him on panel 19E, line 21 of the Vietnam Veterans Memorial Wall in Washington, D.C. Since the names are listed chronologically by date of casualty, he found Eugene Murry on the same panel, just nine lines apart.

"They got him listed that he died the day before," Kuschel says of Murry. "He didn't die the day before. He died the next morning because I was right next to him when he got shot. I caught him when he dropped."

"There's 23 guys on that wall that I served with," Mark Kennedy says. "I finally got out of Vietnam in '69 and was back and spending time in the hospitals. I had a lot of guilt feelings. Why me? You know, I never understood why I survived and all these other guys I knew, they died."

There were mixed feelings of anger and blame within those feelings of guilt.

"I remember the name of a guy nominated for a Silver Star, a squad leader, a corporal," Mark says. "When we found out that he had been nominated, this guy (I'm not going to tell you his name) did not deserve a Silver Star. Several of us went to the platoon commander and said, 'No, we don't believe you're nominating this guy for this. We couldn't even get him to get up and give directions.' We were reacting to the orders of fire team leaders. The squad leader never had anything to say to us."

A few names were mentioned regarding the poor command decisions that might have been made that day, but like Mark, I find no good purpose in stating them here. I will share that at least one officer was reported to have been relieved of command.

"Do you have any theory as to why he got relieved?" I ask.

"I don't really know," Mark says, "but I do know that he didn't order people to go down to the water patrol without weapons. I do know, though, that he was not really, how can I say…he was not really that tactically sound. I don't know how to put it. He didn't know shit, let me put it that way. He just didn't know how to direct people. He was a very good administrative guy."

Though he could be referring to the same person, Antonio uses another name when making the following statement to me.

"They say that {name redacted} was captain—was in a motor transport unit, and then he was transferred to be our captain or something. I never knew him, but supposedly, he was the one out there who screwed up. That's what the word was around, that he was responsible for what had happened. He was the one who sent them out, and he was the one that they removed the next day when the officer flew down. I saw very angry faces because I was at the LZ. I have to help ground the helicopters, wave them in, and all this. I saw the big brass getting off, and then they looked very angry about the whole thing."

In a letter of correspondence from a veteran, I can only refer to as Joe, I find similarities in the story. Joe writes:

> *I remember crossing the river the next a.m. and going into the village that was deserted. It was a good thing that it was because the mood was tight and full of revenge. I have blocked a lot of things from those days, and I can't remember choppers crashing on that occasion.*
>
> *I remember that night the Battalion CO came in on the medevac, and there was a huge ass-chewing of the company CO who was relieved "On the Spot" for setting us in on low ground and sending out the "Water Run" without proper security.*
>
> *I'll never forget hauling those bodies back to the CP on poles. The combat was one thing, but to lose our people because of a shit-for-brains captain was just too much...even today.*

Antonio Ramos tells me that all the guys who died on that day became a part of his life with their deaths.

"I helped put them in the choppers," he says. "It was my job, so I was one of the last to see their bodies. For years, what I named the 'Water Run Ambush' haunted my life. I had heard that 14 Marine brothers died that fateful day, but I also knew that with more than 58,000 U.S. troops killed in the war, that did not count for much. But it haunted me. Did anybody else besides me remember such a 'small' incident?"

It was indeed 14 U.S. servicemen recorded as being killed that day, and possibly more could have died from that day's events if you account for medevaced Marines who might have later succumbed to their wounds. Thanks to Antonio, Mark Kennedy, Richard ("Doc") Kuschel, Joe, and others who shared what they remember, however obscured by the passing of time and the fog of war, those guys and their stories are now a part of our lives too. For the great worth of their death and for all the myriad reasons we have to contemplate war, we have this story now to remember—a "small" incident perhaps, in the grand scheme of the war, but this is what it was, was it not? One day in roughly 7,000 days of a war, one day in roughly 390 days of a thirteen-month Marine tour, this was Vietnam.

For most of those 1st Battalion, 3rd Marines of the newly formed Special Landing Force Alpha, it was just the beginning of what was to come. As it turns out, the battalion's Charlie Company, on the flank not far from Alpha, had also been engaged with the enemy since the day before.

Back on Hill 65, a little more than two miles away, though the night had been filled with the not-too-distant thunder of artillery, it had been uneventful for Delta Company. Delta's young Marines stood watch and slept as they had done the days before. They might've looked upon the stars with an ember of boyhood wonder, distant but still glowing within them—unaware that by the evening of the next day, those embers would be choked out and lost forever.

CHAPTER 15

Cavazos

DOWN ON THE SOUTHERNMOST tip of Texas in the Rio Grande Valley, just a thirty-mile drive north of the border from Mexico, there is a small rural place called Sebastian. Though it's only an hour from the Gulf and from the popular spring break destination known as South Padre Island, Sebastian is as heartland America as it gets. Surrounded by flat farming land for as far as the eye can see, it's the kind of place where the sky will often swallow you up in cinematic sunsets. It's the kind of place that country music cowboys refer to when they sing songs about the heartland and call it "God's country."

Sebastian would be almost unbearably quiet if it weren't for the wind bustling through dry crops of cotton, crickets chirping, and the short buzzing flights of grasshoppers. In the whole town and for miles surrounding, there are less than three thousand people even to this day. You might occasionally hear the highway and the big rig trucks barreling by from out in those farmlands, but otherwise, there's little else to be heard.

Back in the sixties, there was an explosion of electric sound, however. A band called the Bell Boys played rock-and-roll on the lawn in front of the Cavazos family home. Martin Cavazos played rhythm on an electric guitar and sang while his little brother, Daniel, two years younger, and their friend, Mondo, both strummed a bass line. Behind them, cousin Robert carried the beat on his orange glitter drum set. Family, friends, and some neighbors had assembled for the show. Still, other neighbors listened from far away, the music echoing from Silvertone and Marlboro amplifiers.

Martin was a Hollywood-handsome Latino with a star's presence who could speak and sing in perfect English, though most folks around Sebastian spoke Spanish. But even though he had the looks for it and even though he'd already won the Bell Boys some air time on the local radio station, KSOKS, or "K-SOCKS" as they called it, he had no designs to be a star. His goal had been to get a degree and teach young children at the local high school. He'd already finished a full year of college but unfortunately could not yet afford another semester, so when he got a notice from the draft board, he knew there'd be no way around it.

In the yard within the small crowd, Martin's beautiful and dark-skinned Latina girlfriend, Olga, might have fiddled pensively with the ring he gave her. She knew it would be the last time her boyfriend would sing in Sebastian for over a year. Martin's little brother knew it, and their mother and father too. And soon, even the farmers on the outskirts of town would wonder what happened to the band that played outdoors in the summer afternoons. Whatever happened to that talented young man on the microphone, whose voice had once traveled with the wind over their amber waves of grain?

In his wallet, Martin carried a card imprinted with words that he had translated to Spanish when he read the notice to his mother and father. It was printed there, after all, that he was required to carry the card on his person at all times—a message from the Selective Service System and a 1-A classification, which meant that he was eligible for military service and that, whether he liked it or not, the next group to enjoy his musical talent would have to be a squad of Marines.

CHAPTER 16

Sweep

WHEN LIGHT STARTED to break the next morning on Hill 65, Ken received word that he was to pick up a VC suspect who had been captured just outside the lines by one of the company's platoons. It was not his day to carry the radio, so instead, he would have to carry a prisoner by chopper to the battalion command post.

Ken grabbed his rifle, cartridge belt with magazines and canteens, but no pack—only what he thought he needed. The battalion CP was less than a five-minute ride away, so he assumed he'd be returning quickly. He went down to pick up the prisoner—a thin and bony little man, hands bound behind his back—and led him over to a UH-34 that had just come in that morning.

The chopper dumped a supply of C-ration cases and water, and then Ken hopped in with the prisoner. As soon as they got aboard, the chopper's crew chief slapped duct tape over the prisoner's eyes. The crew chief leaned forward and spoke loudly under the chopper's noise.

"If anything happens," he said, "do not shoot in the chopper!"

He pointed at Ken's rifle and then pantomimed an action, bumping the bottom of one fist onto the top of another.

"Use your bayonet," he said.

With the prisoner's hands bound with duct tape and his eyes covered with it, too, Ken did not think the prisoner was going to do anything. The prisoner was shaking and looked pretty scared. Nevertheless, Ken pulled the bayonet from his belt, slid it over the end of his rifle, and then tugged back and forth to ensure it was locked tightly in place.

The crew chief gave him a thumbs-up, and the chopper lifted into the air.

* * *

Meanwhile, back on the hill, Corporal Martin Cavazos was saddling up his squad (3rd Squad, 3rd Platoon) to be the point squad on a sweep through some villes down in the valley. The matter was so urgent that he had his boys drop everything immediately—even the can of fruit cocktail that Jesse Hittson had been holding on to. Of all the C-rats, fruit cocktail was Hittson's favorite, and he'd been hoarding his last can. He was about to open it with his "John Wayne," the little P-38 can opener when Cavazos got him on his feet. Hittson tucked the can up under the edge of a large rock. He could look forward to having it as soon as he got back from the sweep. The last rusted flakes of that can are probably still up right where he left it, though. He would never get back to it.

Cavazos had apparently been given a distinct objective and a deadline for getting there. He kept checking the timepiece on his wrist. It reminds me of the mornings before school when my stepdad would yank the covers off my body as fast as a magician pulls the cloth from a dish-covered table.

"Off your ass and on you're feet," he'd say. "Out of the shade and in the heat!"

Then he'd talk like one of those Hispanic Americans he worked with at the railroad.

"Undele, undele! Let's go, let's go! Rápido, c'mon!"

Jesse shares with me a theory as to why there was such a sense of urgency that morning and also why the operation may have been named Beaver Cage. I'm not sure if it's something he learned from his own research or if it's conjecture, but it makes sense enough.

"Technically, if you think about it," he tells me, "Beaver Cage was nothing more than—they were going to close all the way around the gooks. They knew where a unit was. But then the unit started moving, just like a beaver does. Beaver moves, so you have to move the cage. So, we were fluid. We were in motion. And so the next day, took off, and here we go."

"And here we go," he says, the way you might say at that moment when a roller coaster just leaves the boarding bay. His voice implies that we should hold on because we're going for a ride. Not a fun one, though; he doesn't say it with a smile.

"Now comes the part of this letter of which I'm almost afraid to write," Jim Shipp would later say in the letter to his mom and dad. "I know this will alarm you, but I've got to tell someone, and I guess it's got to be those who mean the most to me."

Shipp's machine gun squad, in Weapons, was attached to 3rd Platoon, so they saddled up and followed down the hill just behind Hittson and Cavazos' 3rd squad on what was to be, as Jim Shipp would describe, "a routine village searching patrol."

"We searched two small villes without mishap," Shipp's letter says. "Between the ville, we had just finished searching, and the next one were open rice paddies for about 200 yards. Me and my gun team were right behind the point squad which was in a wedge formation in the following manner."

When The Gazette reprinted Sipp's letter, they omitted the diagram that he drew for his parents, but Jesse Hittson, who was part of that wedge, describes it again for me years later.

Jesse and I sit at a little table in a quiet room at some hotel near his home in the Texas panhandle. I slide my iPhone voice recorder aside and turn my notebook to an empty page—click the pen in my hand.

"There's a tree line here where the hooches that we just came out of were," he says, reaching over and drawing his finger across the empty page in my notebook. "See, the gooks live in tree lines because it's cooler—protection from the rain, whatever. And the rice paddy is just an open field."

I draw a line across one side of the page, write the words "trees, hooches," and out in the middle of the page, "rice paddy."

Jesse tells me the paddy was dry, but he walked on the berms above the field. He'd been doing the berms all morning.

"I had come all the way across, and Marty got pissed off at me. He said, 'Goddamnit, I told you to go straight.' So, he put Mannion on point, and Mannion started toward this area."

He points to the other side of the page in my notebook—the other side of the rice paddy where, in another tree line, was another ville to be searched.

Dennis Mannion, a nineteen-year-old from Lawrence, Massachusetts, was now on point, leading the squad in a wedge formation across the dry paddy. Hittson followed behind, out on Mannion's right. Cavazos fell back to the left behind the two of them. Then, there were two more of the "H Boys" that had come over on the ship with Hittson and Hicks—Harry Hissong, a 22-year-old from Beecher City, Illinois, and Don Hollingsworth, an 18-year-old from Fort Worth, Texas. About eighteen meters behind the point squad, Shipp had just emerged from the ville with his gun team—Bob Gallo with the M60 machine gun and Jose Gomez, a nineteen-year-old Texan carrying the M79 grenade launcher.

When he got about three-quarters of the way across the paddy, Hittson scanned the hooches in the ville looking for its inhabitants.

Still, no one was seen—no old man leading a water buffalo, no toddlers in the yard running barefoot and naked with the chickens, no old mama-sans watching over. White smoke from an unmanned fire drifted on a subtle breeze in the cool shadow of the trees, but there was no such breeze out in the paddy, in the bright, hot light of the morning sun. Jesse caught a bead of sweat with his wrist before it dropped into his eye. He glanced back to his left at Cavazos, who again checked his timepiece. It was almost nine-thirty.

From within the darkness under the trees, to the left of the approaching squad, a team of NVA regulars peered down the barrel of a heavy machine gun and waited quietly. At an almost equal distance to the squad's right flank, another team of NVA also waited quietly behind the barrel of their gun. These were not Viet Cong in black pajamas, nor even a more organized unit of VC guerillas. In their khaki uniforms and pith helmets, these were regulars of the North Vietnamese Army who are normally better trained and much tougher than rebels from the south.

"And here," Jesse says, thumping his finger directly between the two X-marks I had drawn in the tree line to represent the gun emplacements. His finger tapped directly in front of the little black circle I had made to represent the point man in the wedge, Dennis Mannion.

"Three guns?"

"Yes, three," Jesse says. "This is called a U-shaped ambush. If you're in this area, which is called the kill zone, it's supposed to be 100 percent death because of the cross-fire of the machine guns. They should have everybody covered."

Looking down at the bird's-eye-view drawing in my notebook, I am suddenly reminded of a kind of chute a shirtless Vietnamese child might fashion out of stones in a creek, funneling an unsuspecting school of minnows into a little trap woven from reeds. There was nothing for the NVA to do now but wait. The tip of the squad was trekking straight into the inner curve of the U-shaped ambush. The guns on each side, I assume, turned their aim further toward the back of the squad's wedge. Mannion's fate was already sealed with the center gun, but the longer the NVA waited, the further in their prey would amble. It would be up to Dennis himself to spring the trap, perhaps—his sudden stop and widening eyes betraying his recognition of the enemy waiting just ahead in the shadow of the trees.

* * *

Ken Hicks' flight to the Battalion CP had not taken long. When they landed, he moved the prisoner off the chopper and started looking for someone to turn him over to. It took a while, but finally, an MP sergeant came running up, yelling at him for having a bayonet on his rifle. The sergeant ordered Ken to remove the bayonet and to take the magazine out of his rifle. As he complied, removing both, the MP sergeant continued to yell at him for the duct tape over the prisoner's eyes. Ken tried to explain that the crew chief had put it on the prisoner, but the sergeant would not hear any of it.

Once the MP sergeant had left with the prisoner, Ken reloaded his rifle. He snapped a magazine back in, made sure the weapon was on safe, and then put a round in the chamber—"locked and loaded," as they would say. Wanting to get out of there and back to his company, he turned his attention to the LZ, where he and the prisoner had been dropped off, but the helo was gone. He had no ride back.

Shortly after, the Battalion's 4.2" mortars began to fire, and Ken learned that his company was engaged in combat.

"They were pumping off the four-deuce mortars like crazy," Ken says. "You could see them arcing in the air."

Desperate to return to his troubled company, Ken went straight to the LZ and waited for another helo. He would end up waiting there for the entire day. When helos finally started to come, he could not get a ride; each departing helo turned down his pleas. The only cargo they were taking out was ammo, water, and C-rats, with no passengers.

CHAPTER 17

Ambush

AS SOON AS HE HEARD the machine gun fire, Hittson instinctively dropped to the ground. Mannion had likely not even heard the first shot before he was stitched across the stomach and chest. Four to five of the fifty caliber rounds punched through him before the gun peeled off to find its next target. Mannion's body crumpled lifeless to the ground—his head, arms, and legs all sinking where they fell with no apparent force of life opposing the gravity.

"I was shooting the shit out of them gooks running between houses," Hittson says. "They'd take off running, and I'd bust their ass."

Jim Shipp, Bob Gallo, and Jose Gomez, who had taken cover behind a paddy dike out toward Hittson's right side, started firing over his head at the machine gun positions and into the ville. Other Marines, still in the ville before the rice paddy, moved forward, took cover along a hedgerow, and fired over Hittson and the rest of his point squad, who were all now against the ground.

"They killed Mannion. That's Mannion," Jesse says, pointing his finger to the front dot in the wedge of Marines I had drawn in my notebook. He staggered his finger left and right as he dragged it backward over each dot I had drawn to represent the men of his squad.

"And they killed him," he says with his finger gliding over Martin Cavazos behind him to the left.

"And him," he says with his finger moving further back to the right over Harry Hissong.

His finger moves leftward again and further near the ville they'd searched before moving out across the paddy.

"And him," he says, stopping over Don Hollingsworth.

Hissong and Hollingsworth had also been killed in the first few minutes after the guns opened fire, he assumes.

Martin Cavazos had been hit but was still alive. Not far away, Shipp, Gallo, and Gomez kept popping up over the berm to provide suppressing fire, keeping the NVA engaged and, for the moment, disinterested in Hittson and Cavazos. After all, they were pinned out in the open, and with all the fire going on over their heads, they could not stand and start running even if they wanted to.

The NVA may have left them lying there alive on purpose, for all we know. Pinned out in the open, they were easy targets and potentially bait, so long as they were still alive. The NVA knew that Marines would not leave a living man alone to die, so keeping them pinned but alive may have been a tactic they were trained to execute. Since the Marines had arrived, the NVA and Viet Cong had been studying their ways and formulating such tactics. Another, for example, was expressed in what was now a common adage among them:

"Grab their belts to fight them!"

The NVA and Viet Cong had learned that if they could stay engaged in close combat, the Americans would be unable to utilize their superior air power against them. Perhaps this was another reason to keep Hittson and Cavazos alive up near them in the rice paddy.

Between the momentary lulls of fire and the explosions from grenades that Gomez had been lobbing into the ville with his M79,

Marty cried out for help.
"Corpsman! Corpsman!"

CHAPTER 18

Berkheiser

EARLIER THAT MORNING, when 3rd Platoon set out on the sweep, 2nd Platoon, commanded by 2nd Winfield Spear, moved out on their own sweep in a northwesterly direction, left of 3rd Platoon. 1st Platoon, commanded by 2nd Lieutenant Steve Berkheiser, swept in a southeasterly direction to the right of Third Platoon. By the time they heard the gunfire, Berkheiser's First Platoon was more than a kilometer away from the ambush. Lt. Berkheiser stopped immediately and had his men set up a defensive perimeter while he tried to find out what was happening.

He looked over to Private James Hellyer, his radio operator, who was nearby but never at his side. Since a radio operator, side by side with someone who carried only a .45, would present an ideal target for a sniper; the two never traveled too close to one another. Berkheiser called out to Hellyer as he approached.

"We're still on the company Tac, right?"

"Yes, sir," Hellyer said.

"Any traffic?"

"Nothing yet. No traffic."

Hellyer took a knee with the handset ready, and then, 2nd Lieutenant Chuck Templin, whose Third Platoon had just been ambushed, came on the line.

"Steve," he said, "You've got to come quick! I've got a lot of casualties, and we're running out of ammunition. They could come right out and bayonet us."

"Fuck," Steve said to himself. Though his eyes appeared to be shifting rapidly across the landscape where the sound of the gunfire still came, there was nothing to be seen out there but distance to cross. His presence, rather, was flipping rapidly through the files of his mind. *2nd Platoon is closer*, he thought. *Chuck's probably still got sight of them. Shit, he knows we're further away. He wants the whole company on line.*

In short time, Steve formed the platoon into two columns, about twenty Marines in each—a "column of twos," he calls it. It was the best way he knew how to get his entire platoon "hauling ass" while still keeping it administratively easy to control in case they started taking their own fire, which is precisely what happened as they neared the ambushed Third Platoon.

Steve sketches a map showing where his platoon approached southeast of the trees and the ville that Cavazos' squad had swept through. Cavazos still laid out there beyond that tree line, wounded and in desperate need of a Corpsman. Hittson still lay pinned to the ground in front of him. The bodies of the Marines from the rest of the squad were still out there, too. Marines from the rest of the platoon had been trying to get to them, but their attempts were unsuccessful—fire from the trees and the ville across the paddy was too heavy. Shipp, Gallo, and Gomez were still pinned behind a paddy berm. Neither Steve nor any Marines in his platoon could see this as they'd been derailed by the rounds now firing at them from the southeastern side of the trees.

"As soon as the first rounds came toward us," Steve tells me, "we got out of the column of twos and went on with fire team rushes. You see, a squad has three fire teams, just like a platoon has three squads. Generally, it's a triangular type of thing—three companies, three platoons, three squads, three fire teams. 1st and 2nd squads got online. The third squad was my reserve if something else came over."

Four Marines in a fire team from Steve's First Squad moved while the other two fire teams provided suppressive fires. Once the moving team parked, they and one other team fired while the next advanced.

"There was no particular sequence to it," Steve says. "They just moved as they could by terrain and firing. With each rush, you don't try to go very far—you don't want anyone to be a standing target for very long."

Steve watched and commanded from the 3rd Squad, which he held back with him in reserve as his 1st and 2nd squads rushed forward. In this way, his platoon finally made it up into the trees, through them, and to the southeastern edge of the paddies where they could see the tree line and the ville on the other side from which the enemy fire now came also toward them.

"That's when Corporal McMahon and Corporal Turn, my first and second squad leaders, got killed," he says. "They got killed, and Doc Sovey went out to try and get..."

Steve pauses to clear his throat and looks down at his hands, clasped together tightly in his lap. He speaks softly now, almost in a whisper.

"Well," he says. "I still sent him to his death."

Now, his hands are running up and down his pants along the top of his legs. He presses his back into the lounge chair in his basement, where we talk.

"I said, 'Doc, you got to go see if Turn is alive,' because I couldn't tell if he was moving or playing dead or whatever. But, I said, 'We've got to try and get to Turn.' And so, he goes out. Sovey goes to get to Turn, and he gets shot through the helmet twice. He was crawling out. I mean, he wasn't standing up; he was..."

His eyes are now lost across time, and I finish the sentence for him after a couple of seconds.

"Crawling out."

"Yes," he says. "He was crawling out there when he got shot right through the top of the helmet twice."

Clearly, the NVA had at least one sniper hidden somewhere undercover on the other side—a superior marksman who must have been glassing the lines through a high-powered scope. Evidence suggests that sniper fire was almost as deadly that day as all the enemy's other weapons combined.

"It seemed like there were five to six machine guns they were shooting out of that village, plus that gas-check 50," Steve says. He raises his eyebrows and makes a big circle with the fingers on one hand.

"That thing shot big rounds," he says. "It had white tracers that looked like golf balls flying through the air. This wasn't a small group of two or three guys that I was going to say, 'Well, okay, I'm going to lay down suppressive fire, and I'm just going to move around and get up and flank them and take them out.' The amount of fire was just too great."

With surviving Marines from the rest of Third Platoon directly to his left, along with Spear's platoon, somewhere further west, Steve realized that his men were now on the right flank of the entire company, so he had his Third Squad form a line to cover the flank. Then, Steve learned by radio that Spear's Second Platoon had been held back in reserve by order of the company commander, Lt. Aldous. Though Spear had been able to shuttle some ammunition forward to the ambushed platoon, he had otherwise been told to keep his men held back where they stood in the trees. With so many in Third Platoon killed and wounded, Steve knew that much of the fight was now in his hands and that, as belt-tight as the combat was, he had to get artillery or air support on the scene.

Once he got Marines covering the right flank, he then moved himself to the front to assess the situation and figure out how he might safely direct the artillery and close air support, if it were even possible to use them.

"We tried to get some 81 fire on the enemy, but it just wasn't very effective," he says. "It just wasn't effectively shutting them down at all. I never saw one mortar round short, so my guess was they were firing too long. They were firing back behind the village, not landing on the target. I was glad to hear 81s going, but they were not having any effect."

With artillery, maybe he could overshoot the enemy's position on purpose and then walk the fire back, stopping short of his own men. Still, as it turns out, no artillery battery was available within range. He was left with no option but to call for close air support. He would have to wait for the air to clear, however. A Huey gunship had already been called and was flying low over the valley toward them.

Steve's men yelled back and forth across the open paddy to Shipp, Gallo, and Gomez. Reports were filtering back to Steve that, in addition to the three pinned against the berm in front of the enemy village, other Marines were also still out there alive. Over all that yelling, amidst gunfire and over lots of radio chatter, something of a plan was organically falling into place.

The Huey gunship would rain fire on the village from above and behind. Amidst that cover, a medevac chopper would be set down near the cane field to save Marines. As soon as both choppers were up and out of range, four-deuce (4.2 inch) mortars would hammer the enemy village, followed by a volley of smoke rounds just west of the paddies. The smoke might help direct the jets, and if the easterly breeze was forgiving, it might also give Marines in the paddy just enough concealment to make a run back to the lines while others recovered bodies. Failing that, the jets were to make two passes before dropping their payloads on the enemy—one for assessment, the second as a decoy, and then a third to drop their payloads. If, on the third pass, the NVA were not already fleeing, they'd at least be taking cover. This would be the second window of opportunity for Marines in the paddy to get back to the lines.

But, of course, things don't always go as planned, and in war, I'm told, they hardly ever do. The Huey gunship was now flying low toward the kill zone and overhead of the 2nd Platoon Marines standing by in reserve.

CHAPTER 19

Friendly Fire

AMONG THE MARINES waiting in reserve was Ray (Machine Gun) Kelley, a nineteen-year-old gunner who, by his own admission, felt indestructible and was "full of piss and vinegar." Hearing all the gunfire up ahead and not being able to do anything about it was driving him mad.

"I was standing with the machine gun on my shoulder," he says. "Had one of the bipod legs down. All of a sudden, there were three explosions. One to my left, one to my right, and one behind me."

I wonder if it might have been the 4-deuce (4.2" mortars) that Ken says were shooting off from the Battalion CP. Were they coming in short?

"I thought they were hitting us with mortars, and I didn't even bother to get down," Ray tells me. "I said, boy, these guys are good. I glanced off to my right and saw what I would later learn was a rocket round—bounced off a well and hit Sgt. Brackins in the jaw. Ripped his whole jaw off. The whole bottom jaw. And just at that time, I looked up, and there was a Huey overhead. I put two and two together—our own Huey had opened up on us. He thought that we were the gooks."

Ray put the twenty-three-pound gun against his shoulder and waited for the chopper to circle back around—dead set on taking the bird out of the sky if it shot at the platoon again.[1] Luckily, Lieutenant Spear was already on the radio calling off the gunship.

---

[1] Ray admitted that, in retrospect, this was youthful arrogance and false bravado on his part. "The real heroes were those out there in that ambush," he said.

CHAPTER 20

DePope

JACK ("DOC") DEPOPE, the Corpsman who tended to Sergeant Brackins, thinks it was a large piece of shrapnel from the rocket's explosion that severed Brackins' jaw.

"I was probably twenty feet from him," DePope says. "It just wasn't my day to get a piece of shrapnel because it was all over the place. One of the rockets either shorted out or misfired, but it came into our lines and just blew hell out of the place."

What was left of Sergeant Brackins' bottom jaw was hanging from the skin on one side of his face. His bottom teeth were completely gone, and the bloody dark pit of his throat was fully exposed under the shadow of his top jaw. Blood streamed from the wound and quickly stained the entire front side of the sergeant's uniform. As the sergeant leaned forward to keep the blood from pouring down his own throat, it painted even his trousers all the way down to the knees.

"There was blood all over the place," DePope says. "Just...God almighty. And I couldn't...you couldn't put a bandage on too tight, or he couldn't breathe, but you had to stop the bleeding somehow. So I did the best I could, but he just kept bleeding and bleeding and bleeding."

DePope leaned the sergeant back while wrapping a bandage around his throat, but Brackins coughed with a wet, gurgling moan and forced himself forward. The sergeant's eyes were both wide with horror and dizzy from delirium.

"You couldn't roll him on his back," DePope continues, "you had to lay him on his stomach because if you rolled him on his back, he couldn't breathe. His jaw was just hanging from his skin, and that scared the mess out of me. We put him on a helicopter, and I didn't think he'd make it. I thought…pfft…he's gone. But from what I understand, he's still alive somewhere. He made it."

DePope tells me that veterans sometimes remind him of the times that he patched them or their buddies up for some given wound in some given battle. Still, all these years later, he remembers mostly just nameless young faces—a flipbook montage of fading photos, each blood stained and, perhaps on purpose, a little out of focus.

"But he's the only one I remember distinctly," he says of Sergeant Brackins. "That's the one thing that sticks in my mind and probably will until I die. There were a lot of guys that we put on the helicopter that day who we thought were gone."

* * *

Dr. Teal, a Lieutenant then, recorded the following memory in his diary. It could not be confirmed whether it was Sergeant Brackins or some other Marine that he remembers.

A crying marine,

We could only tell he was crying by his tears……..
because he had no mouth.

He was trying to cry out his anguish....

My corpsman tried to soothe him...........we couldn't tell what he was trying to say!

Because he had no mouth..........

"You're going to be alright! We are going to take care of you! You are safe now!"

*We couldn't put him to sleep........
he would have drowned from the bleeding.....*

I had to put a tracheostomy tube in his airway, so he could live. I gently told him that the tube would temporarily prevent him from making any sound, but that I could now finally give him morphine for his pain...

*We never could understand the words
he had tried to form.....*

CHAPTER 21

Wounded in Action

JESSE HITTSON AND MARTIN CAVAZOS still lay pinned in the rice paddy. Jim Shipp, Bob Gallo, and Jose Gomez were also still pinned behind the berm about thirty yards away from them.

The battle intensified and spread to the right flank, where Steve's 1st Platoon had moved up to reinforce them. It was becoming increasingly apparent that Delta Company had engaged with an agile and well-coordinated NVA unit of formidable size. The Battalion's mortars and the Huey gunship had suppressed the enemy fire, but only for moments at a time. None of this was yet giving Jesse the cover he needed to get back to Martin and then over to the berm with Shipp, Gallo, and Gomez. As soon as the Battalion's mortar fire had ceased, gunfire erupted again from the ville. Likewise, as soon as the gunship peeled away from a strafing run, the enemy gunfire would return within seconds.

In those brief lulls between the action, Jesse could still hear Martin calling out behind him.

"Corpsman! I need a Corpsman!"

Jesse looked back toward Martin, then turned his head and shifted his body around to the right, toward the berm, where he could hear Shipp, Gallo, and Gomez calling back. His movement drew too much attention, though, and he suddenly felt a round slam into the heel of his boot. Another round jerked at his waist with a loud metallic thunk, and his canteen went spinning into the air and across the dirt.

"I finally seen the machine gun—seen the grass moving," Jesse says. "So, I opened up on that grassy spot and evidently shot somebody off of it because it quit firing."

In the lull of the fire, Jesse rolled over, ejected the magazine that he'd just emptied, and snapped another into the rifle.

"When I rolled back over, somebody got on that machine gun, and they was right in front of me, and they ripped my ass then," he says.

He lifts his shirt and shows me a scar on his solar plexus. A bullet went underneath him where his body had been lying flat on the ground. It skinned his chest and then punched a hole just below and between his two breasts. Just after the gut-ripping shock of that punch in the chest, he felt an explosive force on his right forearm, followed by a wave of sensations as his brain assimilated what the stunned nerves in his arm were trying to tell it. His own eyes helped put the pieces together. It was as if he'd been bitten by a great white shark. The muscle of his forearm had been completely torn away and had been thrown back out of place—a large mass of raw meat above a bloody bone that glistened pink in the sunlight.

Jesse grabbed the mass of meat with his left hand and flipped it back on the hinge of the skin from which it hung. He watched it slide away again as he reached back to retrieve a bandage from his first aid kit. He used everything he had in the kit attending to his forearm, but the work was sloppy at best. The final job looked as if some amateur, freaked out and jacked on adrenaline, had hastily and loosely wrapped the arm with only one hand, twisted the bandage carelessly so that parts of it were wound up like rope and wasted, then tucked the very end under the rest, where it would just slip right back out and loosen the entire wrapping until it all just hung half open under the weight of the blood-soaked rag and muscle. The final job looked like precisely what it was—a red-hot sticky mess and a worthless waste of bandage.

Hittson lifted the front of his chest up off the ground and placed his left hand in the gap. He turned his head down and looked at the palm of his hand to see fresh, warm gushes of blood pumping out with each beat of his heart. He pushed his fingers up against his chest, felt them slip inside the sticky open hole, then covered it with his palm and fell back against the ground, pinning his hand there.

The thought occurred to him to just chance it, to get up and run, but since the NVA were no longer shooting at him, he would instead just keep still and, at least for the moment, play dead. He closed his eyes and listened to the ongoing firefight—the chopper overhead, grenades from Gomez's M79, Gallo and Shipp on the machine gun, the NVA screaming foreign words and firing back, and Marty calling out for a Corpsman, though less and less occasionally, until somewhere around two in the afternoon, Marty wasn't calling out anymore.

Jesse felt lightheaded and dizzy. A sudden chill came over him—as if a cloud had suddenly covered the sun over Vietnam and the monsoon rains might soon come pouring down. I imagine that's what the explosions and the gunfire might've sounded like as his consciousness began to fade—like thunder over the distant hills at Khe Sanh, like raindrops on a poncho fading off into one blissfully quiet hour before the morning watch. Like peace and quiet, and finally, sleep.

Though chaos raged around him, Jesse's body was now as still as those of the other Marines who lay dead where they fell. All had gone dark for him. All had gone silent. He was no longer playing dead but actually dying. He fell completely unconscious.

CHAPTER 22

Hittson Enlists

THE VAST PLAINS of Levelland, Texas, stretched endlessly under the summer sun of 1966. Oil rigs hummed and clanked like big steel see-saws in the fields. Dry cotton plants rustled in the winds of the Southern Plains. Heavy old vehicles kicked up dust clouds as they barreled down dirt roads that ran through a patchwork of farmlands. Some were driven by the town's soon-to-be high school graduates. With windows and convertible tops down, they played country and western music on AM/FM radios—steel guitars, fiddles, and tin-can voices from far-away places. Voices like those of Merle Haggard, Johnny Cash, Loretta Lynn, Dottie West, and Kittie Wells.

Among those to graduate was Jesse Hittson, but he had no vehicle of his own and was not, for the moment, out celebrating with friends from his class. His lack of transportation was, in fact, a topic of the heated argument he had with his father. I can imagine him sitting across from the old man at a worn-out kitchen table, Jesse's rebellious spirit flaring up as the weight of expectations hung heavy in the room.

"What are you gonna do now?" was something like what his old man said. "You gonna sit around all day, every day, all summer? High school's almost over, boy. It's time you step up now—get a good job and whatnot."

"Aint got no ride," Jesse would say. "What am I s'posed to do out here, middle of nowhere?"

"You know, that bullshit," Jesse says to me, his voice echoing the rawness of that memory, the casual defiance of youth. We sit in a quiet budget hotel conference room, just the two of us, not far from where he grew up. My iPhone is on the table between us, recording his story and the soft hum of an air conditioner.

Like Jesse, I was born and raised a Texan, so I have no trouble understanding the heavy redneck in his speech and manner—his rich use of distinctly southern expressions and his heavy twang and drawl.

By "that bullshit," he means no disrespect for his father. I take it to mean that he is simply referring to tough love—the kind that is common amongst cowboys and ultimately why they sing "a country boy can survive." But he also refers to a sort of cold steel discipline brought by his father from the Marine Corps.

Though his father's service was brief and came at the tail end of World War II, the discipline, the ethos—it shaped him, and by extension, his son. Jesse's father never saw the horrors of war, but he was, first and foremost, a Marine. And that identity was instilled in Jesse from the moment he could walk—a fighter, a survivor, a man with grit running through his veins.

"You think you're better than me?" Jesse said, his youthful bravado on full display. "Any goddamn thing you did, I can do just as good!"

The old man's eyes held a mix of amusement and disdain. "You? Join the Marine Corps? You'll never be half the man it takes."

"Awe, bullshit," Jesse said. "I'll go over there and get with the best of 'em. It don't make a damn to me."

"Well, alright," the old man said. "What will it take to get you in the Marine Corps?"

It surprises me to hear that Jesse's father challenged him to enlist. By that time, President Johnson had ordered an increase in the number of U.S. troops in South Vietnam, so there was a very real probability that Jesse would be sent into combat. But I had not yet learned about the spirit of the Marines ("esprit de corps" as they call it) or what it really means to a Marine to be one—especially in the time that it was and with Marines being among the grand American heroes of the Second World War. Now, however, having met several of them, it makes sense that nothing might make one prouder than for his son to become a fighting Marine, much less a Marine at all. Besides, if anything could beat some sense into that cocky-ass boy, Jesse's father knew it would be the Corps. He knew they'd tear him down to nothing and then remake him into something new.

"You give me a new motorcycle down payment…I'll go," Jesse said.

And so it was that just two weeks before his high school graduation, Jesse's father signed enlistment papers for his underage son. The next day, he put a down payment on the boy's dream machine—a Honda 305 Superhawk. Then, for at least a few precious weeks, Jesse thundered free on two wheels across the desolate roads just south of the Texas panhandle.

CHAPTER 23

Hittson Makes a Run

MORTAR ROUNDS EXPLODED about 50 meters in front of where Jesse lay in the paddy—close enough to send shockwaves into the ground beneath him and loud enough to buck him back into consciousness. He felt small pellets of dirt and debris pelting over him and then the heat of the noon sunlight cooking the side of his face. His lungs gasped in a reflexive attempt to pull oxygen from the air, and then, as the blinding light of day dimmed in his eyes, he found himself looking at the blood-soaked bandage on his forearm.

His ribs, he felt, were being wrenched apart from the center. He lifted his torso and saw again that blood was pumping from his wound into the palm of his left hand. Realizing again that he'd been shot in the chest, a surge of adrenaline shot through him. His heart raced, and the flow of blood from the wound increased. A large patch of the ground around him had been muddied dark by the blood. He wondered how much he had lost and how long he'd been unconscious.

In a panic, he scraped a wad of the mud into his fingers and stuffed it into the bullet hole to stop the bleeding. He'd used his only bandage to hold the muscle of his forearm onto the bone, and it was soaked sloppy with blood. He didn't want to be seen moving for fear of being shot again, so with his left hand concealed under his torso, he scraped up another wad of mud and pushed it in the hole. This time, he pressed hard with three fingers to pack the mud as tight as possible.

Jesse cried out in desperation—a wordless outburst against his impossible odds. His time was running out, and he knew it. He took a deep breath to yell again, this time for the Marines behind the paddy dike—Shipp, Gallo, and Gomez. His lungs filled with the burn of white phosphorus, and his mouth with the bitter-sour taste of it. He was suddenly engulfed in a cloud of smoke and then drifting quickly again out of consciousness.

* * *

Recruits living west of the Mississippi were sent to San Diego, California, and those living east of the river were sent to Parris Island in South Carolina. All who went to San Diego were called "Hollywood Marines."

"Being from Texas, like your dad," Jesse tells me, "I was a Hollywood Marine."

He flew out of Amarillo on July 5th, 1966, with a piece of paper directing him to take charge of two other recruits and to dial a telephone number when they arrived. As the two other recruits stood by, Jesse made the phone call.

One of them, Thurmon, had already been in college and then dropped out. He had long hair and a casually cool demeanor. Jesse wondered why they hadn't put the college boy in charge instead of himself. Jesse guessed he must have been at least twenty-one—a bona fide man.

The phone answered, and before Jesse could finish his fumble of an introduction, the voice on the other end gave him a shockingly warm welcome. Warm like a bed of coals, that is—a bed of burning embers that some charlatan guru had fooled him into stepping across. Thurmon and the other kid watched with amusement as Jesse's eyes widened to the barking on the other end of the line.

"Alright," Jesse said. "Uh huh… OK…yup…yes…yes, sir. Yes, sir!"

"Hey, you little mother fucker," the voice concluded, "you better be outside and on the goddamned corner standing at attention! Don't be chewing gum, don't be smoking, don't be scratching your ass or picking your nose! Stand at attention!"

Click.

Jessie hung up the pay phone and turned to Thurmon and the other kid.

Did I just really hear all that?

When he saw how they looked at him with timid smiles, he forced a cool smile and shook his head.

"I think we're fuuuuuucked up," he said, drawing out the F word to emphasize the extent of their fucked-uppedness. They were about to learn that he had not drawn the word out quite nearly long enough.

The boys mulled around a bench by the curb until a green Dodge pickup truck with a fiberglass shell on the bed pulled up.

"Well, I guess this is our ride," Jesse said.

Out jumped a surprisingly small man.

"This old some-bitch, barely five feet tall," Jesse tells me. "Hollering and screaming and shaking his head as if the last place he'd wanted to be was there with us shit-fucks."

He threw their bags in the back, then the boys, and slammed the door on the truck bed. As they pulled away from the airport, Jesse leaned forward to look at the top of the palm trees lining the road. They were taller than any tree in North-West Texas—even the oldest mesquite he'd ever seen. Already, he was feeling far from home.

"You know," Thurmon said, shaking his head. "If they ain't no bigger than that in the Marine Corps, I'll just whoop his ass when we get stopped."

Jesse smiled.

"That little man is like a damn chihuahua," Thermon said, puppeteering with his hand as he yapped like a little dog. Then he thrust his right leg out, splayed his fingers, and stopped the barking.

"I'll just step on that some-bitch," he laughed.

Jesse and the other recruit laughed with him as the Dodge headed out toward the Marine Corps Recruit Depot, where, in the darkness of night, they were soon to be greeted by bigger breeds of men—Dobermans and Wolves.

***

"Hittson!" a voice cried. "Hittson, we're coming out to get you, OK?"

It was Jim Shipp, fading in from the paddy berm as Jesse returned again to consciousness.

Jesse considered running back to the lines. When he looked back in that direction, he saw a Marine in the paddy who'd been searching for bodies, which were now revealed in the thinning smoke. Concealment was quickly drifting away. He heard Shipp's voice again.

"Hittson, get ready. We're coming out now, alright? We're almost out of ammo—"

"No!" Jesse said, "The hell you will!"

He couldn't bear the thought of seeing anyone get killed trying to rescue him. As far as he felt, and as far as he knew, he was probably dead already. He'd already lost so much blood that he wasn't sure he could even stand, much less make the run to the dike.

"Stay there," he yelled. "Just stay there! I'm coming to you!"

He had no control of his wounded arm whatsoever.

"It just felt like somebody dropped a sledgehammer on it," he tells me.

Jesse pushed himself off the ground with his good arm, leaving his rifle, and then stumbled into a dizzied run towards the paddy dike.

"Every time I took a step, my stomach hurt," he says.

That agonizing pain, he would later learn, was from the bullet that had pierced through his solar plexus. When the round entered his body, it didn't just pierce the tissue but rather exploded through it and probably went into a ripping spin that left a wake of destruction much larger than the bullet itself. It had tumbled all the way through his gut before stopping somewhere near one side of his lower back.

He dove over to the other side when he reached the paddy dike. Shipp reached out, stopped Hittson's roll, and helped drag him closer to the earthen wall. Jesse let out an audible sigh of relief. There was, at last, a brief moment of hope, but then he saw the distance yet between them and the lines. He turned his bloody left hand away from his chest, exposing the wound, and then lifted his eyes up toward Shipp's, searching for some sense of assurance, but in Jimmie's eyes, he saw only panic and dread.

CHAPTER 24

Bird on Fire

UP UNTIL ABOUT 5:00 PM, it had been "just a typical day" for PFC Steve Bozeman, the door gunner on a UH-34 stationed out of the Marble Mountain Air Facility where the Marine Corps based squadrons of Hueys, 34s, and CH-46s. On that day, Steve's crew had been assigned strictly for medevacs. They'd completed three or four pickups since sunrise, so when the late afternoon call came in for an emergency medevac, Steve figured it might just be the crew's last extraction for the day. Picking up wounded and dead Marines, even getting shot at, after all, was common work for the crew. They left the hootch where they'd been standing, boarded swiftly, and cranked up the helicopter as usual—Captain Arthur Picone in the pilot seat, First Lieutenant Larry Anderson co-piloting, and then a crew chief and a Corpsman in the cabin with Steve. None of them were aware that it would be the last flight the old bird would ever take. For Steve, in particular, it was to be the most memorable and visceral experience in his tour of duty.

The chopper took flight unusually low above the sand and surf along the South China Sea. It passed through the large granite outcrop from which the place took its name—five exotic spires of bedrock rising up from the sand as large as mountains, each weathered by time and now covered with lush green vegetation.

"It was a nice little beautiful place," Steve tells me. "Had beaches out there. Had Marble Mountain over in the far corner, they call it."

Steve refers to the most famous of the mountains, with a marble staircase of 160 steps leading up to an ancient pagoda several centuries old. The mountains are home to several Buddhist and Hindu caves, which may have contained a hospital for the Viet Cong within earshot of the airfield. In his book Brothers In Arms, author William Broyles Jr. described the enemy as having been so "certain of our ignorance [...] that he had hidden his hospital in plain sight."

"And the odd thing about this was," Steve says, "the extraction site was just two or three miles south of Marble Mountain. As we were approaching the zone, I could hear all kinds of activity in my radio headset. Jets were flying here and there before we went in. You know, F-4s."

Since the requesting unit, call sign "Circumference I-2," was in close contact with enemy forces, they were provided with a flight of F-4s for support. However, as Captain Picone described in his after-action statement, "friendly positions were too close to those of the enemy to risk an actual fixed-wing bombing run."

"At my request," Captain Picone stated for the record, "the VMO-2 Huey gunship chase, piloted by Major C. G. REDMON and Major R. C. FINN, co-pilot, instructed the F-4s to make low passes, simulating firing runs prior and during my approach."

I remembered when Jesse Hittson told me about the moments before his final sprint from the paddy dike, where he'd ended up alongside Shipp, Gallo, and Gomez. Marines from Steve Berkheiser's platoon had been yelling out what they were learning from the radio—that the F-4s were first going to make fly-bys and strafing runs.

"They would strafe and make two rounds or whatever," Jesse says. "Then on the third payload, that's the snake eyes—everything, they were going to drop all of it."

Snake eyes on three!

"The situation on the ground at this time was somewhat vague, due no doubt to the closeness of the enemy contact," Captain Picone recalled. "We were able to ascertain that the enemy pressure was coming from the north and west, and with this information, plus the local terrain features, I chose to make a high-speed spiral from the south. Just prior to commencing an approach, I instructed the ground unit to lay down a maximum base of fire, which they did."

"They've got orange or different kinds of smoke coming up," Steve says. "We're going down, and I'm seeing the smoke, and I'm hearing the gunfire. You can hear it before we even get on the ground. We landed in the zone, and I didn't get any fire on my side, but I heard—the Marines were shooting on the perimeter, back and forth. Shooting something out there. I immediately go start helping the Corpsman and the Crew Chief bringing in the wounded."

Captain Picone's statement continues.

> *"While we were in the landing zone, we received a good bit of automatic and semi-automatic weapons fire. The ground unit continued to return this fire while the two medevacs were being loaded. My gunners were unable to fire at this time due to the efforts involved in getting the two WIA's aboard, and the fact that their guns were masked by friendly troops."*

"They brought in this one," Steve says. "He was on a stretcher—big black Marine. We loaded him up and got him on the floor below where I sat. And then the walking Marine, he came up walking in by himself. He'd gotten shot in the leg. So, he walked up in there and sat on the canvas seat next to the Crew Chief."

When Steve got back to his gun position and sat down, he could see the Marine sitting across from him, gritting his teeth and pressing out the pain in his upper thigh above the brutal bullet wound. Perhaps that Marine knew better than to oblige himself a moan or even a groan when the one in the stretcher on the deck was in such worse a condition. Steve turned to his side and looked down at him and the Corpsman, who was already working on him.

"He'd gotten shot in the chest," Steve says. "Had a sucking chest wound. So, all that's going on, and you just… within a split second … you're processing that. Then I get back and I'm looking out my side where I'm expecting anybody to start shooting at me, but I don't see anything where I can shoot back, so I just hold my trigger back."

Immediately, they started lifting off and moving forward while Steve watched on the ground. As they lifted, he could hear all kinds of automatic weapon fire and the impact of bullets piercing the shell of the chopper on his Crew Chief's side. Though Steve could see no targets on his side, his Crew Chief, Lance Corporal Moore, apparently had the enemy on his side because he was just blowing away—the whole time shooting his machine gun during the lift-off.

Since they were already taking on a good bit of fire, and since he was not aware of friendly positions in the immediate area that he could safely spiral up over, Captain Picone elected to make a high-speed, low-level departure using as many evasive maneuvers as possible. The crew braced themselves as their bird angled in the air.

"Approximately 2000 meters from the pickup zone, I heard more automatic weapons fire and at least one explosion," Picone recalled.

Steve felt the explosion above them. Again, Lance Corporal Moore returned fire.

"They struck the upper part of the chopper where the transmission fluid is, where the transmission is," Steve says. "And the transmission was catching on fire—the fluid. Whatever penetrating bullets they had, they punctured the cast iron or the aluminum transmission, and it was leaking fluid, and that caught on fire."

When Steve saw flames dripping down around them into the helicopter's belly, he reported to the crew through the microphone on his flight helmet.

"We're hit!" he said. "We're on fire!"

"My first impression was that we had been hit by a rifle grenade or 57-millimeter type weapon," Picone's statement says. "The aircraft reacted very smoothly and I experienced no loss of power. However, upon applying aft cyclic in an effort to reduce speed and land, I realized that I had lost my primary servo."

"So I look down, and I'm seeing fire dripping down right behind me on the stretcher patient," Steve says. "I turned around to move him out of the way, and then I heard on my headset that we were going to do a hard crash landing. I'm going, 'Shit!'" All that probably happened within a few seconds. The helicopter didn't lose control in terms of hydraulic power. So, he had some control of it as he approached this rice paddy."

"I thought for years until I got Captain Picone's after-action report, I thought we got shot down pretty close to where the Delta Marines were, right there, but then based on what he said, it was almost like 2000 meters away. I'm thinking, OK, we're crashing into enemy territory here. I knew they were everywhere."

Steve unmounted his M60 machine gun, took up a belt of ammunition, and moved towards the door, preparing himself to fight as soon as they touched the ground so long as he would still be physically able. He had no idea how they would crash; he just knew they were going to crash.

"The heat and smoke from the fire was very noticeable," Picone's statement says. "The aircraft, however, continued to remain controllable and I was able to land with about 5 knots of ground speed. Once we touched down, I applied breaks, and Lieutenant Anderson applied full rotor brake."

The aircraft swerved about 90° to the right and began shaking violently. Captain Picone secured the engine by cutting the mixture.

"I could now see flames to my right," he recalled, "but was unwilling to leave until I was fairly certain the rotors were stopping, and there was a minimum danger to the crew or myself being struck by the blades."

"As soon as the wheels hit the ground," Steve says, "I was ejected or jumped out. I'm not sure what happened, but I went out the helicopter door with my machine gun, holding it very tightly, and then rolled like a dice. And it was a soft landing, as far as I could tell. I wasn't cut up or banged up or bleeding anywhere. So then I had my M60 machine gun. The Crew Chief did not get his machine gun. He left his in the helicopter, I learned later. But he got out."

Steve ran about twenty yards to the end of the rice paddy and took cover on his knees with his machine gun ready at his side. He expected the enemy to start shooting or to storm out after them at any moment. He looked back and saw the helicopter still in the landing position. All three wheels were there, but it was now burning with red hot flames licking through a billowing cloud of black smoke—large drops of liquid flames still falling from the top into the bottom. Up in the cockpit, Captain Picone released his lap belt and dove out the right window. The Marine whose leg had been wounded hobbled away from the chopper with the Corpsman. A long plume of smoke rose high in the air—a signal, Steve knew, that betrayed the landing site.

"I looked back toward where I thought the enemy was," Steve says.

Raw adrenaline had sharpened his senses and slowed down time.

"I was expecting just...a whole bunch of shit gon' hit the fan at that moment, but it was all within...probably seconds."

When Steve turned back around toward the helicopter, he saw the hand of the other wounded Marine sticking out of the door. *He was still in there.*

"I still today don't know why, or how, or what, but I immediately just...I left my machine gun right there—jumped up, and ran back to the helicopter to get him out. He was still in there on the stretcher.

He was still conscious when he came on board, but now his eyes were rolling, so I knew he was hurting bad. Thank God, I ran back over there to him. I've thought about it many times. Had I been too scared and hadn't gone over there…it would have been terrible."

When Steve arrived at the chopper, the radiant heat felt like it was searing his face. Flames were licking out the top of the door. He leaned down away from the fire and reached his hand up into the belly, thinking that he would grab the stretcher and heave it out and away with the Marine still on it.

"I'm yanking and yanking as hard as I can," he says. "I'm pulling. And, like I say, he's a big-ass Marine. Black Marine. And then he actually says, I can hear him saying it, he says, "Leave me! Leave me! It hurts too much!' Whatever I was doing, yanking on him—he was hurting. I'm not sure what kind of morphine he had or what, but I was trying to yank him out, and it wasn't working. So, fortunately, my Crew Chief came over about the time I was—I don't know if I was ready to give up or what, but… I'll crawl up in there and find out what in the hell was hanging up on his damned stretcher."

Steve and the Crew Chief reached up further into the belly of the chopper, and that's when Steve saw the Marine was strapped into the stretcher. They released the strap, and then both grabbed him and yanked him as hard as they could out the door and onto the ground. By then, Captain Picone had recovered from his dive out of the window, though he'd lost his chest protector and survival radio.

"This man had received a chest wound and was semi-conscious and completely unable to move," he recalled. "Lieutenant Anderson, I believe, also arrived on that side of the aircraft at this time, and between the five of us were able to carry him clear."

Steve grabbed the Marine's right arm, the Crew Chief grabbed his left arm, others grabbed his feet, and they rushed about 30 yards away from the fire and machine gun ammunition, which had started to cook off.

Their Huey chase helicopter landed and jettisoned his rocket rods. They carried the wounded Marine to the Huey and loaded him aboard. The other wounded Marine was able to get aboard with no assistance.

Steve watched in relief as the chopper carried the two wounded Marines back to Marble Mountain for medical aid. As the Huey banked overhead and broke the plume of smoke from the burning UH-34, he began to feel searing pain from third and second-degree burns over his hands and along his arms.

"I had my helmet on, thank God," he says, "or probably my hair would have caught on fire."

As luck would have it, they had landed just outside the wire perimeter of a Marine CAP outpost near Marble Mountain.[1] The occupants had set up defensive positions inside their wire when they saw the chopper going down and now had sent a squad out to fetch the crew.

"The crew and I were led into the outpost and took cover behind a bunker," Picone recalled. "I then made my way to the radio shack and attempted contact with the helicopter that was now orbiting overhead but could raise no one."

"I don't know why or how they did it, but someone handed me a soft carton of white milk, and it was cold," Steve says. "I was thirsty by that time. You know, I was bone-dry. I was scared shitless, and my mouth was dry, so I immediately sucked that milk down. Then I looked around and said, 'Anybody got any water anywhere?' So, I was thirsty."

The crew stayed there in the cover of the bunker, a sandbagged trench, for about half an hour when another helicopter came.

Captain Picone closed his official statement there.

"By this time," his written statement said, "a UH-34 from HMM-361 piloted by Captain Gregg L Gammack had landed inside the

---

[1] CAP, or Combined Action Platoon, was a squad of Marines combined with two squads of some local popular force (or local militia).

outpost. We climbed aboard and were returned to Marble Mountain."

In trade for that cold carton of white milk, Steve left those Marines at the CAP outpost with an M60 machine gun that he figured they probably needed more than him, and back at Marble Mountain, he was taken to the hospital to be treated for his wounds.

"OK," the doc told him, making short work of it. "You're good enough to go now."

It was late in the afternoon. The sun was falling into the mountains to the west. Choppers were still coming into the strip—returning home from their storied adventures in a wild country. The smell of salt water slipped in on the first cool breeze of the evening, and with a bit of pride welling up on pools in his eyes, Steve thought about the black Marine whose name he never knew and hoped with every ounce of his heart that he would live.

CHAPTER 25

Gomez

BACK UP FRONT, where Jim Shipp was still behind cover with Gallo, Gomez, and now Jesse Hittson, the enemy's machine guns threw bursts of dirt along the top of the paddy dike.

Over the hours, Jim could tell that Martin Cavazos' pleas for a Corpsman were growing weaker, but with the intensity of enemy fire, there had been no way to get to him. At one point, Martin even called out for Jim by name, and all Jim could do was send back an assurance that they were still there and trying.

"Just hang on, Marty! I can't get you, buddy; you've got to hang on!"

But that had been at least an hour or two before, and there had been no word from Martin since.

"It was awful," Jim says. "I couldn't do anything. There was just nothing—no way I could get out there and that...I'll take that to my grave."

Jim admits that being unable to get to Martin was his darkest moment.

"Marty was out in the open field where no one could get to him, and he later died." Jim wrote in the letter to his mom and dad, but he did not mention how close the two had been.

"I knew Marty better than most," he tells me. "He's the only one I went through boot camp with that was over there with me. And he was such a good guy, such a good man."

Though almost out of ammo, Cpl. Gallo kept fighting back—moving his position along the dike between short bursts of fire from the machine gun.

"He would shoot and move, shoot and move," Jim says. "I was doing the same, you know—so the gooks wouldn't know where we were going to come up next and start shooting again."

Jim shakes his head.

"Gallo with that machine gun—that was one of their main targets. They wanted to get him. Definitely wanted to get him. He fired a lot, trying to give those guys some concealment that were out there, you know—firing where their machine guns were, trying to stop them. And so, he fired at them until, basically, he was out of ammo. He should have gotten a medal, a Silver Star, or something. I mean, here they were, zeroed in on him, and he kept firing back, moving and firing. And I mean, we got a lot of fire coming back at us."

Between the volleys of fire, Gomez stood up and exposed himself just long enough to take aim with the M79 and lob a grenade. As soon as it exploded, he stood again and fired his M16. Jim Shipp watched him from below, his body pressed against the paddy dike.

"Gomez," he yelled. "Don't do that! You have to move! Shoot and move! Don't come up in the same place!"

Gomez stood and fired again—a quick switch back to the M79. Jim was astounded by his bravery but unsure that he had heard him. Gomez was pissed off and frenzied, taking careful aim to make each shot count, but at what? Jim had only a split second to find a clear target before they saw him above the dike, and in that short time, he could never find one. As soon as he ducked, the enemy fire thumped against the dike above his head again.

When Jim yelled at Gomez for popping up in the same spot, Jess Hittson watched to see if Gomez would change position, but he did not.

"Third fuckin' time he did it," Jesse tells me, "he caught one right in the chest. They were just waiting for him to pop up, and as soon as he popped up, they got him."

Gomez spun around as he hit the ground, but he was still alive. He'd been shot in the right side of his chest, away from the heart.

"After a while, lying there wounded, he got delirious," Jess tells me. "He really wanted to get up, and Gallo and everyone were just trying to keep him down, but then he got up and started running for our lines out of the clear blue sky—never said a word. It was 102 degrees, extreme heat."

The lines seemed so far away. To make that gamble, Gomez must've known that he was slipping away from the world already and that he had only the choice to at least try or surely die there in the dirt against the dike—his mother and father receiving only an obscure message on a yellow telegram before his body made it home.

Jesse watched as he made the long dash back toward the lines. Gomez still wore his flak jacket with grenades hanging on the front, but a skilled sniper had plenty of time to set his aim. Gomez had little more than twenty meters left to run when the shot rang out, and his lifeless body crumpled forward onto the ground.

Jose's parents, Juana and Teodoro, may never have learned more about what happened than what was typed in a single sentence on a government form.

> *"Died 4May67 vicinity Quang Tin Republic of Vietnam result gunshot wound to the chest from hostile rifle fire while on operation."*

CHAPTER 26

Rocket Man

TOM JALBERT AND HIS fire team had taken cover in a depression back on the left flank at the edge of the village before the paddy field. They'd been "trading pot shots with the gooks" since the fighting broke out but were having trouble locating them.

"We weren't dealing with a bunch of little VC farmers, you know," Tom says. "These were NVA. They were regulars; they knew what they were doing and had prepared the battlefield. It was an excellent place to set up because we went at it all day, and I probably didn't see but half-a-dozen gooks—that's how well-camouflaged and concealed they were."

Usually the point man for the platoon, Tom was supposed to have been first across the paddy field that morning. If he hadn't followed his gut, it would have been him instead of Dennis Mannion who sprung the trap. Before crossing, he had called the Platoon Commander, Charles "Chuck" Templin, up to the front.

"To get to that village, we've got to go across these paddies," he warned Templin. "That's not too kosher if the gooks are set up over there, you know?"

"Well, the Captain's in a hurry, so we've got to get over there," Templin said.

Jalbert had scratched at the stiff stubble under his chin and shaken his head.

"There's nobody around here," he'd told the Lieutenant. "Do you see any people around here? I mean, there are cooking fires in their houses, and there's no livestock or chickens around here. I'm telling you, they moved out. They knew we were coming, so they moved out of here. We're crazy going across these open rice paddies, you know? How about I take my fire team and a machine gun around here to the left? If we take the left and the gooks are out there, I'll have them flanked in case they do open up."

"Yeah, alright," Templin told him, "whatever."

"He was pretty indifferent about it," Tom says. "He was in a real hurry, you know?"

And so Tom had been leading his fire team far out on the left flank when the fire opened up on Martin Cavazos' team, who'd replaced Tom's. When the shooting first began, Tom and his fire team immediately started rushing forward to flank the gooks as he had planned but were stopped short by the squad leader, a Corporal from Alabama named Branch.

"'Jalbert!' he's yelling. He had a really big mouth. 'Jalbert, get over here!' There's gooks out there, and Branch is calling me back to his line, you know? He's yelling so vociferously that I told the guys, 'Let's get back there and see what the hell going on.' Of course, I was pissed off."

"Why the hell didn't you get right back here?" Branch had barked at him. "We're going to get ready to assault that village."

"We're getting ready to assault it? You've already got guys within 25 feet of it dead!"

So, that's where Tom had been positioned with his fire team when he finally spotted a muzzle flash from one of the machine gun nests at the base of a grass hooch on the other side.

Alan Burleson, a 3.5" rocket man attached from the Weapons Platoon, was called forward. He moved up alongside Tom Jalbert in the trench.

"Where they at?" he said, keeping his head down until Tom identified a hooch with a small square window cut out from the side of its grass wall.

"That one there?" Alan confirmed, pointing across the way.

"Yeah," Tom said. "See if you can put a round right through that thing."

"We had guys still out in the middle of the paddy that were wounded, you know," Jalbert says. Like all the Marines fighting from behind the paddy field, his focus was on those stuck out there in front of them, in the open.

"We had a lot of wounded and dead out in front," my father confirms, "but we couldn't get to them."

"Some were wounded and others dead, but you really didn't know," Steve Berkheiser says. Whether responsive or not, any of them could've still been alive. Or, like Jesse Hittson admitted that he'd done himself, "Any of them could have been playing dead," Steve says. "You just couldn't be sure."

Tom Jalbert and his squad were sure, however, that Lance Corporal Mel Allen, a black Marine from Chicago, was alive. Allen wasn't in the open paddy fields when the fire broke out, but during the ordeal, he had bravely maneuvered his way out alone to save Marines, not once, but four times before getting wounded himself. He'd been attempting to retrieve Don Hollingsworth when he took a bullet to the chest near one shoulder.

"Don was a goofy kid," another Marine, Gary Culp, tells me, "but Mel Allen took a liking to him—always called him 'Hammerin' Hank Hollingsworth' like he was some kind of prizefighter or something."

"Hammerin' Hank was what they called Hank Aaron," Ray Kelley tells me. "You know, the famous baseball player—Major League."

Hank Aaron, like Mel Allen, was also black, but Don was a white kid from Texas. The "goofy kid" might've been into baseball, but Mel was more likely the real baseball fan and called Don "Hammerin' Hank" because it also paired well with Hollingsworth. It had a ring to it, rolled off the tongue, and was a fun little way to lighten the monotony of a moment. I can imagine such moments.

"Hammerin' Hank," Mel says out of the blue, putting deliberate play into the words. "Hammerin' Hank Hollingsworth." It's an easy way to coax a smile from the young Texan, and when he sees it on the boy's face, one side of his own mouth raises to smile back—one eye glinting, almost in a wink—it's that "little smile" Ray Kelley tells me that Mel always had on his face.

The smooth alliteration reminds Mel of his two daughters back home, and he also says their names aloud.

"Sonia and Sheree. That's my baby girls," he says. Then he speaks their names aloud again slowly, but this time to himself, bobbing his head as if to the rhythm of a song—as if each word alone is a poem entirely.

"Sonia and Sheree."

Hollingsworth envies the faith and hope Mel conjures, like a magic spell, by just uttering words—how those words appeared to summon sense for the man out of thin air. It seems to do something like it does for the folks back home in Texas, back home in the delta-Nile of the Bible belt, just after they say, at the end of a prayer, "In Jesus' name, amen."

Hollingsworth tries it for himself.

"Tricia," he says. "That's my baby girl."

"What? You?" Mel says, surprised. "Hammerin' Hank? Hell, no! You got a baby girl?"

"Well, she ain't no baby," he says. "She's my dog."

Mel laughs.

"Hey, I love her, just the same."

Mel shakes his head from side to side.

"Hammerin' Hank," he says. "What'd you say, Trixie?"

"Tricia."

Mel chuckles.

"She's a good dog," says Hollingsworth.

And then Mel was lying on his back, up against Hammerin' Hank's dead body, with Jalbert yelling out for him to just "hang tight" while they try to take out the machine gun.

Alan took cover behind the remains of an old concrete building not far from the trench—a weathered remnant of the French occupation. He called his loader, Perry Gosset, who came up beside him and loaded him up as he peered around the edge of the wall.

"I would jump out into the opening and try to fire, but my rocket launcher kept misfiring," he tells me. "The wires would corrode because of the humidity, and you would have to clean them. I tried this a couple times and I think about the third time I jumped out, he shot at me with an RPG."

The rocket-propelled grenade spewed out of the launcher with a puff of white smoke and headed straight toward him, moving across the distance with such incredible speed that Alan thought it might catch him before he even had time to dive behind the wall. He heard the RPG spewing past him as he hit the deck aside Gosset, there behind the concrete. Realizing they'd been missed, he looked up at the small space between the building and a tree where the RPG had slipped through. If it had hit the tree, which was set back just slightly from the building, the blast could have killed him and Gosset both.

He got back on his feet, stepped out, and fired his rocket.

"Your old man was pretty good with that 3.5," Tom tells me. "He put it right through the window of that hooch and it went out through the back. I think it set the back of this hooch on fire."

"Shoot at the base," Jalbert yelled to him. "You've got to hit where it meets the ground—set the whole thing on fire!"

"The adrenalin was flowing with the bullets," Alan says, "so I pulled the rocket and tried another shot. This one worked. I put it right where the RPG came from. Don't know what the outcome was, but we didn't get any more fire from there."

With the hooch now ablaze, Jalbert and his men urged Mel to run for it.

"Allen," they yelled. "We'll lay down a base of fire, and you can run back!"

Mel nodded, Jalbert's squad opened up, and then Mel started sprinting back toward them.

"He made it all the way to our trench when they hit him right in the neck," Jalbert says. "He was right out in front of our position—within reach almost, you know."

Jalbert claims that Mel had gotten so close to his trench that he felt a spatter of Mel's blood when the sniper's bullet hit his neck.

"The Corpsman, as a matter of fact, came over there," Jalbert says. "And he was going to go out in front of my position right there, just four or five feet away, and tend to him. I said, 'Get back in here!'"

Tom was convinced that Mel Allen had just been killed.

"What are you going to do with him? His head!" he said to the Corpsman. "His head is just about completely off! And so he got pissed off at me and called me a coward and stuff. I said, 'Have it your way and do what you want to do.'"

The Corpsman chanced another look at Mel and knew that Jalbert was probably right. He never went out for him.

"I felt guilty about that all my life," Jalbert says. "If he didn't run back to our line, he might still be alive, you know? But, I've felt guilty about that because I was one of those who were hollering for him to run back."

CHAPTER 27

Close Air Support

UP FRONT, ACROSS the paddy, the NVA's machine gun fire continued to punch along the top of the paddy dike. Bob Gallo and Jim Shipp had little ammo left with which to fight, so they kept their heads down and studied the distance back to the lines. Gomez's body was still out there, reminding them both that even if they could provide enough suppressing fire to escape the nearby machine gun, a skilled sniper would have a good chance at one of them, at least.

Jim looked down at Jesse Hittson, who, gripping at the pain in his abdomen, now lay curled up in a fetal position, frightfully still. Hittson's face was pallid, and his lips were cold blue. He was dying, and Shipp could do nothing about it. Jim looked at Bob Gallo and noticed that Gallo had been watching him watch Hittson. Gallo's eyes shifted between them and then to the M60, which he turned sideways in his hand. There was no bend in the small piece of the ammo belt on the side of the gun—less than a dozen rounds remaining. Jim could see that Gallo was calculating the value of that last meager burst and how to use it. Gallo turned and pressed his back against the paddy dike—the burden of the gun dropping in his hand.

Gallo stared skyward with his helmet pushed against the dirt, his mouth open. His chest heaved as he worked to catch his breath but suddenly froze. His head turned quickly, tracing something across the sky. Jim followed his gaze. An F-4 Phantom jet had just crossed overhead, so low and fast that it was barely noticeable, and now it was arcing upward and turning to make another pass. It had come in low, almost treetop level, and Jim had not even seen it before the screaming roar of the jet's engines washed over him. Behind it came a second Phantom. As soon as the roar of its engines passed overhead, there was silence, save the glorious rumble of the two jets' turbines hissing and torching in wide circles around them in the distance. The enemy guns went quiet for the first time since the ambush broke out that morning.

"On three!"

Jim heard Marines yelling out at them from across the paddies. Back at the lines, a Marine threw three fingers into the air.

"Snake eyes on three!" he yelled.

Jim was still processing the moment—the way that Gallo had sighed and dropped his head in relief, bouncing it on his chest—yes, yes, yes! And then he'd looked at Jim, not with a smile, but with relief, with hope—a look that said, *get ready...the tables turn now*.

"On three!"

The first jet came around again and opened up with a 20mm Gatlin cannon. An echoing rip crossed the sky—the sound of countless rounds, each two inches long, snapping supersonic cracks through the air and then drumming into the dirt so stunningly close that it was more felt than heard—a buzzing in the skull like a hand sander on the helmet. Then, only now reaching Jim's ears, followed the sound of the Gatlin gun itself—its barrels rotating so fast, it trumpeting like a low and loud horn. The second Phantom came in after the first, and another horn-like warning signal echoed across the valley.

And then again—silence, save the distant engines torching across the sky, circling back around.

On three. The sheer power of the jets had been so overwhelming they'd pulled even the sense of Jim's self out of his chest for the moment, but now it was coming back to him. He, back to himself. *Snake eyes on three. That's bombs.* "Snake and nape," as they say. *That's bombs and then napalm. That's bombs!*

"Hittson!" he said. "Listen, get ready! Next time that jet comes in here, I'm going to throw you over my shoulder, alright? I'm going to get you back over there. Put your arm around my neck. I'll carry you. I'll get you back!"

Jesse pushed himself up with his one good arm and shook his head.

"Oh, shit, no!" he said. "The hell you will! Two targets are easier hit than one there, my friend. You wanna go back to the line? You go your way, and I'll go mine!"

And then, somehow, by the time Shipp had even heard all the living will exploding out from Hittson's mouth, the near-dead kid from Texas was on his feet and stumbling into a sprint back toward the lines.

"Even before that jet came in there," Jim says, "he just jumps up and starts running. And I still don't...to this day...I don't know how he ran that far, but he ran back at least...I would guess back to where that hole was, at least 50 yards. At least that far, maybe further."

That "hole" that Jim refers to was a deep bomb crater along the edge of the lines that Hittson dove into, only then to find himself nearly drowning under five to six feet of water. The rice paddies had been dry, but along the coast, before you reached the clay soil around the foothills of the mountains, the ground was still sandy, and the water table was high. Jesse emerged from his splash into that bomb crater, coughing up a lung full of dirty, warm water and gasping for air. Then he went under again, the weight of his flak jacket and grenades pulling him down before he finally got his one good hand clawed into the sandy, wet side of the hole and his head above the muck.

A Corpsman leaned through a gap in the upper blast wall and pulled Hittson over. The two rolled over one another on the other side, and then nerve signals from Hittson's arm began to hit him again—a pain so pure and raw, it came pushing between clenched teeth until his mouth broke like a levy and let loose a screaming flow of curse words.

"It was his first firefight," Jesse recalls about the Corpsman. "He had an ampule of morphine and stuck it in my arm—forgot to break the god-danged needle off!"

Ampules of morphine come with a serrated tip that is designed to leave a sharp needle when the serrated edge is snapped off.

"Well, he forgot to do that," Jesse tells me. "Be like, just jammin' that some-bitch in your arm. Yeah, and this was like eight hours after the fact or nine hours after I'd been shot. I said, 'Don't do that again, Doc.'"

"And I thought he couldn't even move," Jim Shipp continues to tell me. He shakes his head at the memory of watching Hittson cross the yards—of watching gunfire spit dirt up around his feet just before he disappeared into the crater. "I thought he was hurt that bad, and he jumped up. Adrenaline, or whatever, got him back there. I didn't even have a chance. He just got up and ran. And then, long story short, I never saw Jesse again after. I didn't know whether he lived or died. I didn't know that. And I didn't know that for thirty years. I heard that he made it, but I was never sure until, thirty years later, he called me."

Back in the flat area behind the tree line, where the second platoon had been held back in reserve, Ray Kelley watched 250-pound bombs drop from one of the jets. The bombs dropped before the jet had even crossed over and sped toward him like spiraling footballs.

"Dumb bombs," Ray calls them. "because, at the time, they didn't have laser guidance systems. When he dropped the bombs, they were so close, I could hear the four fins coming out and 'click, click, click,' they lock in to slow the bomb down, cause drag, and guide it over to the enemy positions."

"Started killin' the shit out of them gooks," Jesse tells me. "Literally. That's what got 'em off our ass. That's the only thing that got 'em off our ass. 'Cause them's bad to the bone."

To the bone, literally. Marines could feel shockwaves from the bombs pass, not just over, but through them—as if the sheer volume of each blast transferred energy through the atoms of their flesh. They watched as five-hundred-pound aluminum canisters of napalm tumbled, end over end, through the air—perceived them in slow motion with brains fueled on adrenaline-super-sense. You can watch them much the same way today on YouTube. They were filmed with high-speed cameras, tumbling end over end as they fell toward the treetops. Though Ken Hicks was not there to see it that day, he tells me that it's how it looks in real life.

"Every time I saw close air support," he says, "it was like watching everything in slow motion. I don't know why, but it was like my brain just processed everything in slow motion."

When the napalm canisters burst open, their contents of gelled fuel continued traveling with the force of perpetual motion. The fuel lit up in white-hot and yellow flames that crawled hundreds of yards across the valley floor. From white-hot and yellow to orange-red, the fire churned and billowed in clouds that eventually went black as they rolled up hundreds of feet from the ground. An agony of screaming, Alan Burleson claims he heard it, from NVA soldiers who'd been too wounded to run, too late getting away, or unable to find the now bomb-blasted entrances into the safety of their tunnels underground. And then a rumbling, crackling roar of everything biological ablaze—of everything recoiling into black coal and then swirling in ash along a long, wide swath of hell-on-earth. In that place, above ground, at least, no singular inch was free.

The Marines may have felt elation in their hearts, finally some sweet crescendo of vengeance, but dolly-shot along the lines, you see few smiles, if any. You see those flames of hell glistening in streams of sweat that crawl and bend paths around specs of debris on young faces. You see the light fading into darkness on eyes wide and glazed with horrified wonder. This is the scene of boyhood vanquished—of new men born in blood and fire—rising up now on weary feet and trembling knees and none yet knowing how long this moment would reverberate, how deep the cost would be, even for them—those still living. This is it then—the blood-red stripe, ever flowing down the outside seams on dress blues—a day to remember through all the years of the rest of their lives, and with more like it yet to come—unforgettable.

CHAPTER 28

Pure Adrenaline

THE CLOSE AIR SUPPORT had given Gallo and Shipp the opportunity they needed to get back to the lines. No living Marines remained stuck out in the rice paddies. The enemy's aggressiveness had been significantly reduced but not entirely subdued.

"I started taking fire when I went out for a Marine," Alan Burleson says. "I tried to get him on my shoulder but couldn't because he was stiff. So, I started to drag him back—back to a landing zone with some more bodies. There were also some wounded Marines who were shot there. And that's when the chopper got hit in front of the hedgerow. And that's when I went out between two hedge rows to get to the chopper."

The Marines had not expected anything to survive the onslaught of the air support, but they were not yet aware of the elaborate and well-prepared tunnel system under the enemy ground. And we may never know how many NVA could have just been arriving in support of their ambush. A full regiment of NVA was thought to be out there, after all, in the valley and in the foothills south of Da Nang. Like my father, Alan, several Marines had started out to fetch their dead when the NVA suddenly returned to the fight.

Alan had just gotten one Marine, stiff with rigor mortis, to the LZ when an approaching UH-34 medevac was suddenly pierced in the engine behind its bulbous nose from machine gun fire.

The chopper turned oddly in the air and drifted clumsily away from the Marines below it around the LZ. A river of black smoke from burning engine oil followed the chopper out and down. Alan traced the dissipating smoke with his eyes. His feet moved slowly toward the wounded bird, pulled like a magnet, faster and faster, until his mind finally caught up to the mission his sprinting legs had already committed to. *We're doing this. Between the hedgerows— out in the open. If those guys are alive, we're getting them back.*

By the time he reached the chopper, the pilot and co-pilot had just slipped themselves out of the side windows above the nose, still billowing with black smoke. They backed themselves up against the front tires with pistols drawn. Alan pointed back in the direction from which he'd just run.

"Our lines are back that way," he said. "Run that way!"

"Our crew chief's still inside," one of them said. "he's hurt bad."

"I'll get him," Alan said. "I'll get him! Now, go! Haul your ass!"

"The gunner in the chopper was still sitting in the chair and strapped in—shot in the leg," Alan tells me. "I threw him over my shoulder. He was screaming in pain."

On the way back to the lines, Alan made a leap down a four-foot drop-off, landed without stumbling, and then kept running—all the weight of the door gunner still on his shoulders and firm within his grip. By then, he was jacked on adrenaline.

He set the gunner down at the LZ, where a Corpsman took over, then went straight back out to retrieve the machine gun from the chopper. Once he'd gotten that back to the lines, he went out a third time to check for more weapons and ammo and contemplated destroying the chopper.

"I was going to set it on fire," he says. "But on that third time, rounds started hitting the chopper, so I hauled ass."

When he got back to the lines, this time, he found his way into the cover of a deep depression carved out of the ground under the cover of a hooch. There, he caught his breath, and when the tunnel vision from his adrenaline-fueled frenzy finally began to widen and subside, he noticed something cowering in the shadow of the far corner of the dugout— a mama-san with a young boy clenched tight in her arms.

He flinched quite dramatically—sort of the way anyone might if a three-inch spider appeared—crawling suddenly over one's right shoulder. Steadying himself in the opposite corner, he noticed a piece of paper trembling in the mama-san's hands and, not knowing what else to do, stepped forward and grabbed it.

"Let me see those papers," he said.

He then proceeded to pretend to read them.

"Mmm hmmmm," he mumbled. With his heart still pounding in his chest, he moved his head up and down to show that he was inspecting the ID card, though if he could've actually read it, such an animated display would not have been necessary.

"Yep," he said. "Looks good."

He handed the ID card back to the mama-san.

"It's alright, kid," he said to the boy, who was also terrified. He fluffed the boy's thick black hair in his hand to let him know he wouldn't hurt him.

Alan crawled out of the hole, stepped out of the hooch, and strolled back to the group—a long, slow sigh.

CHAPTER 29

Ponchos

AFTER THE CLOSE AIR SUPPORT came in, the heavy fighting dwindled into a standoff where both sides continued to take potshots at one another until nightfall.

On the radio, Captain Ed Aldous commanded Steve Berkheiser to pull back in an orderly fashion before Steve could retrieve the dead from his 1st Platoon.

"Hey, I've still got bodies here," he told the Captain. "I know of three bodies right now that are still out here, and we haven't recovered them."

Still, Aldous demanded his return.

"I had to leave, and I was pissed about that," Steve tells me. "I was horribly pissed. I felt like I was letting them down. We don't leave bodies out on the battlefield. Not unless you're just physically unable—radiation hazard or whatever."

Elwood ("Doc") Sovey, Corporal Frederick McMahon, Henry Turn, and several others were to be retrieved later that evening or at the break of the next day.

"I couldn't tell myself 100 percent, 'Well, I know for sure that there was nobody left alive on this battlefield when I walked away from it.'" Steve says. "I couldn't say that to myself, which bothered me."

Corporal Gutierrez, Steve's Third Squad leader, got everyone rounded up and ready and then signaled to Steve with a thumbs-up. Gutierrez saw then, no doubt, how visibly distraught his Platoon Commander was.

I remember Steve recalling the moment Doc Sovey got shot through the helmet. Sovey had been crawling out, as Steve had ordered, to check on McMahon. Steve spoke hesitantly about that moment. I got the sense that it was something he never fully reconciled and made peace with. It is probably naïve to think one could ever make peace with such things.

"Well," Steve had said to me after a quiet swallow, almost in a whisper. "I sent him to his death, is what."

It was Steve who'd put his primary focus on getting the close air support, and ultimately, it was the close air support that ended the fight. All of that, though—all of the frantic hours on the radio, all of the things he might have done "right" that day, for the rest of his life would only be wallpaper to the bodies of Sovey, Turn, and McMahon—everything just a foggy backdrop to the Marines killed. Those few good men, in those few minutes, would never fade from his memory, never get mixed or misplaced—certainly never erased.

He said it with a grimace on his face— "I sent him to his death, is what," —like he didn't want to go back there in his memory again, but that if there was anything he'd learned to accept in all the years, it was that there would never come a time when he could *not* go back there—never a time when he would stop remembering. Even the good in a very good day could often be stained by the old familiar feeling welling up despite every effort to hold it down—that feeling that a good day is something some Marines can never again know—that feeling that someone else deserves it more.

* * *

It is now December 2019, and we're standing on a glass bridge inside the National World War I Museum and Memorial in Kansas City, Steve and I. After a life-long career in the Marine Corps, the museum became his magnum opus, a creation he and his wife dedicated years to. They helped guide the architectural design, managed the unique building reconstruction, assisted in curating and restoring hundreds of artifacts, and helped procure nine thousand blood-red poppies. A common sight on the Western Front of World War I, each flower was carefully placed to represent its combatant deaths. There are nine thousand under the glass beneath our feet—a sea of red that he has brought me here to see.

A small child leans his forehead against the glass near my knees and says something awe-stricken by the sight of them all. His mother tells the child that each flower represents a soldier who fought in the war.

Steve is quiet. It does not matter to him, I can tell, that all the poppies down there represent the soldiers of another war. Doc Sovey is among them—as are Corporal McMahon and Henry Turn.

For the child, they are just flowers. For the child's mother, they are soldiers, nameless and distant in time. But for Steve, they are all Doc Soveys and Corporal Turns, Henry McMahons, and many others who came after. They are not just May 4th, 1967, but every May 4th since, and many more days in between—like the night before, when I waited for him to push the memory of Doc Sovey past a growing lump in his throat.

"A thousand," Steve says as we stroll off the bridge inside the museum. "Each poppy represents not one, but a thousand killed. It was not nine thousand combatants; it was nine million that died. It was supposed to be the war to end all wars."

God, how he wished it would have been.

* * *

"Me and Culp and three others went and got bodies that night," Tom Jalbert tells me. "The lieutenant passed the word down, so we went out and got those bodies, one at a time."

Among those venturing out into the darkness was Gallo. When the air support came, he left the gun so that he could retreat faster, but when he returned to the spot where he had left it, the gun was nowhere to be found. Good thing he had taken the firing mechanism, the trigger housing group, out of the gun so that it couldn't be fired if found by the enemy. He held the housing in one hand now, a .45 caliber handgun in the other.

"We went out for the first body first," Jalbert says. "All the way out. And we could hear the gooks talking."

They snuck out to the furthest point first and carried Dennis Mannion's body back to the body of Martin Cavazos, then Martin's body back to the next, and so forth. In this way, they shuttled each body back further to the next until they'd gotten the job half done. The air was still hot, the work was slow and exhausting, and, according to Jalbert, the bodies had decomposed rapidly in the sun all day.

"It took two guys to carry one body," Jalbert says. "One guy on the ankles and the other guy on the shoulders. That's how we carried them back. I was such a rookie at this stuff that when I went to pick up a body, I picked him up by the arms, and the skin pulled off his arm. And that just sickened me, you know? PTSD—that's a picture that comes back to you. And so, needless to say, I didn't do that again. I tried to just grab his sleeves or something and stand up, basically right up underneath his armpits, because he had the utility shirt on, you know? So we grab them up under the armpits and carry them that way. But, boy, they were heavy. They were heavier than normal, you know? And so, that's how we managed to carry them back toward our lines. But before we got back there, the gooks came out."

Tom believes the NVA patrol was a sapper unit that came out after them. "Jack-of-all-trades of the North Vietnamese Army," he calls them. "They started coming out when we got about halfway back with the bodies. You know, they were a good outfit. They were all dressed in black, and as far as I know, their only weapons were knives. I guess they wanted to see if they could get any more casualties because that was their thing, you know? They didn't care so much about killing you. They wanted to wound you so you could return to the rear or wherever and tell people what it was like."

One of the NVA sappers jumped over a two-foot paddy dike so close that he might've landed on Jalbert had he not been ready with a .45 caliber handgun. The Marines had decided to go out with only .45s and KA-BARs instead of their rifles so they could carry the bodies back more easily. Two men would carry a body, while the other stood guard with a .45, and then they would trade with each other—handing over the pistol to take the next body and vice-versa. Jalbert had just finished his turn carrying and now stood guard with the .45.

"Just while he was on top of the dike, the moon came out," he says of the sapper that surprised him. "It was a real dark night, cloudy, so you could see a little bit when the moon came out from behind the clouds. I saw him just like it was daytime, almost, and was able to get a round off. We killed 3 or 4 in that skirmish."

Even Marines back in the lines encountered trouble that night.

"We had a gook try to come up on us," Ray Kelley says. "He had on a pair of black swimming trunks—that's all he wore. He had a grenade up by his head, and he was going to throw it at us. One of the guys opened up on him and killed him. He let go of the grenade, and he basically blew his own head off. All the flesh and blood and what-not got all over us."

The next morning, the same gook's hand was seen propped up against a helmet on the ground. Someone seemed to find it amusing to prop two fingers of the man's severed hand up against the helmet to make a popular sign of the times.

Peace...mother fucker.

"Beak saw it the next day," Ray says of the helmet's owner, Dave

Brooks, who he claims the Marines called "Beak" because of his big nose.

"To this day, he thought I did it," Ray says. "I didn't do it."

* * *

The next day, Ken Hicks was finally able to get back to the company.

"I already knew what happened," he says. "Word had swept back through Battalion that Delta got hit hard, and I'd been sitting on my ass the whole time, unable to do anything about it."

It wasn't his choice to leave the company to transport the VC suspect, but still, he could not shake the feeling that he'd somehow let them down by not being present for the fight. Ken decided then and there that he wasn't going back to being a radioman for the XO. When he stepped off the first chopper flight to rejoin the company that next morning, he marched straight back to the company CP, but only for his pack. With his pack in hand and without asking for permission, he slipped out to rejoin 2nd Squad Machine Guns—the squad he'd been with in Khe Sanh.

"I wasn't going to miss the next firefight," he says. "The company CP was always set back in relative safety, and I didn't want to be with them the next time. I wouldn't be in the rear when they had the next firefight. Technically, they could've court-martialed me, but they didn't. They chewed me out, but they didn't court-martial me."

The whole company saddled up and then swept back through the area where the battle had occurred the day before. When Ken's gun team moved out with the platoon, they swept through the area where Berkeheiser's men had been shot.

"Berkheiser was out there, moving his platoon through open rice paddy," Ken says. "He was yelling at one of his squads—telling them to spread out. He had tears streaming down his face."

As an eighteen-year-old PFC, officers to Ken were like gods.

"When I saw him crying like that," he says. "it made him human.

It made a real impact on me."

When the Marines reached the charred wasteland where the NVA had been, they discovered the reason the NVA had been able to keep fighting, even after close air support had decimated the area. The NVA had, as Tom says, "prepared the battlefield," and with well-fortified bunkers and underground tunnels, they had apparently been preparing it for a very long time.

"They had a trench all the way across the damned village big enough you could drive a six-by in it," Tom says. "The napalm wasn't hurting them. That's the problem we mostly had with them. They had bunkers or tunnel complexes they could hide in when the planes came. They'd been building them damn tunnel systems since World War II—The Tunnels of Cù Chi, for example. I don't know if they still do it, but you used to be able to take a tour in Vietnam and go to The Tunnels of Cù Chi. I think it was like twenty dollars. You could buy a magazine of AK-47 rounds and fire it off, and you could take tours through the tunnel systems. They were pretty damn elaborate. I've seen diagrams of it, and it's multi-story. They had hospitals, classrooms, barracks, mess halls—they had it all in the ground."

Marines were finally able to retrieve all of the bodies that had been abandoned when the volunteer party got derailed the night before.

"We had all the boys in there by the command post, if you want to call it that," Jalbert says. "It was set up right behind our trench, and we got them all lined up there with ponchos over their bodies."

Since those bodies were tagged when they were retrieved, official records may specify that some of the Marines died on the 5th of May. Veterans who were present that day assure me, however, that it was on May 4th, 1967, that most of these Marines died in service of their country.

- Cpl Don W. Minton from Vidor, TX
- Cpl Frederick A. McMahon from Suffolk County, MA

1st Battalion, 3rd Marines load those killed on
Operation Beaver Cage—May 4, 1967.

Martin Cavazos (K.I.A. 67 May 4), Robert LeBarge,
Ron Marinucci, Bob Gallo, Dennis Mannion (K.I.A. 67 May 4)

Cpl Don Wayne Minton
K.I.A. 67 May 4

Cpl Frederick A. McMahon
K.I.A. 67 May 4

Cpl Henry L. Turn
K.I.A. 67 May 4

LCpl Jose M. Gomez
K.I.A. 67 May 4

LCpl Melvin L. Allen
K.I.A. 67 May 4

PFC David A. Hickman
K.I.A. 67 May 4

PFC Don Ray Hollingsworth
K.I.A. 67 May 4

PFC Harry L. Hissong
K.I.A. 67 May 4

PFC Frank X. Cuozzo
K.I.A. 67 May 10

HM3 Elwood C. "Doc" Sovey, Jr.
K.I.A. 67 May 4

UH-34 choppers return to the USS Okinawa at dusk
after Operation Beaver Cage.

- Cpl Henry L. Turn from Jacksonville, TX
- Cpl Martin Cavazos from Sebastian, TX
- LCpl Jose M. Gomez from Edinburg, TX
- LCpl Melvin L. Allen from Chicago, IL
- PFC David A Hickman from El Cajon, CA
- PFC Dennis J. Mannion from Lawrence, MA
- PFC Don R. Hollingsworth from Fort Worth, TX
- PFC Harry L. Hissong from Beecher City, IL
- PFC Frank X. Cuozzo, from Los Angeles, CA (*Cuozzo had just raised his rifle when he was shot between the eyes on May 4th. He died six days later on May 10th.*)
- HM3 Elwood C. "Doc" Sovey, Jr. from Rockwood, MI

CHAPTER 30

Ghosts

THE H&S COMPANY of the battalion was stationed about two miles away at LZ Cardinal, along with a 4.2" Mortar Battery and an Artillery Battery from the 12th Marines. They'd been told to displace about seven miles southwest to LZ Magpie and were loading a CH-53 heavy lift helicopter when they started receiving enemy mortar rounds.

"Helicopters landing are a dead giveaway," Ken tells me. With the amount of NVA in the valley, it was not unusual for them to show up as Marines were moving out of an LZ.

Gunnery Sergeant Gilbert Gesualdi was responsible for organizing the movement and quickly took charge—immediately organizing troops and directing their fire. Major Billy Thornbury was there and later wrote a statement about Gesualdi's actions into the night. He said that, even as they began to take small arms fire, Gesualdi continued to stand in the zone directing helicopters and supervising aircraft loading.

"Again, we began to receive 82mm Mortar fire," he wrote, "and Gunnery Sergeant Gesualdi continued in his work without regard to the danger involved."

Ken was back at Hill 65 with his old gun squad when he heard the distant rumble of Gesualdi's ordeal. The sound was not unlike that of a thunderstorm brewing over the far hills back at Khe Sanh, only now, there was no cacophony of crickets and frogs rising for the night as usual. In the strange silence of the twilight, the faraway explosions were now a little more like the percussive rhythms of a funeral procession or the beginning of an orchestral lament of sadness. Things were different now.

"The company was blooded," he says. "That's what they used to call it back in World War II when a unit had their first firefight and became veterans of combat—when they had killed people, lost people."

Two of Ken's close friends, Hissong and Hollingsworth, who had been with him on the ship to Vietnam and back up at Khe Sanh, were dead. Hissong had only been twenty-two years old—Hollingsworth, eighteen. Ken would turn nineteen in a little less than two months on the Fourth of July, but now one month seemed so far away, much less the seven he had remaining in his tour. He shuddered at the thought of it and busied himself with his rifle.

I'll turn nineteen here, he assured himself, considering for the second time that it might not be true. The first time had been back at boot camp when the Drill Instructor said, "Now the men," and then read off the names of those assigned to be infantry riflemen.

"Hicks, Kenneth," the Drill Instructor had announced, reading from his clipboard. "Oh-three-hundred—infantry."

Knowing then that they were all destined for Vietnam, Ken had felt a surge of nervous energy and the sudden presence of the heart beating in his chest. 16mm color films played back in his memory—Marines storming the beach at Tarawa, packed and pinned shoulder to shoulder on the beachfront, a field of helmets. Marines on stretchers, Marines dragged behind the cover of tanks, blood plasma administered from hand-held IVs, bloated bodies tilting in the tides. First to the front is what it meant, MOS 0311—the tip of the spear. He was going to be one of those guys.

And now he was.

It's just two months, he thought.

As part of the newly formed Special Landing Force, the company could now be conveniently inserted anywhere they were needed in the northernmost part of the war zone and Ken knew it. This area was home to the Viet Cong and was a prime location for the North Vietnamese Army due to the plentiful food supply from the Que Son Valley. Intelligence reports stated that at least two full regiments from the NVA's 2nd Division had infiltrated the area.

Just two months and I turn nineteen.

Ken did not know that a multi-battalion Marine assault and sweep had been engaged nearby to prevent an imminent attack on a Marine mountain outpost. In that operation, known as Operation Union, Marines engaged with the enemy, drove them out of the village complex of Binh Son, and forced them to withdraw to the North. Most of the grunts in Delta Company had not even known the name of their own operation, much less that another had been underway in the same area. No news of it had filtered down to them. None of them knew of a place called Binh Son and that it was not far from them to the south. But things were different now—Ken knew that. He could feel it, sense it—smell it, even.

"It had the smell of death in the air," the 2nd Platoon Commander, Winfield Spear, recalls of that day. "It was hot, humid, and smelled of death."

Word was passed for Ken to report to SSgt Orlando, the Weapons Platoon Sergeant back at the company CP, so Ken crawled out of his fighting hole and headed alone down the path.

"This is towards dusk, or evening nautical twilight," he says. "It's not dark, but it's not light. It's that in-between where the light is quickly fading. You can still see, but not as well as you think. Distances are hard to determine, and shadows form as the sun goes below the horizon. As I walk up, there's a rock outcropping to my right. I looked over, and on that rock outcropping were all the Marines who had been killed on the 4th."

Hollingsworth was standing there among them. Always a little thin and kind of frail, he was sure it was him standing right there next to Hissong. Martin Cavazos and Dennis Mannion were carrying on like nothing had ever happened. Gomez, Mel Allen, Doc Sovey—they were all up there together on the rock.

"It scared the shit out of me, and I shot up to the Company CP," he says.

By this time, I don't know Ken to be a religious man, so I wonder what he thinks of the experience now—whether he thinks it might have been a dream or some kind of vision—a hallucination, for example, induced by psychological factors like stress and lack of sleep.

"You were close enough that you thought you could identify them?" I ask.

"Yes, I could see who it was, and it scared the crap out of me, and I just took off up the hill."

"It scared you? You didn't think it's just somebody, could have been anybody, standing up there?"

"It wasn't somebody," he says. "I recognized who they were. I can close my eyes and still see them up there, laughing and joking."

He turned his head and hustled away from the outcropping up the hill to find Orlando. To detach himself from his position with the XO, Orlando chewed Ken out "from one end to the other" but then finally ordered him to get back to the platoon and the gun squad. He was no longer the XO's radioman and runner.

On the way back down the hill, Ken ran, never looking back at the rock outcropping again.

"It wasn't a dream or vision," he says. "I saw ghosts."

* * *

At 1935 (7:35 PM), back at LZ Cardinal, two miles further away, Gunnery Sergeant Gesualdi directed the last helicopter down as close to his remaining men as possible. Still receiving heavy fire from the North and the South, Gesualdi stood, a virtual target in the darkness, with two flashlights in his hands. His coolness and determination served as an example to the sixteen men who watched him wave the chopper down. Though under fire, this motivated them all to be brave and work quickly and professionally. The last helicopter was on the ground for only a minimum of time. Gesualdi had succeeded in getting everyone moved from Cardinal to Magpie, under fire, and without a single casualty. He was awarded the Bronze Star with a Combat "V" for that.

***

Back in his fighting hole, Ken listened to the sound of distant chopper blades thumping through the night—Gesualdi's, perhaps, or some other—UH1E Gunships, F-4 fighter jets, and the spooky three-second bursts of Puff's cannons. A stranger in a strange land, he couldn't help but reflect on the surreal reality of war-torn Vietnam, where even ghosts were real. Looking up at the stars, he began to feel alone, lost, and untethered from the world—as if floating away into the cold emptiness of space—into the vastness of it.

He sat up, steadied himself, and scanned the faces of the Marines of the gun squad that he was now again a part of. As he looked at them, each in their own contemplative silence, he felt a kind of love and camaraderie that somehow went deeper than anything he had ever felt with his biological family. It was them, he realized that moored him to the world—his brothers in arms. They were his home, family, and reason for living now. He knew that if he didn't make it to his nineteenth birthday, it would be because he had given everything he had to protect them, and he was fine with that.

Perhaps that's why Staff Sergeant Orlando allowed Ken to return to the gun squad instead of giving him a court-martial or sending him back to work for the XO. Orlando's ass-chewing had been necessary theatre, but the Sergeant knew he wanted Ken in his Weapons Platoon and back out in the front with the people he loved—with the family he'd found amid the war. Perhaps the Sergeant could see in the young man's eyes what Ken had come to be sure of in the day away from his blooded unit—that Ken had found the place where he truly belonged and would do anything to protect it.

CHAPTER 31

Wounds of the Heart

THAT EVENING, the USS Okinawa eased slowly through the South China Sea with choppers parked quietly on the deck, rotor blades folded back. A waning moon shone at less than half illumination through a thin veil of passing clouds, a soft glow cresting each gentle wave across the ocean's surface.

For Lieutenant Donald Teal, the Sr Medical Officer in charge of casualty care, the day had been a battle of another sort. A flood of wounded Marines had been shuttled from helicopters—some limping out on the support of a sailor's shoulder, others carried on stretchers and brought down by the port aircraft elevator platform to a large triage on the hangar deck. From the triage area, the most seriously injured were quickly brought up by hoist to a resuscitation area in the hospital above.

The day had been a frenzy of blood and bandages, shrapnel clinking into stainless steel bins, stitching, and swearing, conducting, calling, coordinating men and movements, gathering supplies, and rigging things. As wounded Marines were transported from the flight deck to the hangar deck, their sweat-stenched and field-worn utilities were searched for grenades, which were then tossed quickly overboard, with one of them even exploding in the water.

By the time the day's work had settled, Teal was exhausted. He stood out near the bridge in the sea-salted breeze and watched for the last casualties to arrive from the battlefield. It was now the dead that were left to come, and it was his job to receive them.

In the crackling voice on the bridge radio, they were called KIAs, Killed in Action, and it sickened him to hear it said that way—human beings reduced to a mere acronym, to a dispassionate string of letters that conveyed no real sense of the horror that had befallen them. To Teal, they were more than just letters on a page; they were more than just statistics to be tallied up and reported back to headquarters. He shook his head to himself—shook off the idea that he might ever feel different, even after a hundred more days like today.

The western mountains were cast in shadow, their rounded peaks outlined in silhouette against a magnificent array of colors. Where the sun began to dip below the horizon, the sky had turned a vibrant shade of orange that faded into soft pink and lavender hues. As the minutes passed on the windswept bridge and the dusk deepened, the colors became richer and more intense, with streaks of crimson and gold intermingling with the softer pastels. It was difficult to reconcile a God that would create such beauty and such ugliness just the same. Still, Teal thanked him for giving him the foresight to prepare as he had and for the USS Sanctuary hospital ship, which was adrift nearby, where the most critically wounded had been flown.

"Normally, the hospital ships operated independently of the Amphibious Ready Group (ARG)," Dr. Teal tells me. "But we had no surgical team when I got out there with the ARG and the Special Landing Force. I had maintained from the beginning that we were not giving our Marines the best care unless we had a surgical team and I took this concern to the SLF Commander, Colonel, and the

Commodore."

"You've got four doctors here," Colonel Conway had said firmly but respectfully. "Can't you elect one of them as a surgeon, one to give anesthesia, and another to do your...what'd you call it?"

"Orthopedics, sir. No. I mean, yes. I'm not saying no. I mean, I can do that way, but sir, it will cost more Marine lives. None of us are fully trained surgeons, and none of us are trained in anesthesia at all."

Where Teal had trained for his internship, there was a big county Hospital, but downtown, there was also a small emergency hospital. If somebody got shot or injured in a car wreck, they would often take them first to the emergency hospital, only to find the injuries so bad that they had to send them out again to the county hospital.

"Well, that wasted tons of time," he recounted to the Colonel and the Commodore. "In the meantime, we lost lives. People would bleed to death or lose their ability to breathe, and so on."

"Commodore McManus was a great leader to work with," Don tells me. "Partly because he looked at me and said, '"Dr. Teal, please tell me what I should do.'"

"Sir, the modern standard for casualty care is to have the casualties go to where the surgeons are, where the fully trained surgeons are," he said. "Ideally, we need the hospital ship with all the specialists on it. Since there's no chance we'll get a surgical team in time for our first combat operation, we need to have the hospital ship work with us and coordinate with us, not out floating 30 miles away like they are now, sir."

"Now that's against the Geneva Convention," Dr. Teal tells me. "The Commodore knew that. The Colonel and I knew it; we all knew it was against the Geneva Convention."

"Wait," I say. "What was against the Geneva Convention?"

I'd heard of the Geneva Convention—heard it mentioned in the movies anyway. It was some kind of treaty or protocol for treating soldiers humanely when they were no longer combatants, but I didn't understand what it could have to do with ships at sea.

"Hospital ships are not allowed," Don tells me. "They don't even carry cryptographic equipment. They're not allowed to communicate except on an open circuit. They're not allowed to have any secret communication with a combat force. I told the Commodore we needed to have an agreement that if somebody was really badly injured, the helicopter pilots and crewmen needed to take them directly to the hospital ship. If they came to the Okinawa first, just for us to have to wave them off to the hospital ship, that kind of delay would cost lives."

To exact such an order, in violation of the Geneva Convention, McManus knew that he would have to be the most senior ranking officer. Of course, as a very senior Navy captain, the Commodore was the ranking military officer of the fleet, and Colonel Conway was a senior Marine colonel. The trouble was that the hospital ship was driven by a senior Navy captain. Moreover, the doctor in charge of the hospital part of the ship was also a senior captain.

"The Commodore spent all afternoon getting his XO to go over all the dates of command," Don tells me. "Everybody, every officer in both commands, Navy and Marines, had a date of rank, and so seniority was dependent on the date of rank. Say, if the Commodore's date of rank was one day earlier than the commander of the hospital ship, then the Commodore outranked the commander of the hospital ship."

"You mean when their rank title matches, then you go next by the date of rank?" I ask. "In other words, if I've got commanding officers on two different ships, the one who outranks the other is the one who became a commanding officer first?"

"Right, and it turned out that our Commodore was senior to the captains in the hospital ship," he tells me. "So even though it was against the Geneva Convention, they had to obey his order. Guess who got to take the orders to the hospital ship?"

The Commodore gave Teal a satchel containing the orders to carry to the USS Sanctuary. Teal never read the orders, but he hoped the

Commodore had worded them so that he would actually succeed in getting the needed support. So, before Operation Beaver Cage had commenced, Teal flew over to the Sanctuary with the satchel in hand.

"I met the captain and the helmsman," he says, "and I met the commander of the hospital on the hospital ship. They were all smiles and cordial, you know? To them, I was just a nice young officer coming over there from the Okinawa. They didn't know yet what the orders said."

But then the captain opened the satchel that Teal had brought over. Teal watched the captain's face turning flush as he read—his mumbled dictation suddenly quieting and slowing to a stop. His hand dropped with the orders, and his head rose, with lips curled and one eye twitching on a nerve—a laser-piercing glare that split Teal from groin to head.

"You've never seen anybody literally almost explode in front of your eyes," he tells me.

The captain erupted in a madly censorious tirade, something about somebody's "goddamned bright idea" and "who in the hell" or "what the hell" and "the goddamned international law" and "MY goddamned career!"

As spittle flung from the captain's mouth, Teal centered his focus on the left common carotid artery, bulging from his neck, and in the transillumination of light, he saw even a streak of blue bending around the man's mandible—the kind of pressures that could trigger a brain aneurysm or a cardiac arrest. At least they were on a hospital ship.

"I thought the next thing was going to be, you know, 'Make him walk the plank' or something," Don says. "That was kind of famous. After that, the 'play nice' was done with. He had no choice, he knew he had no choice, and he knew he was breaking the Geneva Convention, but his senior officer had ordered him to do so."

Teal was happy to return to the LPH alive, feeling much better knowing they had the Sanctuary as their primary hospital and that he would only have to take the lesser injuries on the LPH. He had his chief work with the crew chiefs of the helos and with several sergeants in the battalion to explain where the critical injuries were to go.

Still, there was the problem of getting a trained surgical team to work with him on Okinawa, but at least for the time being, he'd done what needed to be done.

As the sun set that evening during Operation Beaver Cage, on the fifth of May, he wondered if they had saved lives. Just one would've been worth it—worth everything, in fact. He would've liked to call over on the radio to find out, but even if it wasn't on an open circuit, they weren't exactly "friends."

In the distance, against the shadow of the mountains, the choppers' green and red navigation lights finally appeared to bring in the dead. Teal made his way down from the bridge to ready himself for a second shift of work that he would soon come to call his "night job," performing the somber job normally known in the military as Graves Registration.

"The bodies never arrived in a body bag," he tells me. "They would arrive with a tarp thrown over them. Just thrown in the helicopter, you know? They didn't come in on stretchers. We had bearers that would take stretchers out to meet the helo, and they put the body on a stretcher there, but they still weren't in a body bag. So, we would go back down to the hangar deck and then forward into these three bathrooms."

Those killed in combat were always brought onboard separately, on the starboard elevator, on the opposite side of the ship. Teal and his crew of Navy corpsmen worked discretely and made every effort possible to ensure that no Marines, especially the wounded, could ever look over to the stretcher next to them and see a dead comrade.

The sun finally gave way to darkness as crewmen washed out the chopper bays and Navy sailors swept blood-stained water from the deck. The choppers' blades were folded back, then rolled aside for the night, leaving two empty spots where Thunder Eagles had been parked the night before. Pilots and crewmen of the SLF's HMM-

263, the Helicopter Marine Medium squadron, settled into their bunks where they lay, each too long awake, no doubt, still reeling from the day's events.

In the trauma bay, intravenous fluids were checked and refilled, pain meds were delivered, pulses were checked, and lights were dimmed. In the mess hall, sailors whispered in the night light while gazing pensively over cooling cups of coffee. There was often a certain friction and competitiveness between the squids and the Marines, but on this night, only quiet contemplation and respect.

From the large open bay on the hangar deck, one might have seen a trail of dancing light from the crescent moon pointing across the sea and shrinking away to a vanishing point, precisely wherever one looks. And more than one would be looking, I imagine, at that angel in the distance glowing pristine white in the moonlight with three large crosses painted on her side—the USS Sanctuary.

"To this day, the smell of wintergreen makes me ill," Teal says. "It is just one of many such awful memories."

Outside of the head on the hangar deck, before opening the door, Teal and his assistants soaked their masks in oil of wintergreen. The three forward bathrooms he'd referred to were makeshift morgues—this being the first, with two more soon to be required. After stacking bodies along the bulkhead of the first, they'd soon have to take over two more and connect the three with big fans because only the third head had a porthole to the outside air. None of this was known to him yet, however. All he knew at this point was that the morgue in Da Nang he'd been told about did not yet exist.

Before deploying to WESTPAC, Teal had asked the Senior Doctor in the Marine Amphibious Forces what protocol they were to follow for handling the bodies of those killed in the field of combat.

"The number of fatal casualties will be light," answered this Navy Captain, a medical officer. "Those that occur will be taken directly to the morgue in Da Nang, so you're not to be concerned."

But, when the Task Group arrived on the combat line, Teal learned otherwise.

So, Teal and his boys gathered white plastic sheets and body bags, pages of medical forms on clipboards, and ink pads for fingerprinting. In a somber procrastination of the job they had to do, they prepared these things, then donned their oil-soaked masks and nitrile gloves and stepped inside to do a job that was to take them all night to finish.

In a short personal memoir that Don shared with me, he wrote that he remembered how, before he entered "the morgue," he felt like he had to shrug off his soul as if it were a garment that he didn't want to be soiled by what he was about to see and do.

> *"I remembered carefully hanging up my soul on a hook outside the morgue, and then I would slowly enter night after night.*
>
> *Later, I would pick up my soul as I left the morgue and return to my duties. Faking it as if nothing had happened......*
>
> *Not wanting anyone reading my anguish in my face. I wanted to be solid as a rock, able to absorb any emotional trauma to protect my crew. Trying always to look and act normal—to carry on.*
>
> *I became that rock...*
>
> *But that rock had eyes. My eyes gave me away."*

The room was cold and cramped, illuminated only by the soft glow of weak fluorescent lights over stainless steel sinks with exposed P-traps and pipes running into the floors where the bodies lay.

"It would take all night to clean them up," he tells me.

They stripped off the uniforms and made sure there were no booby traps or live weapons, cleaned up the bodies, and then, as Don tells me, "did preparations that I won't go into."

Teal knelt down and placed a gentle hand on one Marine's shoulder as if to offer a final comfort to the lifeless form. With a careful touch, he lifted the Marine's arm, studied his wounds with a clinical detachment, and then marked them on the outline of a mannequin on the page. His attention then turned to the Marine's hand, which was soft and bloated with gas—darkened black from a day in the sun. He took it delicately in his own, holding it with the utmost care as he pressed each finger to the ink pad and then onto each of the thirty-three pages in his clipboard. It was a solemn ritual that Teal would have to perform all too often, but each time he did it, he would do so with reverence and respect for the life that had been lost.

"I was just seeing the most horrible things," he says. "I still have the side effects from running the morgue. Every single Marine that was killed in that nine months, I was the doctor who signed their death certificate. I was the one who examined the remains of their bodies before I signed the death certificate. For each death certificate, I had to sign 33 pages. I signed my name around over 3,000 times for the Marines that had been killed. That's a memory that I'm still seeing a counselor for."

This, of course, he did not yet know.

After gently wrapping each Marine in a white plastic sheet, they placed them in body bags and carried them through dimly lit passageways to the ship's food lockers. There, they lay in the frigid air alongside the boxes of food that would soon be shoveled onto trays in the mess hall for hungry sailors and Marines.

I write of this scene from Don's brief memoir, which I am honored to have read.

> *"This scenario was certainly not even remotely resembling the dramatic return of the war dead in rows of silver coffins, each one neatly embellished with an American Flag.........."*

The memoir is unpublished, as far as I know. Printed on tattered paper, and tucked away in a drawer.

CHAPTER 32

Sanctuary

When the medevacs came for Jesse Hittson, it was getting close to dark, and there were six other badly wounded Marines waiting there with him in the landing zone. A UH-34 arrived and began its descent but suddenly veered away when it started catching rounds. The pilot had been caught by surprise but was still determined to save the men.

"I'm laying right next to this radioman who's talking to the pilot," Jesse tells me, "and the pilot said, 'This is going to be the last chance. I will come in hot, and you have your people ready to go.' And buddy, when he said 'hot,' he freakin' meant hot because he came back in at tree-top level, and you couldn't see anything. He was running them wheels through the top of the trees. He turned around, came in, and just squatted—just threw that front end up. The first thing that hit was the ass-end, and the wheels fell. They got us all on the helicopter, and then we took off and went to the Sanctuary."

Thanks to the work done by Commodore McManus when Don

Teal had requested a hospital ship, the USS Sanctuary was now only fifteen to twenty miles off the coast.

"The Marines were so far north that they had to have some support up north," Jesse says. "You know, we weren't down by the hospitals and all that other shit. We were out in the boonies. We were out in the sticks. So, they'd set up medical on those ships, the Sanctuary and the Repose, which many people don't know."

The USS Repose would also serve many wounded from the Special Landing Force in the coming months. Operating mainly in the I Corps area, she would serve more than 9,000 battle casualties and 24,000 inpatients while deployed, earning her the nickname "Angel of the Orient." The USS Sanctuary operated off the coast for at least fifty days at a time, with availability and upkeep periods at Subic Bay in between. By April 1968, in just one year on that schedule, she would admit 5,354 patients and treat another 9,187 on an outpatient basis. Helicopters were to make more than 2,500 landings on her deck that year. The Sanctuary's official motto was "Copiae Servamus": *We serve the troops,* but her unofficial motto could be seen on a large banner hanging off the rail for all the pilots and helo crews to see: "You Find 'Em, We Bind 'Em. Open 24 Hours."

Jesse describes a few of the other wounded who had flown to the Sanctuary with him that day.

"One of them," he says, likely describing Sergeant Brackins, "had gotten shot through the jaw, and he was holding his face on because if you come unhinged there, what've you got? Nuthin'. One guy had gotten shot in the back, and the bullet was lodged in his neck, and he had a blood blister."

He makes a circle the size of a large tomato with his hands.

"About that big around," he says. "Another guy got shot through the knee, and it had hit the thigh bone in the other leg. You know, it was just all kinds of shit."

When the wounded were unloaded, they went first to a triage area to be evaluated and prioritized for surgery. The beds, Jesse claims, had gyroscopes on them to keep them level in those times when the sea was rolling. As a nurse cut into Jesse's clothing, fifteen to twenty little piss ants crawled out and zig-zagged across the pristine white bedding. The doctor was quite bothered by them and worked intently to clean them up.

"And boy, he tore me a new one for stuffin' mud in that bullet hole," he says with his finger on his solar plexus. "He said that was the dumbest damn thing I could've done, but hell, what was I s'posed to do? I was bleedin' out!"

Jesse tells me that, like the Marines, the doctors were all young and often had to be innovative to save Marine lives.

"You've gotta have guinea pigs. You've gotta have somethin'," he says, "so they're trying everything in combat. They're doing all kinds of shit. In fact, a lot of the stuff we got now, you know—triage, emergency room, and all that shit was learned from vets and passed over to the civilians."

Jesse went into operation and stayed on the Sanctuary for about six weeks. Since all of the tendons had been severed in his arm, his hand had coiled into a claw. The doctors "sewed all that shit back together" and then put a gadget on his wrist with rubber bands that kept his fingers pulled back and tension off the newly sewed tendons.

When he regained as much use of his hand as they thought they would be able to achieve for him, Jesse was transferred to another hospital ship, where he stayed for another three weeks of rehabilitation. From there, he was sent to the safety of Okinawa, Japan to finish the remainder of his tour doing odd jobs and work details in support of the Marines stopping to do training and those in transit.

"And I was there for about three days," he says. "They were doing all of these inspections. You know—hair cut, uniform, this, that, and the other, and I said, 'I can't do this shit.' So, I went and seen the doctor and they had what they call a profile. It's called a PULHES. Your hearing, your eyes—everything is evaluated by itself, within itself."

PULHES is a US Military acronym used to qualify an enlistee's physical profile for each area in a set of core military skills. Each letter in the acronym is paired with a number from 1 to 4 to designate the service member's physical capacity for a given MOS. The PULHES acronym stands for and rates along the following areas:

P. Physical condition
U. Upper extremities
L. Lower extremities
H. Hearing (ears)
E. Eyes
S. Psychiatric / Stability

Given that Jess was a right-handled 0311, a rifleman, he'd needed a U-1 to return to combat.

"Well, on my arm, I had a two," he says. "And they told me they couldn't send me with that. So, I signed a waiver, and the next day, I went to Vietnam; I went back."

"Wait," I say, "you went back into combat on your own volition? After all that? Why?"

"Well, you know," he says, "I felt like I'd learned something. I had crossed a line between being green and knowing something. And there in Okinawa, all these new guys were coming through to go out, and I felt like I could help them somehow. But also, I wanted to get some payback."

"I got back in the country about a week later, and we were still helping out with that deal up there," Jesse says, referring to Operation Buffalo. "In Lima Company, I became a squad leader because I had some experience. And promoted to Corporal. And then was promoted to sergeant before I left. But yeah, I was no longer with the Special Landing Force. All the faces changed."

From there, Jesse went with Lima Company to Con Thien, "The Hill of Angels," and participated in the Siege of Con Thien, during which relentless artillery shelling was the norm.

"I'd jumped out of the frying pan and into the fire!" he says. "When I got to 3/9, them some-bitches was... the NVA was after us."

Indeed, in his book Con Thien: The Hill of Angels, author James P. Coan confirms:

"In one nine-day period," he writes, "Con Thien was hit with more than three thousand rounds of mixed artillery, rockets, and mortars. Operation Neutralize responded with 790 B-52 Arc Light missions 'right in front of Con Thien' during September, dropping twenty-two thousand tons of bombs. The III MAF artillery units fired 12,577 rounds at known or suspected enemy positions in the region; ships of the Seventh Fleet fired 6,148 rounds at the same area. Marine, Navy, and Air Force jets flew fifty-two hundred close air support missions in support of Con Thien."

Six or seven months after joining Lima 3/9, Jesse ran into some of the guys from 1/3. Jesse inquired about what had happened after he left, and they told him the names of those who were killed that day, others killed on May 9th at Hill 110, and still others in operations that followed. So many friends lost, so many names, so many faces, and yet, by then, for Jesse, from 3/9, there had been more. But through all those months, there were also many he'd fought alongside, and fresh Boots had learned to survive from him and his hard-earned lessons—boys who went home alive. Jesse had done what he set out to do—he got back into the fight, helped his fellow Marines, and got some payback. As the saying goes in Texas, "he gave it hell."

Before shipping to Vietnam, he had told his father, "I'll go over there and get with the best of 'em. It don't make a damn to me."

By the time he took that freedom bird home, he had done exactly that.

And then some.

CPL. Jesse D. Hittson wears a flak vest and delivers mail to a muddy bunker at the U.S. Marine Con Thien outpost two miles south of the DMZ in South Vietnam on Oct. 4, 1967. (AP Photo/Kim Ki Sam)

CHAPTER 33

Into the Que Son

ON THE MORNING of May 6, Ken saddled up with his gun team and set out from Hill 65 to sweep in a westerly direction, further from the sea and up into a valley that, at the time, he had no name for. It was just "that way," just "out," as in, "we're moving out." Where to and why? For Ken, a grunt, the answer would be the same for the rest of his tour: wherever Delta's going, to find and kill gooks. And on this morning, in particular for the whole company, it was hopefully to get some payback.

Today, Ken knows it as the Que Son Valley (not to be confused with Khe Sanh; it's pronounced "Qway Son").

It was a beautiful place. In his book, Road of 10,000 Pains, Marine veteran Otto Lehrack wrote that "from the air, the valley glows with fairytale beauty." But he also noted that in 1967, "it was one of the most dangerous places on earth,"—a fact that Ken knows to be true now, but for his own reasons and not because of Lehrack's book.

This valley, among all places in South Vietnam, was strategically important to the NVA for various reasons. The mouth of the valley, there just beyond Hill 65, was only 21 kilometers (about 13 miles) inland from the beach where Ken had landed with Delta Company in the amtracs only nine days before. Although the company had since been choppered further inland, it was a distance that could be covered in a hard night's march by experienced NVA emerging from the Ho Chi Minh Trail, and this, as Lehrack wrote, "could threaten the isolation of the five northern provinces of South Vietnam." That would sandwich the US Marines between there and the DMZ—Marines at Da Nang, at the Marble Mountain Air Facility along the beach, in the high country at Khe Sanh, and around the four corners of Leatherneck Square (Con Thien and Gio Linh up at the trace, Dong Ha and Cam Lo down along the Cua Viet River). A "shit sandwich," to borrow a phrase from Ray Kelley. I suppose it could've boxed in and tied up the Marine Corps in the North while the NVA infiltrated further down into the South along the Ho Chi Minh, but I'm no military strategist.

What I do know is what the map shows. The valley is a wide corridor between two mountain ranges, like fingers jutting toward the sea. It goes about four and a half kilometers (almost 3 miles) before curving southward against the western front range. On average, it seems to be about one to one and a half kilometers wide—two kilometers (or one and a quarter miles) at its widest, side to side, with a tributary snaking gently down the middle basin. That's enough naturally irrigable land for twenty-five farm fields and rice paddies arranged in adjacent patterns, long and short, across the distance, side-to-side. I counted that many in modern-day satellite images stitched together over Google Earth. And there are rows upon rows of the same going all the way in from the mouth to the western wall. The point is that the valley was, and apparently still is, a rich and fertile land for farming. Tons upon tons of rice could've been harvested there—provisions enough to feed battalions. Rural as it may have been, all those farms also supported farming families—many with young men and women of fighting age—volunteers and conscripts to be Viet Cong, guerilla rebels, and allegiant allies to the NVA.

History tells us that advance elements of the 2nd NVA Division were in the valley—an entire regiment, or about two battalions, if not more. When Ken had set out from Hill 65 to move into the valley with the rest of Delta Company, Bravo, and Charlie, it had been only nine days since the NVA had been driven out of the village complex of Binh Son and forced to withdraw to the North. To the North was the valley that Ken and the Battalion Landing Team were now moving into.

History also tells us that since that first skirmish, up to the end of 1967, the bloodiest series of battles in the Vietnam War would be fought here in this valley.

"...truly to be the Valley of Tears."

Those are the words, remember, that Jim Shipp would soon be penciling under the letterhead of the USS Bayfield and sending home to his mom and dad—ominously prophetic words, looking back on it now, for he could not have known that nearly nine hundred Marines and Corpsmen, and over six thousand enemy would die in the fights that were just beginning there now with them. By the end of the year, more would be lost in the Que Son Valley than around the better-known battlegrounds of Hue, Khe Sanh, or Con Thien.

It pulls the biblical Psalm out of poetry and song and lays it across the tall, dry grass before a staggered line of sweating, sweeping Marines:

> "Yea, though I walk through the valley of the shadow of death..."

From his vantage point, Ken tells me that it did not always appear to be a valley. A Marine's eyes, when not carefully watching for the best place to plant his boot on rugged terrain, are often scanning just ahead—in and around the hooches in a ville, along tree lines at the edge of rice paddies, at a suspiciously random haystack, on the roofless and weathered remains of some old structure from the French plantation days, at bends downstream and on rises overlooking the water they crossed with M16s held high above their heads.

The cool stream water didn't last long. The air was so thick and hot that it was soon after just warm and wet in their utilities and all the more chafing against their skin. And since water was in short supply, most Marines were forced to drink from the streams.

"In the next few days," says Don Bumgarner, a mortar man from Charlie Company, "a lot of guys got dysentery."

That means that in addition to thirst and hunger (they were also short on C-rats), diarrhea, fever, nausea, vomiting, and stomach cramps would have to be endured. Then, of course, there were the skin-scraping folds that one would have to wrench into his beltline because of the consequent weight loss.

"We ran out of halazone tablets," says Ronald Stroud from Bravo Company's 3rd Platoon. "We had no way to purify the water, we just drank it straight out of the streams. We were tired, and we started getting diarrhea. Your immune system just starts breaking down. We still had a lot of guys getting medevaced because of heat exhaustion. I had one of my guys in the water one time, baptizing him. Not spiritually, but I was trying to get him to cool down, and I kept dunking him under, holding him a bit, and bringing him up. He made it, only to get hurt later on."

On that same day, Stroud led his Second Squad down to wade through another stream that was only ankle to knee deep so they could put their helmets in the water and pour them over their heads to cool themselves down.

"I had a C-ration cup in my flak jacket," he says. "I would just take it and dip up the water and drink. Well, one time I did that, I tell ya, I couldn't describe how bad that water tasted. I said, 'Oh my...agh! I hope there's not a dead guy in this water ahead of us!'"

They continued to move upstream, and then, around a bend, they came across some Vietnamese kids washing water buffalo.

"The buffalo were pissin' streams," he says. "Not just in the stream, I mean streams of piss were coming out of them into the water, and they were doing the other thing too—crappin' everywhere. Most of us were drinking that stuff, and we didn't know it. The water was bad. I mean, everybody was sick."

On that first day sweeping into the valley from Hill 65, all three companies encountered signs of the enemy's presence and light contact, mostly in the form of sporadic sniper fire. It started as early as 10:00 AM.

Bravo Company had traveled at least three miles west when they spotted six VC digging in. They radioed an artillery mission on the VC's position with unknown results.

At 11:25, Charlie Company received sniper fire from the stream just south of Hill 65. Two Marines were wounded, and the company answered with 60mm mortars.

At noon, Bravo Company encountered small arms fire. Two of their Marines were also wounded, and they answered with 3.5 rockets, which took out at least two VC.

Five hours later, Bravo's rear element got harassed by 15 VC that opened up on them from behind. They turned around and fought back with their M16s and an M79—killed maybe five VC.

An hour later, one kilometer further west, Delta Company received a little sniper fire, but it was of no consequence.

By 8:45 PM, Charlie Company set in on a northern hill overlooking the valley while Delta Company set in a little further west near the base. Bravo, still just outside the mouth of the valley, settled in further to the east.

It had been a long hot day on Search and Destroy, and the humping had been slow and hard. The water was gone, and resupply was sparse with the choppers working medevacs for the wounded and sick. I also imagine that Command might've held back chopper traffic in the mouth of the valley as it would alert enemy forces of the Marines' approach. And yet, with high ground to the North and South, and with the fights that had broken out during the day, surely by now, the NVA and VC would've known the Marines were moving up the valley.

Perhaps that's why, by 1:45 PM on the next day, all companies were ordered to turn in their flak vests. The Marines were losing the element of surprise. Command needed to relieve the exhausted Marines, decrease medevac traffic, and pick up the pace.

With increased mobility and decreased load, Delta Company crossed the stream and headed up into the hills on the south side of the valley. On the back side of Hill 110, they found a tunnel complex and, as the declassified after-action report says, "some items of intelligence value."

Maps of the area? Plans for future attacks? Communications equipment? To the grunts, it was no matter. The tunnels themselves were enough to prove the enemy regarded the area with enough importance to meticulously and laboriously carve a hidden complex into the hillside. The tunnels showed they were prepared to fight a protracted war. They were also a reminder that Charlie, the enemy, was always watching and waiting and could strike any time.

Finding intelligence was a small victory for Delta Company, but hastily abandoned tunnels produced mixed feelings. On the one hand, they gave the sense that Delta had Charlie on the run and that soon, the boys might get their payback. On the other hand, they indicated an enemy who was cunning, operating on a prepared battlefield and on his own turf.

After finding the tunnel complex, the company spent the remainder of the day sweeping back around the front side of the hill facing the valley and followed a trail that went up into a saddle between the main hill and a smaller one. In their area, the hills were not covered with canopied jungle, but rather, a dense and waist-high shrubbery, like scrub oak—similar, Ken thought, to the hills back home in California where he grew up. Ken could see, however, that the lower portions of the shrubs had been trimmed clean in certain areas. A glance back at the Marines behind him confirmed that they had also noticed—they were humping through prepared fields of fire.

"They had cut the lower branches of the vegetation so you could still see the tops but couldn't see where they had cleared the bottom," Ken says. "They could see you, but it would be hard to see them. The tension level went up several degrees."

Still, the enemy was nowhere to be found, and the sun was setting, so they dug in for the night in the saddle.

Later that night, an enemy battalion of about three hundred men was spotted about a mile and a half east on the same side of the valley where Delta had dug in. As fire missions were being run, Delta also reported movement to their west, and then, just thirty minutes later, they were being fired upon with mortars. Nowhere to be found in the day, the enemy, like nocturnal animals, came alive at night.

"We didn't hear the mortars fire," Ken says. "The only warning we received was the whistling of the mortar round just before it hit the ground and exploded. As soon as I heard that whistle, I was down on the ground, as flat as I could get, waiting for it because we could barely scrape out ranger graves, maybe 6 inches deep, as long as your body, for each individual. The ground was just rock hard."

"The first rounds, as I remember, missed by quite a ways," Jim Shipp tells me, "but then the next ones got closer and closer. They had a spotter and just walked them right in on top of us. And we couldn't pinpoint where they were coming from."

In a lull of silence between the mortar rounds, the voice of a Marine called out from somewhere up the line.

"Corpsman! Corpsman up!"

"We thought there was probably going to be a full-out assault by the NVA to follow," Shipp says. "We were expecting an assault."

The company's 60mm mortars fired illumination flares. Dark shadows swayed from side to side under the shrubbery as the white phosphor flares swung in the air under parachutes.

A few more scattered mortar rounds hit the hill, and then word came down the line that Sergeant Milton Hall from Lieutenant Spear's Second Platoon had been killed. A mortar had exploded so close that the Corpsman could do nothing for him; his death had most surely been instant.

By this point in the operation, 30 Marines had been killed. 55 had been medevaced out of the field. 30 more had been wounded but not evacuated.

"We're sitting there, and the next thing I know, I see this red beam come down from the night sky," Ken says. "It's like a solid red line coming down. At the end of the beam, it would sparkle a bit as the tracers burned out, and then you hear Brrrrrrrrrrrrrrrrrrrrrrrrrrrrrrr."

Puff had been called into the valley.

"It was fascinating to watch," he says. "The mini-gun cyclic rate of fire is 6,000 rounds a minute. You see the red tracers in a single glowing beam of light, then the sound of firing a few seconds later: Brrrrrrrrrrrrrrrrrrrrrrrrrrrrrrr. Then he starts to push out flares, and he's got the really powerful ones that light up the valley. He shoots for a while more, and then there were no more mortar rounds."

And luckily, the expected NVA assault never came, but needless to say, there was not much sleep to be had.

The next day, on May 8, the company came down off the hill and started pushing their way up towards the end of the valley.

Again they were mortared from somewhere across the stream. A few Marines were wounded, but not bad enough to be medevaced.

By noon, about a mile further north, Charlie Company also got mortared. Three of their Marines were killed, and eight medevaced from the field. They called in a Huey Gunship and a fixed-wing air strike—took out the mortars and killed five enemy.

Pushing further up into the valley, Delta Company came upon the weathered remains of what appeared to have been a French-owned plantation. Ken and his squad inspected the main building, which was which was overgrown with brush and vegetation. The plaster walls stood two stories tall, but the second floor was gone, and there was no roof and no glass in the windows.

"There was an additional row of one-story buildings behind the main building, which I assumed were for the plantation workers," Ken says. "Again, no roofs on these buildings, either."

French colonialism in Vietnam lasted more than sixty years, and by the late 1880s, Vietnam, Laos, and Cambodia were all controlled by France. Exploited for production, profit, and cheap labor, Indochine Français as it was called by the French (French Indochina), became one of France's most important colonial possessions.

Vietnamese land was seized and brought under collective control for large rice and rubber plantations. Local farmers were forced to work on these plantations in difficult and dangerous conditions. In the 20 years between the two world wars, one rubber plantation recorded 17,000 deaths.

The landscape of Vietnam was changed by the era of colonialism. Long-standing indigenous temples, pagodas, monuments, and buildings, some of which had endured for a thousand years, were deemed dilapidated and demolished. In their stead, structures reflecting the architectural styles of France were erected. The original Vietnamese names of cities, towns, and streets received French names. Important commercial activities, such as banking and trade, predominantly took place in the French language rather than the local tongues. Had it not been for the distinct climate and the Vietnamese locals, certain areas of Hanoi and Saigon could easily have been mistaken for parts of Paris.

But then, inspired by Chinese and Soviet communism, Ho Chi Minh's Viet Minh rose up against the colonial rule and ignited a war that went on for eight years before the French were finally defeated. On the day before, in the very same month, 13 years before Delta found themselves sweeping through the dilapidated plantation houses, the French were crushed at the Battle of Dien Bien Phu.

Shortly after that, the country was split, with Ho Chi Minh and his Vietnamese Communist Party ruling the North. Where the United

States had once been supporting the French in their war, now they were supporting South Vietnam to stop the spread of communism. By 1957, however, communist rebels, called the Viet Cong (VC), started terrorizing and assassinating government officials and related parties in the South.

At the end of 1960, the communists in the South announced the formation of the National Liberation Front, a political arm of the Viet Cong. Village guerrilla units made up of part-time combatants who lived at home and farmed by day continued harassing government, police, and security forces with booby traps, raids, kidnappings, and murders. The communist insurgency continued to grow in the South until, by the middle of 1960, it was clear to the U.S. that the South Vietnamese army and security forces couldn't cope with the growing threat.

Meanwhile, infiltration from the North kept increasing. Men who had once been natives of South Vietnam, most now Communist Party members, filtered back down to reoccupy their old homelands. As the corrupt Diem regime of the South started losing control to the communists, the U.S. increased its support, eventually committing military assistance with helicopters, armored personnel carriers, American advisers, technical experts, and a limited number of U.S. combat troops. Likewise, China supported the North Vietnamese offensive and supplied weapons and personnel. Even the Soviets sent aid to the North.

In June of 1965, Westmoreland predicted a likely collapse of the South Vietnamese army and called for a rapid dispatch of U.S. troops to go on the offensive against the Viet Cong and North Vietnamese wherever they were found in the South. President Johnson authorized the dispatch of 100,000 troops immediately, and in 1966, he authorized 100,000 more, one of which was Ken Hicks, an 18-year-old Marine who peered now through the empty door frame of the obscure history that led him there.

There, in what his country was reluctant to call, but very much was a full-scale war. There, in a valley where many of the people he was enlisted to protect were farmers by day and rebels by night. There, in a rural valley through which the Suoi Cho Dun stream flowed, as well as a battalion of well-trained soldiers from the North.

The boy, his hand against a plastered wall, leaned in and looked about with curious wonder. He was there to stem the tide of communism. That's about all he knew. After eleven straight days of Search and Destroy, he also knew that the South Vietnamese people, who the Marines were supposedly there to help, did not seem to want them there at all.

"Late that same day, instead of moving into a perimeter, we move alongside a hill and stop," Ken says.

The company sat there against the side of the hill until it was dark. With no electric lights in that rural valley and no moon above it, it was a kind of natural darkness of night that newer generations have probably never experienced. It was so dark, in fact, that when word was passed down the line to get ready to move out, each Marine had to hold onto the pack or E-tool of the Marine in front of him.

"We start moving herky-jerky," Ken says, "and we start and stop, start and stop, start-stop, as we slowly move along. The column stopped a couple of times because one Marine had lost contact with the one in front of him. It was so dark that if you lost physical contact with the Marine in front of you, and they kept moving while you stopped, they simply disappeared into the darkness."

Unlike in the movies, keep in mind, there was very little chatter among the men, if any. Ken tells me, for example, that while occasional radio squelch and chatter was a familiar sound while on patrol, Marines would rarely ever be hollering up and down the line as you see in the first five minutes of Oliver Stone's 1986 movie Platoon. On a dark night such as it was, in hostile territory, if any word was passed up or down the line, it was passed in a whisper from ear to ear.

One such whisper shared the discovery of luminous bits of dead vegetation on the trail. Whether it came from the plant's natural bioluminescence, bacteria on the plants, or some chemical decay process, some pieces of vegetation under their boots were dimly lit.

"Word was passed to put some of it on the pack of the Marine in front of you," Ken says. "It helped a little, but not with the start-stop, start-stop, start-stop. We go a couple of hours, we're moving along slowly. We stopped at some point, and then the word was passed to sit down in place. No mortars that night. We did the same thing the next night and there were no incoming mortars then either."

With the death of Sergeant Hall, the company had learned to move as soon as night fell in case they'd been spotted where they settled and then to take advantage of the cover of darkness to make distance toward their next objective. In this way, they made it all the way up to the end of the valley, where it curved south against the western front range and was soon closed up by small southern hills. The trade-off had been sleep, so in addition to frequent pains of thirst, a hunger that could never be fully satisfied, and a plethora of sicknesses and irritations, the Marines grew increasingly exhausted, which added to their growing list of agitations: irritability, reduced alertness, weakening motor skills, and attention problems.

But, at least they'd reached the end of the valley, and by 10:30 PM on the evening of May 9, a frag order had filtered down, confirming they'd be turning around to start heading back east toward the coast. By the time word had filtered down to Ken and his gun squad, no part of it included mention of the fact that they were now going to be playing the role of the anvil in a hammer-and-anvil tactic. Unbeknownst to them, 1st Battalion 5th Marines (1/5) were also in the valley and would be playing the role of the hammer. 1/5 would be sweeping west, driving the 2nd NVA Division further into the valley where they would eventually be stopped and crushed against the anvil, 1/3. Or so it was plotted on some map in the cool conditioned air of a control room in Da Nang, or perhaps even on the USS Okinawa, amongst the smell of hot coffee and cigarette smoke, an almost constant hum of radio traffic, the calling out from operators relaying key signals from the noise—situational reports, reconnaissance, enemy sightings, enemy contact, air traffic from Klondike Gunships and fixed-wing air strikes. Maybe even the strangely ill-fitting fill of low-volume music from a little transistor radio grabbed for a steal on the streets of Da Nang.

The plan had probably been drawn up, further up the chain of command, on the map on the table in the more regal office belonging to Colonel Wickwire, Commanding Officer of the First Battalion, Third Marines, Ninth Marine Amphibious Force. Wickwire had, as the low-ranking grunt, Ray Kelley, couldn't help but notice, a big, comfortable leather chair. After the operation, he tells me, he would later be invited along with six other Marines, to visit Wickwire in his office and consult over a large map on the table, spotted with colored pins. The Colonel would point at this pin and that pin, and this way and that, and then finally lean his hands against the edge of the table and look up at this small group of rag-tag Marines he'd pulled straight from the field, tufts of hair pulsing in the breeze of a ceiling fan, and say, "So, what do you think?"

And Ray would deliver a reply that could've ended his military career had it not been for the support of his close superiors who knew of his deeds and for, perhaps, a little compassion from the Colonel.

"What do we think?" Kelley replied. "What do we think? You don't give a fuck what we think!"

He was, then, as he would say, more "full of piss and vinegar" than he was when he first entered the war.

"Those pins on that map are people!"

Wickwire stood up straight, fists against his waist, head cocked to one side with his lips pursed, listening as this kid from the field continued to lay into him. Ray didn't tell me whether the Colonel said much in reply, but I imagine he did not. He just shook his head as he watched four of the others drag the young Marine writhing and swearing all the way out the office door.

"What were you thinking," I say, "a Private, or whatever you were at the time, talking back to the Colonel of the whole battalion like that?"

"What was I thinking?" Ray says. "What do I have to lose? He wants to know what I'm thinking; I'm going to give it to him. These people are trying to kill us!"

I admit that, at first, it sounded like a bit of a tall tale to me, or at least embellished by the old veteran Marine, but that was before I knew the whole story of what the grunts had experienced by the time that meeting had occurred and also before I'd come to trust Ray as a friend and become sure of his honest nature.

It was also before I knew what it felt like on that next day in the valley on May 10, to be the bloody anvil upon which the First Battalion, Fifth Marines were driving a battalion of the NVA.

CHAPTER 34

Sebastian, Texas

DANIEL CAVAZOS WAS sitting on the front porch with his girlfriend, Mary Gonzales, when a friend of his pulled up in a black, four-door Chevy Impala, stepped out and delivered the news that his brother Martin had been killed in Vietnam.

"I cried," Daniel tells me. "I cried right there."

Daniel's friend told him that J.D., the county judge, escorted two Marines to the house to deliver the news to his mother, but those two Marines spoke little if any. When she saw them beyond the doorframe standing on each side of the judge in their dress blues, Daniel's mother knew why they had come, and one look at the sorrow in J.D.'s eyes confirmed it. Before he could get a word out, she turned around, wailed, and then disappeared into the house—her long, loud, and high-pitched cries moving frantically from room to room. J.D. took a brief look in the eyes of each of the Marines at his sides, no doubt, and then followed their nods of encouragement to go in and console her.

"You better go to the house," Daniel's friend told him. "Tu madre... your mother's going crazy, man. She's not taking it well at all."

Danny said a brief farewell to his girlfriend and then drove himself the fifteen minutes back home from Raymondville to Sebastian—the road blurring up quickly again and again after each time he wiped the tears from his eyes. His foot pushed heavy on the pedal, weighted by the need to be close to his family and a half-hearted hope that he could soon find out that it was some kind of mistake, that somebody had gotten it all wrong, that Martin wasn't really dead.

"When I drove up, and this is the truth," he tells me, wiping the memory from each eye with a finger, "all of Sebastian was there. And the whole town was still, you know? Like you could hear a pin drop."

When Martin's body came home, his mother put on a black dress, and they buried him in the small cemetery not far from his house there in Sebastian. Marines removed the flag from his coffin and ceremoniously folded it into a tight triangle. One Marine officer pressed and checked the fold under pristine white gloves. He turned sharply, stepped over to Martin's mother, knelt before her, and presented the flag.

"Como representante de la rama de servicio de los Estados Unidos..." the officer said, his eyes locked squarely on hers. "As a representative of the United States service branch, it is my high privilege to present to you this flag. Let it be a symbol of the appreciation this nation feels for the distinguished service rendered to our country and to our flag by your loved one."

A lone bugle broke the silence with Taps, a military funeral honor song that harkens back to the Civil War. Not many know the song has lyrics, for they are rarely sung.

Day is done, gone the sun,
From the lakes, from the hills, from the sky;
All is well, safely rest,
God is nigh.

"Way back in those years," Daniel says, "when somebody died, the mother would wear a black dress. Nowadays, when you wear a black dress, you take it off the day after. She wore that for years, and years, and years. That's how it affected her."

In the years that followed, she was overwrought with a depression that manifested itself not only in the black dress but in a growing variety of illnesses.

"I want to say that she was 100 percent depressed," Daniel says. "But you know how moms are. They can be sick, and they're not going to tell you. They're not going to worry you. She had it all inside."

The town doctor witnessed her decline, the way she looked and felt, until one day, he took her hands into his own, looked her in the eyes, and gave her the only medicine he could find for what she had. He told her that she must stop wearing the dress.

"You're never going to forget," he said to her, "but you have to let it go."

And she finally did.

When Daniel was 19 or 20, he came home at night after his parents had gone to sleep. He stood quietly in the hallway between their bedroom and his own and put his hand around the door handle, remembering the many times in childhood when he'd dashed in and crawled into the warm cocoon of safety and love between them. But things were different now. They were different now, and so was he, or at least, he was supposed to be, but he didn't feel that way.

He felt very much the same as in all those times in boyhood when he'd been terrified of the night.

Now a young man, Daniel let go of the handle and fetched a pillow from his bedroom. He lay down with the pillow under his head in the hallway, his body pressed against his parents' bedroom door, and went to sleep.

"As big as I was," he assures me, "I still laid down on the floor because I knew my mom and dad were there. I just didn't want to be alone by myself in the room."

It wasn't the first time he'd slept there since his brother Martin had been killed, and it wouldn't be the last.

CHAPTER 35

Union

EARLY ON THE MORNING of the 10th, 2nd Lt Winfield Spear's Second Platoon took up the front, leading Delta Company east down the valley, back toward the coast.

Lieutenant Spear was with the point squad when they came upon a running stream. Several of the Marines, desperately thirsty, approached the stream quickly but cautiously—shouldering rifles and drawing their canteens while Lieutenant Spear, smelling cordite in the air, ambled curiously upstream.

"When you're in the field, and you've got artillery that's gone off," Spear tells me, "or when bombs have been dropped, if you're in close enough, within maybe ten to fifteen minutes or so, you're going to smell the cordite in the air. That alerts you to the fact something has happened, you know? Something. So I was wondering, 'Where is this coming from?'"

About ten yards upstream, he spotted the large, dark mass of a water buffalo lying dead in the water. The sun had dried the top of the muddy buffalo to a dusty gray that turned dark black only at the wet edge above its legs, which were submerged. Had it not been for the striking contrast of the animal's pink viscera, he might have mistaken it for a large boulder. A bomb had gutted the animal, and Spear could see brain matter being gently pulled by the stream from between the horns on its cocked head.

"Of course, the Marines at this time are trying to get to that water. So we started screaming and hollering, as many as we could, 'Don't get the water! Don't get the water!' We couldn't drink it. We couldn't fill up. And we needed water very badly, let me tell you. We were not getting our water supply that particular day. Sometimes, you just couldn't get water to a moving unit. They couldn't get in."

He might have been able to walk his men upstream of the buffalo to draw uncontaminated water, but about that time, a senior officer who had just come in by helo showed up—a man Spear had never met.

"I didn't even know the 5th Marines were there," he says. "I didn't know what they were doing. And there's this lieutenant colonel. He's standing there, and he says, 'You see that hill there?'"

"Yes, sir," Lieutenant Spear answered.

"I want you to take your organization and move up that hill."

Even though Spear was twenty-eight years old, comparatively an old man amongst the rest of his men, the officer commanded him with indifferent authority.

"Sir," he said, "I'm with the First Battalion, Third Marines, Delta Company."

"I don't care what organization you're with," the officer said. "I need you to take your men straight up that hill."

"And see," Spear tells me, "officers in Delta Company wore their insignia upside down, or we didn't show it. You'd be the first one they would shoot, so we didn't show that we were officers. We had it pinned under the collar."

"I'm Lieutenant Spear," he said, proclaiming his rank. "I'm with Delta Company."

"I don't care," the officer said. "I want you up that hill. Now, take your unit and go up, goddamn it."

"Aye, aye," he said.

The man had not masked his insignia, which clearly outranked Spear's.

"He was either a Major or Lieutenant Colonel," Spear says. "But I'm wondering, who the hell is he? Does he know what he's doing? I do what I'm told; I'm a Marine. So, I pass the word to my squad leaders and say, 'Guess what? We're going up that hill.'"

The hill was very steep, and it was very hot that day, so Spear's thirsty Marines were very pissed off, but they started up the hill.

"And the next thing," he says, "I get a radio call, and it's Delta Six. That's Captain Ed Aldous. He said, 'Where are you?'"

"I'm going up the hill."

"I don't know what hill you're up, but get the hell off," Aldous told him. "The battalion is on the move."

"Well, that's when the battalion came under the operational control of the 5th Marines, and we were sent down to be the anvil," he tells me. "They were going to push these guys right over this hill into us. And that's what happened."

Even as a platoon commander, Lieutenant Spear had not known the 5th Marines were in the valley, much less that they were pushing the NVA toward his company.

"All I was told was to reverse course, to get off the hill—the battalion's on the move. Well, hell, I've got to stay with the battalion. So, I followed the last order. I don't know whether you've been told that, but in the Marines, you always follow your last order."

"Reverse," Aldous told him. "Reverse course."

"You don't think I didn't piss off a bunch of my men?" Spear says. "We're going up the hill. Now, we're not going up the hill; we're going back down, right? That kind of thing happened a lot, you know."

As Spear took his platoon back down the hill, Charlie One Five began maneuvering their way through the thick scrub brush up two sides of Hill 110. One of their squads was soon in pursuit of an unarmed Vietnamese who'd suddenly popped up from the brush in front of them and started running. Another was following the blood trail of a combatant they'd shot after he'd lobbed a grenade down toward them, and soon after, they were all being fired upon by several enemy soldiers from up top.

At about 0900 to 0930, Charlie One Five's Captain Caswell called in a fixed-wing air strike. F-4 Phantom jets dropped bombs on the enemy positions at the top of the hill, and as soon as the strike had lifted, Caswell had his men assault up and over it from west to east. One Five advanced aggressively but met resistance from VC combatants who appeared out of spider holes all over the hillside, firing AKs and pitching grenades. While the VC occupied the aggressive Marines, hundreds of NVA were flooding down the other side of the hill toward the valley floor where, just across a field of short grass, they disappeared into the cover of a large cane field.

In the book Charlie One Five by Nicolas Warr, One Five's Sergeant Hillous York was quoted as saying, "That turned out to be the enemy's 'wall of steel.' When we got just short of the cane field, the enemy really started to put it to us."

With Charlie One Five's forward movement stopped against the enemy's defense and with the three companies of the SLF in the valley around and beyond the cane field, the battle for Hill 110 had begun.

Though Winfield Spear, now Captain Spear, was not aware of the big picture then, he can provide perspective now. He says:

> *"They were tough little bastards. They could go without their rice. They could go without their water, I think, for longer than we could. They didn't hump the loads that we humped—that's another thing. So when you were fighting these guys, and they decided to disengage, they were very,*

very expert at getting away from you. And many times, you didn't even realize they were disengaging because they always left back a cadre of people to put up a fight. You know—a couple of machine guns, some rocket-propelled outfits—and they would lay some stuff on you. You think you're still engaged with the whole outfit, but you're not. Maybe, say, two-thirds of the organization is pulling out. They were experts at that. And they would take their wounded and dead with them. So, many times, you didn't know how many you killed.

Now, Operation Union was different. On Union, you see, the 5th trapped them, and we wound up being more or less the anvil. The 5th pushed them up here on 110, and that's when they decided they'd had enough, and they decided to turn and fight—they weren't going anywhere. But then, when they started losing so many people, and they got hit so bad, they finally began to pull out, and that's when they ran into us.

So we didn't assault. It was the 5th Marines assaulting. We just caught them on the run. That was the big picture, but to be honest with you, I didn't know what I was out there for. I knew why I was out there on Operation Beaver Cage, but when Union started, I didn't know what it was all about."

CHAPTER 36

Hill 110

THAT MORNING, at about 7:40 AM, One-Three's Bravo Company was walking in a column down the valley along the northern side of the river with a mountain range and Hill 110 just across the river to their right. Charlie Company was further out among the hamlets in the middle of the valley.

Michael Wynn, a squad radioman for Bravo Company, tells what happened next.

"Another company was walking on the other side of the river, and all of a sudden, it just really hit the fan," he says. "We started getting automatic fire—rear ambush—mortars, snipers, the whole box and dice. We hit the dirt, of course, and I remember looking across the river and seeing Marines go down just all over the place—guys falling in the river."

Wynn says it was another company on the other side of the river, but I could not corroborate that claim. It seems more likely that Bravo Company was spread out on both sides of the river, and he was simply unaware of it at the time. The Marines he saw tumbling down into the river were likely from his own company.

"That whole side of the valley just seemed to come alive with gooks," he says. "It was the first time I'd ever really seen...well...I call them gooks, it's probably not the best thing to say now, but it was the first time I had ever seen the gooks...the first time I'd ever really been fired at directly like that. Mortars were hitting all over the place, and I got a slight wound that day from mortar fire."

The "gooks" he refers to were said to have been infantry from Lt. Col. Tran Kim Tung's 3rd NVA Regiment. Some were already well entrenched on and around Hill 110. Others descended the hill toward them like an army of ants pouring out of a mound. At the base of the hill, they engaged with Bravo Company from a cane field and from various prepared spider holes, trenches, and tunnels.

"The guys across the river were getting hit, and so were we," Wynn says. "They were firing through them toward us. They must have had it all figured out because the mortars were landing on our side where we were. They had the distance knocked out beforehand before they ambushed. They knew there were people on both sides of the river because we were getting hit as well with a lot of mortars and sniper fire. We had a lot of casualties, but the other side certainly was hit worse."

Within ten minutes of the engagement, Bravo and Charlie companies sent their mortars and rockets back at the hill. UH1E Huey Gunships were called to work over the hill, but it would be another twenty-five minutes before they arrived. As it turned out, the artillery battery that should have been in range was on the move and unavailable.

Charlie Company's Captain Jerry Reczek tells me that he had an ominous feeling when they got up that morning to turn around and start heading back out of the valley. As he moved his company down the valley with Bravo to his right and Delta to the rear, Bravo's Company Commander, Jerry Shirley, called him on the radio.

"Jerry," he says, "you're getting ahead of me. Hold up."

So Reczek stopped and passed the word. He told his men, "You better grab whatever chow you can right now because I'm not sure we're going to be able to eat again."

So, they sat there for a few minutes, and that's when the fire from Bravo Company started.

"Bang, bang, fire, bang, bang," he says, mimicking the sound of the distant fire.

"Jerry calls me and says, 'I got something going here, but I really don't know what it is yet.'"

"Well, I can see from where I am," Reczek said, standing up. "I can see the muzzle flashes coming from the middle of Hill 110, below Hill 110. I can see those muzzle flashes."

Reczek continued to watch the muzzle flashes with the radio in his hand until Shirley came back on.

"I need help right now," Shirley said. "I can see them in khaki uniforms. I need help!"

Bravo was engaged from their front, now facing the hill. With Delta to their right and Charlie behind them, their left flank was wide open, and Shirley reported seeing VC moving into the gap. He immediately made radio contact with the battalion Operations Officer, reported what he knew and requested that Charlie Company link up on his left flank and Delta Company link on on his right flank.

"So that's when I took Dick Chapa and 3rd platoon," Reczek tells me, "and I said, 'Go real quick around this left flank of Bravo Company. Get out there because they need our help.'"

At the same time, Reczek took the 1st and 2nd platoons, got them up, and ran across the open area towards where Bravo Company was engaged.

"As we were moving, we were taking rifle fire in that patch," he tells me. "I told Ron, my XO, I said, 'Ron, we're going to keep the mortars here."

Reczek radioed back to Shirley that they would be firing mortars on the hill where they'd seen the fire coming from and left his XO with the mortar team to fire the 81s.

"So we go up there, too," he says. "1st Platoon and 2nd Platoon. 3rd Platoon is flanking around Bravo's left. We find this huge trench line already dug when we get in there. Big fighting position—a trench line dug all the way across. It's like a berm, and down the other side of the berm, it is like a dry riverbed or something. A lot of growth down there. So we get in there, and first thing, I look below us, and there's this damn NVA soldier, or Viet Cong, stripped down, no shirt, but he's got this camouflage on his back. And he's trying to scurry away from us. The troops stood beside me, and I said, 'There's one right there. Get him. Get him!' They couldn't see him. They didn't see him, so I grabbed the guy's rifle right next to me, and I fired three or four shots right at his back as he was going away. Whether or not I killed him, I don't know. Or even whether I hit him, I don't really know."

Captain Billy West, the artillery forward observer, was in the trench line with him. He noticed the mortar rounds were being walked in to calibrate on them—one behind them, then one in front.

"They got us bracketed," he said to Reczek. "We got to get out of here. We're bracketed!"

Reczek caught a glimpse of the smoke from a mortar tube on the hill when Chapa from his 3rd Platoon on Bravo's left flank came on the radio.

"I need help," Chapa said. "We're going to be overrun!"

"There's me and two radio operators," Reczek says. "We grab whatever we can. I should have gone down into that damn river, or I should have taken a machine gun from one of the gunners over there and blasted the shit out of where I saw that mortar coming. But my first concern was to get over there where Chapa was."

Reczek pulled his pistol and tried to load it. The ammunition was old, so it jammed up, but he finally loaded it and ran over to Bravo's left flank.

When he got there, he saw one of his squad leaders crouching behind a hedgerow. The squad leader had gotten detached from the rest of his platoon. He shrugged at Reczek.

"Move on," Reczek said, urging him forward.

"No, no," the squad leader said. "They're out there."

"Oh, bullshit," Reczek said.

"So I go charging out there, right? It's open," Reczek says, "and there's a hedgerow. I didn't see anybody there, so I jumped over the hedgerow. And when I get over the hedgerow, I see two Marines laying to my left over there."

One was John Michael Reid. He was lying dead on his back, and right next to him, five yards away, was Lance Corporal James Bishop, an M79 gunner. Bishop was still on his knees in the firing position with his M79 cradled in his arm — bullet wounds on the right side of his chest and one through the right side of his head.

"I went over to Reid and looked down at him," he says. "He had real blue eyes, and they were just staring straight up into the sky."

In his book Road of 10,000 Pains: The Destruction of the 2nd NVA Division by the U.S. Marines, 1967, Otto Lehrack wrote of Reid's actions just before Reczek had found him dead:

"His platoon was going at it hammer and tongs with the enemy when mortar fire wiped out one of the Marine machine gun teams, and fire pinned his exposed platoon. Reid ran across the open ground to the gun, picked it up, and ran toward the enemy, firing all the way until he found a place that suited him, then set up and laid down heavy gunfire on the enemy's guns, silencing them and enabling six other members of his unit to reach covered positions. When the enemy attempted to overrun him, he stuck to his gun, stacking up enemy bodies until they killed him."

Reczek moved away from them and got up to the trench line near the stream bed, where he found Dick Chapa and the guys from 3rd Platoon.

"And just before that, or just about that time, is where Corporal

Sanders had jumped into one of those trenches with a machine gun where a bunch of NVA were, shot them all up, killed them, but then they killed him."

Charlie Company's 3rd Platoon was, as Dick Chapa had reported, being overrun. They were in a vulnerable position and taking numerous casualties. Corporal Thomas Sanders was an African-American machine gun team leader, and when his entire team had gotten wounded, he knew it was up to him to protect them and the rest of the platoon. He moved himself into an exposed position and fired on the enemy, suppressing their advance long enough for the rest of the platoon to take cover in the trench. Then, when enemy troops got into the trench where his platoon had taken cover, he placed himself between them and the enemy. The NVA got to within six meters in front of him as he delivered machine gun fire down the long axis of the trench, which killed at least two NVA and wounded three more before the enemy finally killed him. Still, he'd bought his men enough time to get repositioned, where they could fight back with grenades and M79 fire.

Both Sanders and Reid were posthumously awarded the Navy Cross for their initiative and courageous actions.

"So, what we did then when I found the third platoon," Reczek says, "we tied in with Bravo Company—our first and second platoons. We had 3rd Platoon in there and tried to line them up. And then Delta Company was told to come down and reinforce me, help me."

At some point during all of this, Reczek had looked over to see that his XO, Ron Sutton, had returned. Just as Reczek saw Sutton approaching, an 82mm mortar round exploded, knocking Sutton unconscious and taking off the leg of Reczek's 1st platoon squad leader, Cpl. Alfred Brown.

"I thought Sutton was dead," Reczek says. "Cpl. Brown died from shock before we could help him."

Both Marines were rushed away to a casualty collection area.

"Lt. Billy West, our Charlie Company FO, helped to unload

ammo that landed next to us, and some casualties were also loaded," says Reczek, "When he finished, I told him to go back and check on Ron Sutton. They were close friends—Sutton, a Georgia Bulldog, and West, a Georgia Tech Yellow Jacket. West came back and told me that Sutton was still alive but covered up under a pancho, mistaken for dead."

In his extraordinary book, On Full Automatic: Surviving 13 Months in Vietnam, author William V. Taylor wrote about this event, describing it as it was described to him. The entire left side of Sutton's face and body were fully covered in blood, he wrote, but there was seen a glitter of moisture in the slit of Sutton's right eye, a tear, and fresh blood dripping from his wounds.

"My God!" West yelled back to a Corpsman, "He's still alive! Sutton's still alive!"[1]

Doc Eastman bandaged Sutton up, and several Marines carried him onto a medevac under heavy fire, where he was then flown to the USS Sanctuary hospital ship.

* * *

Ken Hicks' platoon had been further up the valley trailing behind Bravo when the sounds of the battle reached them. They paused only briefly as the sounds registered and then quickly dropped their packs and rushed forward through a small field until they hit the river. They crossed the river, up to their chests, and then rushed across another small field and into a tree line on the edge of an embankment several feet high. There, about 50 to 75 meters beyond the tree line and another small field, they could see Hill 110.

They had only been in that position briefly when they heard yelling

---

[1] In the book, On Full Automatic, Surviving 13 Months in Vietnam, author William V. Taylor Jr. wrote that Dick Chapa discovered Sutton still alive. Reczek told me that it was Billy West who found Sutton alive—a correction, for the record. "Dick Chapa had his hands full with his third platoon," he said.

and firing from the hill not far in front of them. About 20 meters up the side, running parallel to the field, Ken spotted an NVA soldier. He tracked him briefly, watching the soldier's head and occasionally his chest bobbing over the brush as he ran. About fifty feet behind him, one of the Marines from One-Five gave chase.

"Everyone along the embankment opened up on the NVA, on full auto," Ken says. "I went through a couple of magazines, and the NVA continued up the hill. We were all shooting, but then we stopped because of concerns about the Marine who was chasing him."

Seconds after they stopped firing, an explosion erupted on the hill, but Ken could not tell if it had been from the NVA or from the Marine.

Ken was told to go back to the platoon CP for more ammo, so he ran along the embankment with his head down—one hand on his helmet and the other on his M16. When he arrived at the platoon CP, he was given no ammo but instead was tasked with escorting a wounded Marine back to the company CP and finding more ammo there.

Perched against the embankment was a Marine who'd just received a Corpsman's wrapping around his face. Fresh as it was, the bandage was already soaking with blood and loosening around the wounded Marine's cheeks.

"There's no battle dressing that really fits your face," Ken says, "but the Corpsman did the best he could."

A bullet had entered the soft fleshy side of the Marine's face just above the jawbone, took out a few teeth, and then exited with a slightly larger hole on the other side. Ken cocked his head at the wound, careful not to perform a noticeable grimace, and then shrugged his shoulders as if to say, "That's nothing. You're damn lucky." And all things being fair, the kid really was, though his eyes said otherwise.

Ken transferred his rifle to his left hand and then held his right hand out and open.

"You ready?"

The wounded Marine took Ken's hand but paused on a knee and leaned forward with an open mouth to let a dark red stream of blood and saliva pour out—enough, it seemed, to fill a ration can.

This time, Ken grimaced. He studied the direction back to the company CP with one eye burning in a drip of sweat. It would be a long trek back across the river, across open grass fields, and then somewhere in the paddies further back from the fighting. And then, of course, he'd have to return alone and hopefully with the ammo he set out to get in the first place—ammo that his gun team was still waiting for, plus "5.56 and 40 Mike-Mike for the M79 if he could get it."

"C'mon," he said, speaking more to himself than the Marine who held his hand, "Let's get going."

The wounded Marine stood up lazily. Ken took him up under his right arm, and they started down the line and back toward the river.

The wounded Marine leaned into Ken for support, and they both stumbled sideways. Ken was not a small man at six feet three inches, but he was weak from hunger. It had been several days since they had rations. After dividing his last can of peanut butter into thirds and sharing it with his gun team, they'd only been eating raw shrubbery when they could find it in the farmers' fields—fibrous gourds, sugar cane, and barely ripe pineapples. The sugar cane was good for a quick rush but left him feeling even worse when he came down from it. The small pineapples they'd found were sour, acidic, and the worst thing he could've put into his empty bowels. An immediate regret, the fruit had wrenched at his stomach. It had rumbled down his gut, pushing a new wave of diarrhea against his sphincter, which he clenched as he chucked the damned thing away from him. His gun team had all done the same—little green fruits, like grenades, thumping and rolling through the grass away from them.

Ken stepped against the weight of the wounded Marine to upright them both, but then the man's knees buckled, his body weight tugged down on Ken's arm, and he struggled to hold him upright, lest they both start stumbling now to the side. He could tell the Marine was not only weak from his own hunger but also going into hypovolemic shock. The Corpsman, he thought, had probably given him a shot of morphine, too. Either way, the kid was out of it.

"I'm going to need your help here," Ken said. "Come on, we've got to move."

The wounded Marine attempted a reply, but his words were incomprehensible and broken. He mumbled a word or two but then lost the air to finish. He took a quick, deep breath, but then again, only a word or two came out before he was gulping for air again like a fish. Lethargic and confused, the Marine pulled the two of them heavily down the river bank, and Ken struggled to keep them both from stumbling clumsily over one another into the water.

When they stepped in, Ken struggled to hold onto the Marine while navigating some unseen rocks at his feet. The wounded Marine lost his footing and tumbled heavily out from under Ken's arm. Ken shuffled around the unpredictable shapes of the large rocks until he found a footing and caught his own balance. He then reached out to take the Marine's arm and pull him back out of the water onto his feet. The boy came up coughing—a brown and pink stream of water ran over his chin and neck. The water-soaked bandage began to move down his wet hair off the top of his head and over one eye.

"Here," Ken said, stepping in front of him. "Get on my back. Put your arms around my neck and hold on. It gets deeper."

The Marine put his arms around Ken's neck. He didn't have the energy to hoist himself onto Ken's back, so Ken lowered himself to get the bend of the boy's elbows over his shoulders. He then pressed the Marine's arms against his chest and leaned forward to drag them both across the deepest part of the stream—his left arm still raised with the rifle in hand. Ken could feel thick blood from the Marine's wound gushing over the side of his neck and down onto his chest—unmistakably warm in contrast to the cool water on his body. A metallic smell of iron then overpowered the earthen smell of the brown river water under his nose.

When the two had gotten out of the river and above the bank on the other side, they had to rush across an open field to get to the cover of a tree line. Ken could hear the fight intensifying behind them. Automatic weapons fire cracked into a chorus, like a hundred strands of Black Cat firecrackers going off along the lines at once. There were occasional breaks in the fire, occasional explosions, but then it would erupt again into chaos. He needed to get back with ammunition for the gun, and from the sound of it, the company desperately needed it.

He pulled hard at the Marine with his arm, dragging him forward with all the force he could summon until he had the boy running fast through the tall grass (or falling ever forward under their momentum) until they reached the tree line. They both tumbled through the underbrush in the shade of the trees. Ken hoisted himself back to a knee, using one of the trees for support and catching his breath as he watched the wounded Marine roll over with dead pieces of vegetation now stuck to the blood and bandage on his face.

He got the Marine on his feet again, and they paralleled the tree line until it ended. To his right, where the tree line ended, the field opened up. He could see Marines across the field, but they were several hundred meters away. He traced the open ground between them with his eyes and then followed an imaginary sightline toward where he knew the enemy to be. The ground was open—completely clear to the base of Hill 110.

Ken attempted to lift the Marine into a fireman's carry, but he had not realized how weak he'd become and how hard it would be with little assistance from the wounded Marine, who was himself about as tall as Ken. He got the weight of the Marine over the back of his neck and his right arm around a leg.

Ken searched with one hand to find the Marine's arm so that he could grab his wrist and pin it to the leg. By the time he got upright, he still hadn't found the man's wrist, and so the weight of the wounded Marine's body slid off Ken's shoulders and pulled him backward toward the ground on top of him. With the M16 in one hand, Ken only had one to work with.

They tried the fireman's carry again, but on the second try, Ken overcompensated and found himself leaning too far forward over his own center of gravity before getting steady on his feet. The weight of the wounded Marine pulled him down toward his knees, and he stumbled forward until the rim of his helmet bit into the ground, and both his helmet and the Marine rolled onto the ground.

Ken had his helmet back on his head, the Marine back up over his right arm, and the both out in the open, hobbling across the field before he realized what his body was making him do. Across the way, one Marine caught sight of them and began to wave his arms over his head. Another Marine joined him, and so two Marines waved their arms in wide arcs over their heads. Both were yelling at them, but Ken couldn't understand what they were saying.

When they finally reached the other side, the company's Senior Corpsman ran out and took the wounded Marine into his care. It was then that Ken learned the waving Marines had not been trying to get him to come to them but rather to get them to stop and turn back. A sniper on the hill had just taken out two Marines in the very field they had just crossed.

Ken noticed a row of dead Marines several yards ahead, ten to twelve of them, covered with ponchos on the ground—boots protruding from under the poncho of one, a tuft of hair protruding from the next. He could smell them no sooner than he saw them—not the putrid smell of rotting flesh, but more like a meat locker. Death has a very distinct smell. It was well over one hundred degrees, so Ken knew they had all been killed very recently.

He hurried to find ammo, strung it on bandoleers across his chest, Poncho Villa style, and then headed back toward his men. There was no other way to go except the way he'd come, but by then, the UH1E Gunships had arrived and were working the side of the hill.

***

"I saw a cane field over there across from where Reid and Bishop were," Rezcek continues. "But I focused on the right, the stream bed and everything, because I felt that's where all the fire was going. But apparently, there was still NVA in that cane field. Because later on, a few minutes later, we had a helicopter come in, bringing a resupply of ammo. And I'm standing there with one of the machine gunners. He's standing right next to me, and all of a sudden, he gets shot right through his damn arm. He goes, 'God damn, that's hot!' He was a squad leader, I think. I don't remember his name. But yeah, they were in that cane field. And we didn't sweep that cane field."

Reczek moved most of the line back away from the trench and the river bed and on the way to some higher ground, which would be a good marker for close air support. Then, he started calling in A-4 Skyhawks and controlled strikes in the riverbed to the front of them.

An OE observation plane arrived on the scene—a small fixed-wing aircraft like a Cessna they called a "Bird Dog."

"I had a Lance Corporal, TACP man, a Tactical Air Control Party man," Reczek says. "And I would say, OK, this is where we want to strike. He would call up to the aerial observer and say, mark where we want it."

The Bird Dog shot air-to-ground rockets with target-marking smoke bombs from its underwing pylons. By about 10:30, the jets were dropping snake and nape (Snakeye bombs and napalm).

"I remember Major Dick Ossenfort, our battalion's S-3 Communications Officer, saying to me, 'Look up.'" Reczek says. "What the hell is he talking about, look up? During that time, when everything was going on, I saw these people up on top of Hill 110 who were part of the 5th Marines. This is after all the action we were involved with. They showed up on top up there. I didn't know that part of 5th Marines was right there on my left. And we're running airstrikes in there!"

When One-Three transitioned from Operation Beaver Cage to Operation Union, control of the battalion shifted to One-Five, and communications were poor from that point. Company and platoon commanders had little awareness of One-Five's presence, much less their positions and movement.

Unfortunately, one of the air strikes hit close to One-Five's Alpha Company, and their unit received casualties, killing five and wounding 24.

"We didn't even know they were there," Reczek says.

"The jets were coming by dropping napalm in the river valley, and everything down there just got burned to shit," says Michael Wynn. "That's when, behind us, the helicopter got shot down. Before we went back up the hill to get to higher ground, a chopper behind me was shot down. I don't know what happened to them, but we got up on higher ground, and we could still see the gooks down the valley, and then the napalm hit them. It got rid of quite a few of them."

Wynn may be referring to one of the choppers in a 40-man Sparrow Hawk sent after noon to reinforce the men.

Author Otto Lehrack quoted Captain Jerry Shirley's description of the moment.

"Battalion decided to send the Sparrow Hawk reaction force out there, and in the meantime, Jerry Reczek came up on the left and made contact with my northernmost platoon. The Sparrow Hawk platoon came out in a couple of Hueys and started to set down between my unit and the enemy position, and I saw what he was going to do and threw a red smoke grenade to try to warn him off. He didn't get the message, and the enemy put twenty-one rounds in the helo and wounded one of the pilots, but the troops made it off the helo. One of the choppers lifted up and slowly moved behind me but had taken so many rounds it couldn't fly."[1]

---

1   Jerry Shirley asked for me to correct the record here, saying that he was either misquoted or that he may have misspoke in his interview with Lehrack. "The helicopters were UH-34s or CH-46s as our sup-

The declassified Command Chronology reports that "the platoon met such resistance that further use of helicopters in the area became impractical."

At another point during the battle, a UH-34 had landed to drop off a couple of ammunition boxes and take some of the wounded back. They'd only been on the ground for one to one and a half minutes before they were back in the air, and when they got back to the ship, they counted thirty-four holes in the chopper. By that point, dozens of the Marines had been wounded, at least twenty-three from Bravo Company alone, but they would all have to wait.

Among those wounded was Tom Harrison, from Weapons, who was injured when Charlie Company's 2nd Platoon was moved forward to tie in with Bravo Company.

"They called rockets up," he says. "so I stood up to load, and the Corporal had it on his shoulder ready to fire, and that's when I got hit in the left leg with a piece of shrapnel. I don't know if it's from a grenade or a mortar round, but I didn't hear the explosion go off. You're just intent on doing your job."

The shrapnel went deep into Harrison's inner thigh just above the knee, where X-rays show that he still carries it to this day.

"I made it back to where the wounded were, and me and another African-American guy, he got hit. The bullet pierced his helmet, went completely around the inside of it, and came out about an inch of where it went in. He had terrible headaches sitting there, laying in the sun and stuff."

Many of the wounded Marines would have to bear their wounds for the entire day.

"It was dark when we got medevaced out of there," he says.

By 3:30 that afternoon, the enemy's backbone had been broken. After the air strikes, Bravo Company reported that NVA were retreating to the east. By 4:00 PM, remaining contact was light, and all three companies of the battalion started consolidating positions

---

porting helicopter squadron did not have Hueys," Shirley told me.

and tying together in a perimeter for the night.

"We spent that afternoon in our positions overlooking that stream bed where we figured we had the NVA trapped in there," Reczek says. "That day, there was not one cigarette to be found in the whole company. All the guys smoked. I smoked. There was not one man; nobody had a cigarette there. But nobody really missed a cigarette."

One of the platoons brought up a prisoner they had caught. Dressed in black pajamas, the prisoner was, as Reczek describes, "sturdy, strong, and young." The prisoner had big scars on his shoulders where you could see that he'd been carrying heavy loads for a long time. The prisoner stared directly at Reczek with arrogant contempt.

"So, we kept him overnight," he says. "That night, we were told by the 5th Marines to hold our positions and run night patrols because they wanted us to try to catch them leaving, catch them trying to escape the trap down there. So, we ran some patrols under illumination, but my guys were exhausted already."

"Word passed to pull from our position back across the river," Ken says. "We set along the stream's edge; previous fighting holes had been dug, and we reoccupied them. We had dropped all our packs when the fighting broke out, so we only had what we'd stuffed in our pockets. We were still at 100 percent watch. Everybody's up—nobody's sleeping. We had no idea what phase the battle was in. As far as we knew, anything could still happen."

Before dark, a patrol from another company ambled through their lines, going out. Just after dark, Ken could sense they were returning because he could smell the bodies before hearing the patrol. He and his team watched quietly from the sandy ground where they sat as the patrol carried bodies back through the lines on ponchos to wherever they'd come from. Only the eerie distant hiss of white phosphor could be heard—illumination rounds fading as they fell into darkness.

"Movies do not capture that element of a battlefield, the smell of rotting bodies," he says. "If there is one thing that will take me instantly back to Vietnam, it is that smell."

The next morning, the Marines brought the prisoner back up to Reczek.

"I don't know where they found this damn truck tire, but they had this truck tire draped over his shoulders," he says. One has to wonder how the night had gone for that prisoner under the watch of some very pissed-off Marines.

"His demeanor was changed big time, I'll tell you," Reczek said.

"That morning, we went back across the river," Michael Wynn recalls. "We couldn't get to the dead that day. It was just too much firing. We couldn't pick up the dead that day. So the next morning, when everything was sort of over, we went over there and had to retrieve the dead. I'll just never forget a number of things. There are a couple of things that stick out in my mind, and the number one is how bloody quiet it was there. There wasn't even a bird chirping. Everything was just so quiet and just so amazing. The day before, it was so loud. After all that, we went across the river, and there wasn't a sound. There were just bodies everywhere, gooks and Marines."

Wynn says they also had to count the dead NVA and search them.

"A lot of times, they put grenades under them with the pin pulled," he says. "If you move the body, the grenade will go off. So, we had to get grappling hooks and rope and get away before we moved the gook bodies."

"When we went over and scoured the battlefield to see what was left up there," Steve Berkheiser says, "we found scoped SKS rifles that were very capable—rifles for people trained well enough to make 500 yards or more. They didn't have second-rate equipment. They were well-funded and well-supplied. They were tough, well-armed, and well-trained. After Beaver Cage and Union, I would never say they were poor shots. Their snipers were damn good."

"We also found a lot of freshly dug graves when we were over there," Wynn continues. "They tried to bury their dead at one time or another."

The Marines could see indentations in the soft ground where shallow graves had been hastily dug at some point in the afternoon or in the night, so the Marines went over to a nearby village and rounded up a bunch of the women.

"We never saw any men in the village over about 12 years old. They were all gone, but there were a lot of women, kids, and old men. They took the women over, gave them E-tools, pulled out a 45, and made them dig these graves up. They were full of, we call them 'crispy critters,' full of the NVA that had been hit by the napalm. It was quite a sight, you know…what that looks like."

In the war of attrition that was Vietnam, America did not fight so much to gain ground or to hold it as to kill more of the enemy than they killed Americans. Washington and the upper echelon were always interested in body counts.

"The other thing that sticks out in my mind that I still think about today is the Marines," Wynn says. "I have images still to the day of the Marines stacked. The dead Marines under ponchos, stacked like firewood. Then, at the end, it was open, and all you could see sticking out were the jungle boots. It just really got me. You know? They brought them over the river, and then they just stacked them. Maybe three high, just stacked like firewood."

When Ken saw the dead under the ponchos the day before, he had only seen them in a single row, ten to a dozen men, not stacked. By the next day, however, all the Marines had been accounted for, and 22 had lost their lives. 88 had been wounded. As for the VC/NVA KIAs, 86 were confirmed.

The battle-worn and exhausted Marines continued moving east toward LZ Quail, where they would soon return to the ships at sea. For Ken, the next couple of days were "kind of a blur"—a slow and listless march back to the relative comfort and safety of the ships.

At one point, he recalls, they passed through a village where there had been an airstrike.

"There were dead animals everywhere, and you could smell the napalm," he says.

One of the dead animals had been a bloated cow—its legs stiff straight in the air from rigor mortis. For Ken, it brought back memories of the Taft High School class of 1966. His high school's athletic nickname had been the Toreadors (the bullfighters), and their senior graduation gift had been a large, black fiberglass bull rolled out on a wheeled platform in a chorus of cheers and feet thundering on bleachers.

It had not even been a year since he graduated, yet it already felt like a lifetime ago—the boy he had been there, a stranger to himself now. Back then, he knew that if he ever wanted to achieve a different life for himself, he would have to be a different person, but he needed help.

He hadn't succeeded in changing himself; he just couldn't get around his shyness. His parents were so tied up in themselves and their own issues that they neglected his needs. The school had brushed him aside. His grades weren't good enough for college, and since his mother hadn't let him get a driver's license, his mobility was limited. To get away from home and on his own path, joining some branch of service seemed like the only logical option. So, when recruiters showed up at Taft High in the last semester of his senior year, he joined the assembly in earnest.

All male seniors were gathered in a large multi-purpose room where staged upfront, were recruiters from the Army, Navy, Air Force, Coast Guard, and Marines. The Army recruiter stood first, introduced himself, and delivered his pitch in a way that reminded Ken of a door-to-door encyclopedia salesman. He talked about how, in the world's most powerful army, you might find yourself anywhere in the world. He said you could go to Europe, for example, to Heidelberg in Germany. You could get to France, Spain, Italy, and Switzerland by train but then come home to a self-contained community complete with an all-American school, cinema, and church—hot dogs and American football. Even American automobiles—any make, any model.

The Army recruiter wasn't lying. Everything he said was true, but Ken couldn't help noticing that one quintessential fact had been suspiciously avoided. A conflict had been escalating just below China, on some long, vertical sliver of continent called Vietnam. He'd seen it on the CBS Evening News with his father. Although the US Congress had not formally declared war, television news reporters were assuring the American people that the conflict in Vietnam was nothing less.

"The United States is indeed at war," Walter Cronkite had said. "…a full-dress war against a formidable enemy."

While not as salesey as the Army recruiter, the Navy and Air Force men also skirted around the elephant in the room. The Navy recruiter had talked about atomic submarines, aircraft carriers, and electronics. The Air Force recruiter had talked about fixing airplanes and the advancing technology in America's state-of-the-art aircraft. Like the Army recruiter, both emphasized the variety of trades and skills that would be learned and that could lead to lucrative careers. Whatever the Coast Guard recruiter had said, Ken could not recall. His attention was drawn to the Marine in the dress blue Charlies.

The Marine recruiter was a thin, wiry man a couple inches shy of six feet tall. He wore blue trousers with a scarlet stripe down the outside seams of each leg, or "blood stripes" as they were called. He wore a khaki long-sleeved shirt with a khaki necktie, and, over his left breast, he wore multiple rows of colored ribbons representing his service in WWII and Korea. His white dress cover had been removed when he entered the building, and his flat-top, crew-cut hair was short and clean. He introduced himself as a First Sergeant and then gave a decidedly brief speech. He had no sales pitch. His attitude conveyed that if you didn't want the Marine Corps, the Marine Corps didn't want you.

"I'm not going to promise that we'll send you to school or that you can go live and work in some exotic country," he said. "All I want to promise you is this: If you want to be a Marine, we will put you through boot camp where you will be pushed and tested to prove yourself twenty-two hours a day, seven days a week. If you make it through boot camp, if you make the cut, then you will be a goddamn Marine."

The Marine recruiter sat down with his head and back as straight as a ramrod. Ken was slightly stunned at his frankness but knew the man wasn't selling anything. He wasn't giving anything away. He wasn't promising those boys anything for just showing up. The indication was clear: what he offered had to be earned. Ken was persuaded, not by his words, but by the no-frills truth that everything about the man and his words conveyed. He had reached down into the boy and grabbed hold of something, as if by the collar, that had been there all along—pulled it upright and forward. The answer to his need and the question of his life had been there all along; the first sergeant simply shined a light on it.

He was destined to be a Marine, and he was willing and ready to earn it, sure as the sunrise.

Now, he was in some exotic land with foreign soil smoldering under his boots. He'd seen things men aught never see, and more death than most folks back home would ever see in a lifetime. He'd never been as thirsty, hungry, sick, weak, or pushed to the limits of mental and physical endurance as he had in the days passed, but still, he felt a certain pride—a certain something hard-earned and inexplicable. It was what the veteran Marine from WWII and Korea had promised but did not endeavor to explain.

The shy boy he had been back in high school was a stranger to him now, unrecognizable. All he could relate to was the sense that he had, the feeling that whatever that old salt was selling, that's what he wanted. He had wanted that.

And so, though weak and weary, he smiled as the words echoed back because he was beginning to understand what that old salt meant when he had said it.

"You will be a goddamn Marine."

"The Mike Boats take us back to the Bayfield," Ken says. "No one's doing much talking. We're just standing in the Mike Boats—quiet and filthy. We're really filthy. Torn utilities. Most of us haven't shaved in a while. We pull alongside the ship, and I look up. I don't know if I can get up there. I have my rifle slung across my back. I keep staring at the cargo net, thinking there is no way I can climb up to the ship. We form into groups of three and get in the queue to go up. You grabbed the vertical ropes so no one above you could step on your hands, and we started climbing up. The Mike Boat is banging up against the Bayfield because of the swells. Once you get above the Mike boat, it becomes more steady because you're not constantly moving back and forth and up and down. I'm exhausted, and I'm sure the two Marines beside me are just as exhausted. I'm pulling myself up, and I must have had that look on my face because as I'm climbing, I'm looking up, and I'm about within arm's length of that sailor up at the top. He just reached down and grabbed me by my straps, and pulled me up. The same happened to the Marines I was climbing with."

A sailor in dark blue dungarees and a light blue shirt had pulled Ken up and set him down on the deck. Ken looked across at the cargo hatch and saw a mountain of 782 gear from all their dead. They had dropped packs in the Que Son Valley, and all that stuff had been sent back to the ship, along with all the blood-stained gear from their dead and wounded.

"I looked at it," Ken says, "and that 782 gear hit me harder than probably anything else. I had friends who were killed. Hissong was a good friend, and now a KIA, Hickman was KIA, and Hittson was wounded and gone. I didn't know whether or not McKeon, who we called Ricky Recon, was OK. He had been medevaced as a bad heat casualty. I don't know what happens when heat strokes are that bad. The company—we had 12 dead and about 40 wounded. The sailors were very…they didn't push us around, didn't say anything, they were very quiet around us."

CHAPTER 37

In Memoriam

MEMORIAL SERVICES WERE held for those killed during the operations. One service was held on the flight deck of the USS Okinawa, where Alpha, Bravo, and Charlie were held. Another smaller service was held aboard the USS Bayfield for Delta Company.

The Marines stood at parade rest—with left foot ten inches from the right and their hands behind their backs. It had been three full days since they returned to the ships, but they were still exhausted from fifteen grueling days in the field. 201 men had been wounded in action, so many of them were sore from shrapnel that had been dug from muscle tissue and from where their skin had been stitched. Others, with more critical wounds, were aboard the USS Sanctuary hospital ship or up in Teal's hospital ward on the Okinawa. Additional Marines, not counted among the wounded, suffered still from various illnesses—exhaustion, malnutrition, dehydration, and a variety of gastrointestinal infections from the pathogenic organisms in the waters of Vietnam. At least now they had the comfort of their soft covers and clean utilities.

"A couple of Marines passed out during that service," Reczek tells me, one of which was Ron Asher, who wrote the following in his diary that night.

> **16th** *I am back aboard the Oki now, we had a memorial service on the flight deck for Marines killed on the op, I passed out and was taken to sick bay. I was there for a few hours, and the doc said it was just exhaustion and I should rest a little and drink liquids. Tonight we are anchored in Da Nang harbor, I am real tired, guess I'll catch a few winks.*

In front of the rows of Marines, the large aircraft elevator platform rose to meet the flight deck. On the platform were laid four long rows of helmets—58 for Marines killed, 3 for Navy Corpsmen, and 4 aviator helmets for the flight crew who'd drowned when their chopper crashed into the sea.

Behind the rows of helmets, in between a row of standing officers, Navy Chaplain Lieutenant Paul Uhles approached a podium and performed an Old Testament reading from Psalm 27.

"The Lord is my light and my salvation—whom shall I fear? The Lord is the stronghold of my life—of whom shall I be afraid?"

Though authoritative and sure, the chaplain's voice was no doubt obscured by the lingering echoes of madness still reverberating somehow in the silence of the salty breeze. Intense sights, sounds, and smells were still flashing off the edges of frayed nerves and filing themselves into various new compartments of mental cement. New weight to be carried—along with all the 782 gear.

Of all the Marines I talk to, few remember anything about what was actually said during the services. James (Jim) Cook from Delta Company's second platoon remembers only that the chaplain on the Bayfield read from Ecclesiastes 3.

> *"To every thing there is a season, and a time to every purpose under the heaven,"*

The men, many just boys on the cusp of manhood, were all still decompressing and processing what in Hell had just happened to them. Cook's twenty-third birthday came the day after they returned from the operations, but I can't imagine he mentioned a word about it, considering the circumstances. Like all the rest, he had his mind on the things he witnessed—things he didn't quite know how to file, moments that would come back to him again and again for the rest of his life. He tells me of two, in particular, that he never forgot.

"There were two Marines that were dragging another out on a poncho, and his legs were inverted," he says, "They were bouncing across the ground there, and he was hollering, 'Kill me! Kill me!' He'd been hit with a machine gun, and it blew his legs off. That was after Sergeant Hall got hit in the chest with a mortar round. The mortar fire missed my spot and went over to First Platoon and killed him. He was laying behind his fox hole."

"A time to be born, and a time to die," the Bayfield's chaplain continued, "a time to plant, and a time to pluck up that which is planted; A time to kill, and a time to heal..."

The Okinawa's chaplain continued from Psalm 23.

"Though an army besiege me, my heart will not fear; though war break out against me, even then I will be confident."

On the outside, each memorial was tranquil and quiet, but for my father and for all the Marines and Corpsmen, the silent pauses between each stanza were undoubtedly the noisiest that perfect silence in the ocean breeze would ever be.

"I never heard such screaming in my life," Burleson says, remembering Hill 110. "Blood-curdling. We kept calling the F4s on the hill, and they did a lot of damage. It was like a nightmare, so much screaming."

Ray Kelley remembers it, too.

"When the napalm was being dropped in there," he says, "I will never forget the screaming."

Nor would he forget seeing Sergeant Brackins' jaw, hanging from his head on a sliver of skin, running to reinforce Bravo Company and seeing Marine and NVA bodies in so many places that he looked, and the bodies and gear he helped load onto the chopper after the ambush on May the 4th.

Brackins had been one that Winfield Spear could never forget as well.

"The only time I got sick in Vietnam was when I spoke to Sergeant Brackins," he says, "telling him we were with him and he would be okay. When you look down a man's throat and see only the tongue and upper teeth, your mind does not want to comprehend that awful wound."

Stanley Wilson from Delta's First Platoon will never forget just how close he came to dying—the incredible punch against his helmet when a round went in, rattled around, and sent him flying through the air.

For Steve Berkheiser, it was seeing his two squad leaders, McMahon and Turn, killed, each within five minutes of another and then Doc Sovey getting killed trying to get to Corporal Turn. It was the pain of having to leave them out there overnight and a certain guilt for not having disobeyed the order to fall back.

"I was sure they were all killed instantly," he said, "We couldn't get to them, but we should have at least stayed and watched over their bodies through the night."

For Tom Nollman, it was seeing Louis Tilton get hit and then dragging him back to the lines under fire with help from Tom Jalbert and Bottom. And then, seeing Mel get hit and how enraged it had made him, he'd immediately jumped up and started spraying the area with rounds until the Right Guide Sergeant got him out of his crazed fury and back down under cover.

For Jim Shipp, it was seeing Dennis Mannion, Marty, and the

H boys go down in the rice paddy on the 4th—hearing Marty call out for a Corpsman and unable to get to him.

Ken Hicks would never forget the chopper going into the sea—the sound of the klaxons and the searchlights on the surface of the dark waters. He would never forget the inexplicable scene of killed Marines on the rock outcropping, like ghosts, but as real as if they had never died. He would not forget the Marine bodies laid in a row on May the 10th, the smell of bodies passing through on that night, or the bloody mountain of 782 gear stacked on the hatch cover when he rolled off the net ladder back onto the Bayfield. Though he was young, he no longer felt the invincibility of youth. He wondered if he could make it, at least to the Fourth of July, to see his nineteenth birthday.

The young Marines had returned to the ships forever changed and already, their new experiences haunted them. They had literally walked through the valley of the shadow of death, and they had joined the rich history of their brethren in doing the noble but god-awful job that Marines are called to do. For most of the Battalion Landing Team, it had been their first combat experience, and most of the Marines still had from four to nine months left in their tours—those that were to survive and avoid severe wounds, that is.

Beaver Cage/Union marked not only a drastic increase in the tempo of the war for the battalion but also a mental turning point for its men. After that May, their average combat days would shoot up to twenty-two per month. The Special Landing Force, of which they were a part, would be heavily relied upon for the remainder of the year. Up to Christmas, there would be twenty-three more back-to-back operations with no more than a week of rest on the ships between each. The Marines commonly describe the months to come as a long and arduous "blur" during which one operation flowed into the next.

On the Okinawa, there was a New Testament reading from John, Chapter 14, prayers, a blessing, and three volleys from a firing squad.

On the night of the 14th, when they had arrived back on the Bayfield, Shipp had to express what he was feeling in some way. He sat in the dim light of the mess deck and wrote his sanitized description of the May 4th ambush in the letter to his mom and dad. He stopped once to quickly blot a single tear off the page, something he would hate for them to notice, and then continued writing.

"We lost many fine men on that day and I saw more courage in a few hours than I've seen in a lifetime. All were good friends of mine, and I must say that I only hope these guys' parents realize how bravely they died.

I'm up for a Bronze Star for helping a wounded man out of that living Hell, but I doubt that I get it. There are many who showed more courage that day than I'm capable of. I'm sure that if it were possible, every man who gets a cheap piece of metal would gladly trade it in to have one of our beloved Marines back. They later said we dealt the NVA severe losses. That doesn't mean a thing to me, as the life of one American is worth more than 1,000 filthy gook lives.

Later on (several days) we lost some more by mortars, and finally the full battalion was engaged in a pitched battle with a full regiment of NVA on the 10th. Delta Company suffered only a few casualties, but some of the other companies were hard hit. I do know that we annihilated that regiment. 200 bodies were found, and that means about 400-600 were actually killed. Once again, my life is God's life.

Now, onto more happy things. They brought us back onto the ship today, so I'm very, very safe and sound. We had a large mail call, and I got my Miss America picture (all the guys were amazed, as was I). (A friend of Jim's had arranged for Miss America to mail him an autographed photo. Ed.).

I also got a Playboy and lots of letters, so I'm in great spirits. Everything will be alright, just keep praying, as I am now a witness of the fact that you have been. We are supposed to be on the ship for several days, but I guess time will tell. I've got less than four months left now, so start working on a menu and on that menu have nothing but ice drinks. Okay?

Not much else at present. Take care, and keep 'em coming. These next few months will be tough, but when the going gets tough, the tough get going, and be proud of the U.S. Marine Corps, because there's no tougher or courageous outfit in the world. I must go.

All my love, Jim."

In the morning, only two days after the memorial services, the Marines were served steak and eggs for breakfast—yet another meal Ken does not recall actually eating.

That same morning, a familiar dreadful voice came over the loudspeakers. The Battalion Landing Team's next operations, Beau Charger and Hickory were beginning.

"NOW HEAR THIS," the voice said.

"BATTLE STATIONS!

BATTLE STATIONS!

LAND THE LANDING FORCE!"

Aligned across the deck USS Okinawa (LPH-3) are helmets of those who gave their lives on Operation Beaver Cage and on Operation Union.

IN MEMORY OF
(BLT 1/3)

2nd LT Thomas W. Mallon
SSgt Elpidio A. Arquero
Sgt Milton L. Hall
Sgt Donnie D. Jacobs
Sgt Reinaldo A. Castro
Cpl Luciano P. Plesokov
Cpl John W. Urick
Cpl Frederick A. Mcmahon
Cp I Martin Cavazos
Cpl Don W. Minton
Cpl Henry L. Turn
Cpl Thomas Sonders
Cpl Alfred L. Brown
Cpl John M. Reid
Cpl Sterling S. Woods
L/Cpl Eugene Murry
L/Cpl Eugene D. Spicer
L/Cpl Troy M. Carnline
L/Cpl Melvin L. Allen
L/Cpl Jose M. Gomez
L/Cpl Michael M. Gukich

L/Cpl James E Lakey
L/Cpl William M Shaw, JR.
L/Cpl Harold T. Gillis
L/Cpl Delaney D. Tolbert
L/ Cpl David M. Hart
L/Cpl James M. Bishop
L/Cpl Blenn C. Dyer
L/Cpl Gene Vaughn
L/Cpl Ronald K. Pennington
PFC Phillip D. Munday
PFC Clarence J. Simmons
PFC Robert J. Rose
PFC David Verbilla
PFC Joseph R. Larose
PFC Mounty D. Button
PFC Tommy E. Dickerson
PFC John E. Sweesy
PFC Donald W. Falwell
PFC Rickey M. Gilbertson
PFC Dennis J. Mannion
PFC Don R. Hollingsworth
PFC David A. Hickman
PFC Harry L. Hissong
PFC David L. Rowell
PFC Albert J. Darling III
PFC Donald A. Pittenger
PFC Allan F. Berweger
PFC Frank X. Cuzzo
PFC Jomes R. Cooper
PFC Thomas L. Foy
PFC Brian C. Hewitt
PFC Randall R. Grueber
PFC Kenneth W. Mcgee
PFC James C. Riley
PFC Russell P. Miller
PFC James A. Benton
PFC Samuel W. Osborne JR.

(HMM-263)

Capt Jefferson J. Chesnutt
1stLT Jon D. Baker
L/Cpl Richard H. Dallas
Cpl Phillip R. Vanasse

SHADOW OF THE VALLEY

(NAVY)

HM3 Elwood C. Sovey
JR. HN Jomes I. Bolch
HN Steven D. Chambers

Epilogue

Operations Beau Charger and Hickory

```
Beau Charger: May 14 - 31, 1967

Hickory: May 18 - 28, 1967
```

On May 8, while 1/3 had been sweeping the Que Son Valley on Beaver Cage/Union, the catalyst for their next combat operation was already in motion. NVA ground forces on the southern side of the Ben Hai River attacked Con Thien, just below the DMZ. Farther east and south, they also struck Camp Carroll, Gio Linh, and Dong Ha. The enemy assaulted, sometimes engaging the Marines in hand-to-hand combat, and then headed back across the DMZ, where they knew they could not be pursued by the Marines.

At the time, the U.S. adhered to the Geneva agreement restricting military forces from entering the DMZ, but clearly, the NVA had been exploiting the area. Because of this, General Westmoreland authorized the entry of U.S. troops into the DMZ just south of the Ben Hai River (the Ben Hai was generally the centerline of the DMZ). In four simultaneous operations (Hickory, Lam Son 54, Belt Tight, and Beau Charger), 5,500 troops from the 3rd Marine Division and the ARVN (Army of the Republic of Vietnam) 1st Division were to sweep the area, route the enemy, and evacuate civilians. Once the southern half of the DMZ was cleared, it would become a "free-fire zone" where anyone could be considered an enemy combatant and fired upon with no required coordination or approval from headquarters.

The Marines of 1/3 had only six days aboard the fleet to rest and recover from their first combat operation before they were called to make their second amphibious landing under the code name Beau Charger. That morning, on May 18, a duel started along the coast between Navy fire support ships and NVA shore batteries. Ten salvos from the NVA batteries bracketed the USS Point Defiance but hit no vessel. After return fire silenced their shore batteries, the landing proceeded without further incident or opposition on the beach.

1/3's heliborne force experienced a different situation, however. Marines from Alpha Company set out from the Okinawa on UH-34 helicopters from Marine Medium Helicopter Squadron 263. Only 6 miles from the North Vietnamese border, resistance was expected to be heavy at the landing zone, LZ Goose.

The lead chopper, piloted by Lt. Col. Edward Kirby, the squadron's commanding officer, took off at 0800 and pushed his UH-34 low and fast over the DMZ. When he attempted to set down at LZ Goose, machine gun fire ripped into his helicopter as well as into the co-pilot, crew chief, gunner, and three of the five Marines aboard. A fourth Marine fell out of the chopper to his death.

The injured gunner fought back while Kirby worked hard to lift the helicopter off the ground again. Since his radio was destroyed, he couldn't alert the other pilots about the situation, so as Kirby rushed back to the Okinawa, the other choppers continued toward the LZ, unaware. When Kirby got his damaged chopper landed on the deck, he ran to tell the SLF's commander about the carnage at LZ Goose. The commander immediately moved the second wave's landings about 875 yards south to LZ Owl, but it was already too late for the first wave. They had unloaded all their Marines in the "hot" zone at Goose and gotten six more choppers shot up.

Those who survived the landing set up a defensive formation and fought for survival. With the odds stacked against them, Alpha Company Marines pleaded for naval gunfire. However, the request went unserved since nobody could pinpoint the enemy's position, and the ships feared their shelling could hit the Marines.

By 0855, the second wave had landed at Owl and moved in double-time to support the aborted assault at LZ Goose. Lance Cpl. John Galluzzo was in one of the second-wave helicopters from Alpha Company's 2nd Platoon. In the December 2014 issue of Vietnam, Galluzzo wrote about the carnage he and his squad found when they reached the area around the first LZ.

Corporal Richard Land, PVT Ed Christensen, Lance Cpl. Paul Doyon, Corporal Russell Keck, PFC Mark Dagliesch, PFC Charles Anderson, "another machine gunner I didn't know," Rebel (Corporal Stanley Godwin) and Doc Smitty (hospital Corpsman Michael Smith) were dead.

"Larsen, Wallace, Funk, Storey, Godwin, Sgt. Martin, Pete Gobaliewski & McEvoy had all been injured. We had an 11-man platoon. We found 3 more, safe, so now we had two 7-man squads, and I was made 1st squad leader."

Several of those injured were of little use in combat.

"Sgt. Martin's okay, Ski may lose one or both arms, Larsen & Wallace are going home, Tex probably will go home, Funk, Storey & Chase are okay. T.W. Godwin was shot through the pack…Tex was not only shot three times, but his pack stopped seven rounds from hitting his back."

While Alpha Company had been landing into the hot LZ by helos, Delta Company had come ashore with amtracs and a platoon of five M48 tanks (four with 90mm main guns and one with a mounted flame thrower instead of a gun).

"Once on the beach," Ken Hicks says, "word was passed for 3rd Platoon to mount up on two of the tanks (called a 'light section') and head out to link up with Alpha Company. Along with Bravo Company, a day of heavy fighting ensued."

The fighting remained fierce until the enemy was finally subdued by close air support, but by then, many Marines had already been killed and wounded.

One of the battles fought that day was to be the most memorable of Ray Kelley's tour. It was so memorable, in fact, to those who witnessed it that more than fifty years after his actions on that day, they would together petition for him to earn the Silver Star Medal, which is the United States Armed Forces' third-highest military decoration for valor in combat.

* * *

"There was a beautiful little pond with lily pads," says Kelley, who recalls a patrol they were on that day. "We turned to switch back near this pond and this bombed-out house, and I'm looking ahead at a little rise, like a sloping hill."

On the hill, Kelley saw what looked like a dark-skinned Puerto Rican with thick hair. Kelley stopped and turned to his A-gunner, Glenn Close.

"Is that a gook up there?"

Before Close could respond, the man on the rise opened up on them with a 30-caliber machine gun. Kelley and the Marines beside him dropped to the ground and moved quickly out of the open to the bottom of the rise. Once at the base of the hill, the enemy gunner started throwing down CHICOMs—the Chinese Communist grenades, the ones with wooden handles.

"I look up, and I can see them tumbling down at us in slow motion," Kelley says. "So we're yelling 'Grenade!' and we curl up in a fetal position and boom, boom, boom—they went off all around us. Myself, Glenn Close, and this kid, McKeon, who was a rifleman, then decided to charge up the little rise."

Kelley fired his machine gun from the hip as he, Close, and McKeon charged up the hill.

"I'm bangin' away, and these two guys are firing, and we drove the gook out of his fighting hole," he says.

The hill was a 50 to 60-foot slope. When they got to the top, there was a depression past which they'd driven back the NVA. After the depression, the ground sloped back up a bit, and the gooks were up above. The enemy gunner had built a fighting hole in the sand with a shelf that still had two or three more grenades on it, so Kelly, Close, and McKeon took position in the hole.

At some point, Kelley locked horns with the enemy gunner and stitched him from groin to head—every fifth round in his gun, a tracer that punched like a laser through the NVA. Spiked on adrenaline, the scene was vivid.

"He went to see Buddha," Kelley says. "It was pretty intense. You know how they say an athlete can be 'in the zone?' Or if you've been in a car accident, everything's in slow motion? Same thing here. Those NVA were actually from the 324th A & B Division—they were trained by the Russians and the Chinese. They had all modern equipment and uniforms. I could also see this other uniformed gook—he could've been a lieutenant, a captain, I'm not sure. He popped up because he didn't know where I was. He stood up, I opened up on him, and I could see the bullets leaving the machine gun in slow motion. He dropped down just before they got to him, and they went right by him. I just missed the bastard."

Ray makes the sounds of machine gun fire and, with his hands, he indicates the bullets cutting closer and closer to the NVA, the NVA ducking just in the nick of time, and the bullets passing over the spot where the NVA had just been standing.

"Amazing," he says, the moments still as clear in his memory as when they happened. "Amazing."

"We were on their left flank," he continues. "They actually had a horseshoe ambush set up, and if we would have been maybe another 150 feet in that direction, they would've swallowed us all. So, we basically caught them by surprise. They tried to overrun us on the left flank, so we were firing down there to keep them from overrunning the company, and, of course, we were engaged with the gooks in front of us, and the shit's hitting the fan."

McKeon, who was fighting just to the right of Kelley, was shot in the back of the leg. An alarming stream of blood gushed out of his leg with each heartbeat; the bullet had severed his femoral artery.

"McKeon had earned several scholarships—football scholarships for college, but he decided to join the Marine Corps," Kelley says. "He was a pretty chunky guy, so I said to him, 'Mac, you're going to have to push with your good leg!' So, Close took over the machine gun, and I took McKeon down."

All the while, bullets were going between Kelley's legs, past his head, behind his head.

"Bark was flying off the trees," he says. "There was smoke curling up the trees. If anybody ever tells you they got shot at and they heard 'whoosh,' well, you know they're a bull-shitter because when you're shot at, and the round's close enough, it cracks. That bullet's passing you at the speed of sound. Just like if you step on a dry twig or hear wood pop in a fireplace—you hear crack, crack, crack. That's what it sounds like when you're being shot at. Believe me. I had shit going by me. I got slightly wounded when a bullet bounced off the machine gun, but I still don't know how I didn't get shot."

"On my first trip down, dragging McKeon down, one of our guys down there had been shot in the helmet." Kelley continues. "The round went around his helmet and took off the tip of his ear. And he's stunned, so, on the way back up, I went to him, and I said, 'These people are trying to kill you! They want to take your life! Wake… the…fuck…up! Pull your shit together! You wanna fall apart later, great…but let's hold it together now!"

With McKeon back down in the care of a Corpsman, Kelley returned up the rise to rejoin Close. But while he'd been gone, Close had been shot below the leg. Kelley found Close lying on his back with his right foot flat on the ground and turned impossibly sideways.

"I grabbed him, and I drug him back," Kelley says. "And he and I were very close (excuse the pun), but when I was pulling him, he was screaming. So, I put my hand up underneath his chin. I didn't want to hear him, you know, crying in pain like that. I also gave him my pistol."

Other Marines from the company watched as Kelley drug Close off the hill. As the gooks advanced toward them, Close shot with Kelley's pistol to hold them back. When Kelley got Close down the hill, he went back up, completely alone.

"I grabbed the cocking lever on the machine gun and pulled it back, but it came straight back with no resistance."

Lifting the feed cover on the gun, Kelley peered inside to see the bolt was gone. Close had put it in his pocket! Kelley left the gun and went back to the bottom of the rise, gathered as many grenades as he could, then went back up again, running on full automatic as other Marines watched in awe.

"The gooks were so close I could hear them talking," he remembers. "I could still see them up there. There's like a three to five-second delay on the hand grenade. You pull the pin, and you let the spoon fly. There's a fuse in there, and it burns until it hits a blasting cap, and then the grenade explodes. The gooks were so close, I'd hold the grenade like a baseball, let the spoon fly, count, one-thousand one, one-thousand two, and then I'd throw it. Because I didn't want them to grab it and throw it back at me."

As Kelley threw the grenades, a prop-driven A-1 Sky Raider plane, piloted by ARVN, suddenly appeared overhead and began peppering the enemy with cannon fire.

"I think they were 20mm canons they had," Kelley says. "That's when the gooks finally broke."

In that encounter, the company was taking so much fire, they had to bring amtracs to take the wounded Marines out; they couldn't bring in the helicopters.

"There was a tanker sitting outside of the tank, with the upper part of his body exposed, you know, from the waist up," Kelley says. "And Skipper Spear told him, 'You should get inside that tank.' He didn't listen to him, and later that day, that tanker took one in the chest, and it killed him. So, it was just…you know…there are so many things that happened."

* * *

Ken Hicks' 3rd Platoon rejoined the company late in the afternoon with one tank towing another, which had run into a mine that blew off a road wheel and snapped the track. They completed digging in before nightfall.

Because of their casualties in April and early May, the platoons were short of riflemen, so Ken was tasked with joining one of them to man an LP (listening post). Every platoon put out a listening post or two at night to provide an early warning in the case of a night attack.

The terrain was basically flat, with very light-colored sand and many small scrub pine trees.

Ken quickly cleaned his rifle and checked his frags, making sure the pins were bent over the spoons and that he had tape around the top in case the pins came loose and fell out. He checked his magazines, bayonet, and KA-BAR and made sure his gear was quiet.

Just as it was becoming dark (it is called Beginning Evening Nautical Twilight), Ken and the 3rd Platoon rifleman, a Marine named Tildon, moved slowly and quietly out in front of the platoon.

"It was like we were walking on pins and needles," Ken says. "We stayed in the shadows and very close to the scrub pines. We would move a few meters, take a knee in the shadow of a tree, listen, stand up in a crouch, move a few meters, and repeat the process all over again."

Ken also carried the radio, with the volume turned way down and the radio on squelch, so it made no noise.

They found a couple of scrub pines close together, where they could move into the shadows and sit back to back. There would be no sleeping.

They were in place for about an hour when they heard movement and very soft murmuring. Earlier that day, an ARVN unit had rounded up several hundred civilians, and those civilians had been kept outside of the company's lines. Ken and Tildon had no idea if the sounds they heard were the civilians or NVA. Ken radioed the information to the company command post.

They were starting to get movement all around them, but because of the density of the scrub pines, they could not see anything. They pushed as far back into the two trees they were under as they could, took their rifles off safe, and prepared to fight their way out, if necessary.

The company radioed for them to move back to the company perimeter. Easier said than done. They had no idea what was around them or who. They extracted themselves from under the two trees and sat there listening. With adrenaline pumping through their bodies, their brains were telling them to get out of there, but they could not merely jump up and run back to the perimeter.

They waited for everything to quiet down and then slowly got up and began their movement back, repeating what they had done when they had left the perimeter: move a few meters, take a knee next to a tree, listen, wait, and move again. They made it back, going through the challenge and password before they entered the lines, and Ken started back to his gun position. For him and Tildon, the experience had been terrifying.

As Ken moved down the line, he noticed the company was at 100 percent—everyone in their fighting holes, armed, with gear on, and awake. He was told the same thing at each position: "There is a hell of a lot of movement and noise out there."

"Tell me about it," he thought.

He was still strung out on adrenalin from the LP and the movement back to the company lines.

Ken reached the gun position, slipped into the fighting hole, and brought his squad leader, Bob Gallo, up to date about what they had seen and heard. Ken's gun squad was down to six Marines in two three-man gun teams. The Table of Organization (TO), which defines how many Marines are in a fire team, squad, platoon, etc., calls typically for nine Marines in the gun squad, so they were three men short. As far as the night watch was concerned, everyone would have to do double duty.

As time passed, the adrenaline began to wear off, causing Ken's hands to shake. Well past midnight, the word was finally passed to go to a 50 percent watch. They went to a one-third watch since they had a three-man gun team. But within three hours, they returned to 100 percent as they always did an hour before sunrise. It had been a very long night.

An hour before sunrise (known as Beginning Morning Nautical Twilight), they returned to 100 percent and waited for daylight. As soon as it became light, they went to a standard watch. The extraction of civilians continued. From his position, Ken could see civilians grouped together outside the perimeter along with South Vietnamese police.

The next day brought oppressive heat and humidity, as it was every day. Ken's fighting position was out in the sun with no shade, so when he came off watch, he moved behind their position to get some shade and sleep under the trees.

Just as he lay down, he heard the "pop, pop, pop" of artillery being fired. Before he could react, the first rounds came screaming in, exploding just behind him. He scrambled back into the hole, putting on his flak jacket and helmet while moving.

"Incoming artillery is not like in the movies where you hear a whistling sound and an explosion, which is not very loud," Ken tells me.

> *"In reality, the rounds scream in, and I mean scream: sounding like a jet engine at full throttle. The explosion is a sharp, thunderous CRACK, and you hear the shrapnel buzzing and snapping all around*

you. There is nothing you can do but sit tight in your fighting hole and take it. Between rounds, you are up and looking for a possible ground assault.

There is nothing, and I mean nothing, as scary as incoming artillery. You have no control. In a firefight, you can shoot back and protect yourself with your rifle. With incoming artillery, there is nothing you can do but wait for it to stop and hope a round does not land in the hole with you. I've seen the results of when that happens. And I've seen men lose control of their bladder and bowels because they were so afraid. Anyone who says they were never scared in combat is either a liar or crazy. Courage is never the absence of fear, but simply action in the presence of fear."

According to an after-action report, they received 132 rounds of Russian 85mm artillery fire. Ken has no idea who was counting it; he knows he sure as hell wasn't. The company had 3 KIAs and 8 WIAs.

One of those killed was PFC Willie Brown.

"He had joined us in either March or April. He was 18 years old when he was killed. I was also 18 but felt older since I had been with the battalion since December 1966. I don't think Willie had a mean bone in his body. If you look him up on the Virtual Wall, it says he died of a gunshot wound. He didn't. It was shrapnel. His death affected us because he was just a hell of a nice kid and hadn't been with us very long. In combat, though, it doesn't make a lot of difference whether you are good or not or just got there; you are still dead."

Still, the company had been lucky. For the amount of shelling they received, there could have been a lot more casualties. The fact that they were dug into the sand, which tends to absorb some of the blasts and shrapnel from the exploding rounds, probably contributed to their relative luck. It would not be the only time Ken would experience incoming artillery.

"To this day, when I hear artillery being fired, like when I'm at Camp Pendleton," he says, "my hands begin to sweat, and my pulse rate goes up, as does my respiration. That's also the case when I hear jets flying low or when I go to the range to shoot. There is that initial moment of thinking about Vietnam and the memories those sounds bring back, the sweaty hands, increased pulse, and respiration rates before I am finally back in the grove."

Mail came in that day. Ken had stopped reading any mail he received from his mother—often wondering if she had any idea what he was doing. He had also stopped writing home.

"I had nothing I could talk about—nothing," he says. "I could not figure out a way to explain what it was like watching friends killed, maimed, killing, the smell of death, the smell of fear that we lived with...and always, in the back of my mind, the reality that it was just a matter of time before I was to be wounded or killed."

That day, he tore the top off the small C-ration meal box and addressed it to his family. He wrote "Free" in the upper right-hand corner, his return address in the upper left-hand corner, and then, on the reverse side, "I'm okay."

From mid-May on, he never wrote another letter home—never discussing what he was doing or seeing.

They continued to receive sporadic artillery as the evacuation of civilians continued, and they noticed that none of the artillery ever landed on the civilians, only on the battalion.

By the end of May, the operation was over, and they pulled out. The company boarded amtracs and moved south, down the coast. The Marines rode on top of the tracs, and the tracs ran in the surf line because of the concern for mines. After moving a couple of miles south along the coast, they moved inland and established a company perimeter. They received more incoming artillery in the form of air bursts, but they were obviously at the extreme range of the guns as they were very inaccurate. A few days later, they moved back to the ship.

While they were ashore, Delta Company had been moved to the USS Okinawa, a definite upgrade from the Bayfield.

* * *

According to a tally in U.S. Marines in Vietnam: Fighting the North Vietnamese 1967 (Telfer, Rogers, and Fleming), the combined American and South Vietnamese operations killed 789 enemy soldiers, destroyed many installations, and captured or destroyed tons of rice and military supplies. 142 Marines were killed (85 in Beau Charger), and 896 had been wounded. 22 of the South Vietnamese were killed and 122 wounded.

With the operation still reeling in his head, Galluzzo wrote home about operations still ahead:

> *"I hate to say it, but, I hated more to hear it, yup, we're going on operation again on May 2 [he probably meant June 2]. Somewhere north of Phu Bai from what I can gather. I've been praying very hard and ask the same from all back home. It looks so far away now and like such a hard job, but I'm giving it my all to make it back safe & sound someday. With God's will, I'll make it.*
>
> *Mom, Dad, you'll never know how bad war is. You get tight with guys, some I've been with now, 6 months, and, in a second, they're gone. 2nd plt. has taken the worst beating. Seems to always be there at the wrong time. You can't let it, or try not to let it bother you, but so many so fast, it gets difficult at times. It's gotten to a point where every time you hear a round go off, you cringe. We left Okinawa with 42 enlisted, 1 officer and are down*

to 14 and 1 of the original. I don't know anyone."

Galluzzo also wrote about a machine gunner who had survived the landing at LZ Goose but who had three men, actually "20-year-old kids," die in his arms.

> "This time, he saw Keck & Mark & Anderson get it. He cracked. When they found him, he was sitting in the sand, whimpering, draining sand through his fingers. No one could get through to him. I don't know how he is now.
>
> I don't have any more joyous news to tell. I don't write this to make you worry or because I enjoy it. I have to get it off my mind, and at the same time, I want you to realize what is going on over here."

Less than a week later, Galluzzo interviewed for and accepted a clerk's job aboard the USS Okinawa, handling correspondence for his company. In his new role, he was spared the dangers of the coming operations, and he eventually made it home alive to attend the second game of the 1967 World Series with his father. For a year after the war, he had trouble sleeping indoors, however, and his family would find him asleep under trees in the yard with one leg kicking from a nerve still gnawed by a grenade fragment that was never removed.

* * *

On May 18, 2018, 51 years later, Ray Kelley was awarded the Silver Star for his actions on Operation Beau Charger. Captain Winfield Spear (USMC ret.) had put in the paperwork for Kelley to receive a Bronze Star, but the paperwork was lost, and the award was never given. Hence, he and other Marines from Delta Company worked for twelve years to get Kelley recognized for what he'd done in combat that day. Instead of the Bronze Star, Kelley was awarded the Silver Star Medal. The ceremony was held at the National Marine Corps Museum, so I traveled to Triangle, Virginia, near the Marine Corps Base Quantico to meet Ray and to bear witness.

When I arrived, I went to the museum's theatre, where I assumed the event was to be held. When I asked a young usher, she confirmed there was to be a ceremony in the theatre, so I took a center seat at the highest point in the back and waited. Over the course of an hour, every seat in the theater filled, including all seats in the back row to the left and to the right of me. Even the space between the stage and the front row was filled with wheelchairs. Others stood on the stairs along the edges of the aisles.

The lights finally dimmed, and a speaker took the podium. Behind the speaker, white lettering on a black slide appeared:

Memorial Service
1st Battalion
7th Marines
Vietnam
566 KIA

I realized that I was in the wrong ceremony, but before I could get up and excuse myself through the people in my aisle, the presenter began reading the names of each of all 566 Marines from 1/7 who'd been killed in Vietnam. Of course, pushing my way through the aisle and out of the theater would not have been appropriate while that somber procession of names was being read, so I stayed put. Reading through so many names took such time that I would have to miss the hour of Kelley's Silver Star. I had traveled across the United States to see it but would have to miss it on the foible of trapping myself in a crowded theater for an entirely different ceremony.

But, I see this now as a kind of lucky grace. It reminded me that the battalion I covered in this book is just one of many who served in Vietnam. For every Marine and combat experience I was learning about, for every heroic death, there were many, many more. It was as if God had set me down in that theater and had me listen to the names of 566 Marines so that I could better understand the scope of the war and its consequences.

As I sat there listening to the mournful sobs of family members, it occurred to me how lucky I was to get my father back at all. I was not the only son, and ours was not the only family affected by the war. Both sides considered, the true scope of loss is almost unimaginable.

In another room, somewhere else in the museum, Ray Kelley was also moved to tears. After 51 years, he found himself overwhelmed with a tsunami of emotions. He took a minute to gather himself before making his acceptance speech. Sitting in the audience were the wives of two Marines that Kelley served with—husbands who'd written witness statements for Kelley before they died of cancer. As one who had already felt guilty for surviving, Kelley felt like he was two inches tall looking out at those widows and their children, but he cleared his throat and accepted the award for the whole company and for all who served.

> "I'm dedicating this medal to all of the guys that I served with in Delta Company, First Battalion, Third Marines. This isn't mine. It belongs to them. I also want to dedicate it to anyone who served in Vietnam for what we all went through. As you know, we came home, and they swept us under the rug. They called us 'baby killers' and 'dope addicts,' and that's not true. You're not going to find any more honorable men in the world..."

51 years after the incident on Operation Beau Charger, Lance Cpl. Raymond Kelley (center) is awarded the Silver Star. Captain Winfield Spear (left of Kelley) presents the award.
(Photo courtesy of the National Museum of the Marine Corps)

Operations Bear Bite, Colgate, Choctaw, and Maryland

```
Bear Bite: June 2 - 5, 1967

Colgate: June 7 - 11, 1967

Choctaw: June 12 - 23, 1967

Maryland: June 23 - June 27, 1967
```

"The night before the start of Operation Bear Bite, it was quiet in the compartment. There was no false bravado by anyone. We had all been blooded. Everyone was lost in thoughts of what would happen the next day and the days after. What would the next operation be like, and how many casualties? In the back of our minds, we all knew that death was always there, waiting for us."

—Ken Hicks

Between the end of April 1967 and the end of May 1967, a period of just over 1 month, the battalion had suffered 387 casualties, 87 killed in action (KIA) and 300 wounded in action (WIA). The rifle companies (Alpha, Bravo, Charlie, and Delta) bore the brunt of the casualties. Squads had been reduced to 5, 6, or 7 Marines instead of the usual 13. Replacements were not coming in and the wounded were returned to combat duty.

The operational tempo was to increase in June and continue at a faster pace until December. The battalion was about to participate in four operations in 30 days (instead of just over 60 days, which was the average for other battalions).

June would also be the last amphibious landing Delta Company would make. Since they'd been moved to the USS Okinawa, all remaining assaults were to be by helicopters.

The four operations, Bear Bite, Colgate, Choctaw, and Maryland, would take place primarily in an area the French called the "Street Without Joy," and an incursion or two to Phu Bai and the 4th Marines rear area, Camp Evans, off Highway 1, north of Hue City.

The Third Marines had entered the Fourth Marines' Tactical Area of Responsibility—a land of booby traps, punji pits, snipers, and abandoned Catholic Churches with high-reaching steeples.

Ken's memories of the month are somewhat blurred because they were constantly on the move, getting by on very little sleep, and physically exhausted from walking in sand all the days long.

"Boredom interspersed with moments of terror," he says.

Regarding "The Street Without Joy," Ken says he never saw a "street."

"There were a lot of booby traps, punji pits, and scattered small arms fire," he says. "You learn very quickly (if you don't, you're dead) when to get down or ignore the firing. When someone is aiming at you and shoots at you, the sound you hear is not a "bang." What you hear is a loud "CRACK." That is the bullet breaking the sound barrier as it goes by. Now you know the SOB is aiming at you and trying to kill you. If the round is really close, inches, you can feel it go by. The sound changes as the rounds move away from you, left or right from your position, eventually just being a 'clack.' Nothing to worry about."

Being fired upon had become so common the Marines inherently absorbed the science of the gunfire acoustics.

The Bear Bite operation lasted for several days, and then Delta

Company was airlifted by helos and taken to Fourth Marines' rear area, Camp Evans—just off Highway 1, north of Hue City and south of Quang Tri. From there, they were ordered to move to the airfield at Phu Bai by foot. They had been operating in a sandy strip of land between the coast and Highway 1 to the west, where the foothills and mountains began (with their double and triple canopies typical of Vietnam as you went inland into the mountains). The most notable terrain feature between the coast and Highway 1 was that the ground was all sand.

That morning, the men were resupplied with water and C-rats. They would move 17 clicks (each "click" 1,000 meters) to Phu Bai, a distance of a little over 10 miles.

"It was hot and humid," Ken says. "And I mean really hot, triple-digit hot, with no breeze. The ground was sparsely vegetated and sandy. To this day, I hate walking in the sand. It was white, and the heat just reflected off of it."

Because he was in machine guns, Ken and the Marines in the team carried heavier loads than the typical rifleman. He had his helmet on, a flak jacket, 5 canteens (one and a quarter gallons of water—each canteen a quart), 200 rounds of 5.56mm M16 ammo in 10 magazines, a 140 round bandoleer of 5.56mm ammo, a KA-BAR Marine fighting knife, 4 fragmentation grenades, one smoke grenade, 400 rounds of 7.62mm machine gun ammo in four 100-round belts (each belt weighed 7 lbs, with the belts carried crisscrossed over his shoulders, "Pancho Villa" style), 2 days of C-rats stuffed into his spare socks and put in his pack (the boxes were broken down and only the cans went into the socks), a 2 lb block of C-4 for heating the C-rats, cleaning gear for his rifle, a double-edge razor for shaving (someone else carried the shaving cream), toothbrush and toothpaste, and two ponchos. If he sat down, he had to have someone help him up.

"It was an all-day movement in terrible conditions," Ken says. "Walking in the sand was miserable. Two steps forward and one step back, or so it seemed. There appeared to be no end as we could not see our destination. We could see the mountains way off in the distance but couldn't see Phu Bai. It could be a mile away or a hundred miles away."

They were several hours into this movement when a Marine named Jenkins stopped, started yelling like he was in pain, and began to dance around and literally tear all of his gear and clothing off. He had a prickly heat rash.

"It's not funny, but at the time, the men thought it was," Ken says. "I used the last of my water to cool Jenkins off. He was not the only one suffering from the prickly heat; we all were to varying degrees."

When they finally dragged themselves into the airfield at Phu Bai, the company was filthy, tired, and pissed off. It had been a long day, but at least now they were inside the wire, and they only had to dig holes (not fighting positions) in case of mortars or rockets.

At that moment, unknown to them, their Battalion Commander negotiated to get the battalion into the Phu Bai mess hall for hot chow. Ken heard that their Commander had threatened to shoot the place up when he was told they could only use the mess hall if they were bathed, clean-shaven, and wearing clean utilities and shined boots.

"We got hot chow that night," Ken says, "but the difference between the rear echelon Marines and grunts was like night and day. I guess they must not have seen a lot of grunts in their mess hall. They were quiet around us and simply stared at us. I guess it didn't help that we had our weapons with us. We must have looked a little wild to them."

* * *

The battalion started Operation Colgate on June 7 with a helo lift from the Phu Bai airfield at 0600. They were up much earlier, moving to the airstrip by foot.

The operation was about seven miles east of Phu Bai. They, again, ran into a lot of booby traps, punji pits, and snipers. The Alpha and Bravo companies ran into a firefight, and things were hot and heavy for a period of time for those two companies before contact was broken.

On the second day, Delta Company moved into position to dig in for the night, and Ken, along with several other Marines from the company, gathered up canteens to get water from a well just outside their perimeter. As he was heading towards the well, he encountered some combat engineers who had discovered a booby trapped punji pit. Ken walked up to take a look as the engineers kneeled around the uncovered pit. A trip wire had been strung across the pit and attached to a CHICOM fragmentation grenade.

"The pit was just big enough for a boot to fit in," Ken says. "The punji stakes were on the side, angled down and into the trap's center. If you stepped into it, your boot would pull the trip wire, removing the pin from the grenade, and as you tried to pull your boot back out, the punji stakes would embed into the side of your boot, preventing you from removing your foot. The grenade would go off and take your foot with it."

The engineers were excited about what they had found. Ken was a couple of feet away from them, listening to what they were saying, watching what they were doing, when he heard a "pop" and a sizzling and saw smoke from the fuse burning.

One of the engineers yelled, "Shit!"

Ken immediately dove away so that the bottom of his boots faced the pit and any potential explosion, with his head away from it.

He waited for the explosion, but nothing happened. The fuse stopped sizzling. Ken looked back and saw the smoke dissipating as the fuse stopped burning. It was a dud. They were lucky.

"Curiosity, this time, did not kill any of the cats," Ken says. "But I decided that the next time I saw engineers playing with a booby trap, I would just keep on walking."

At the end of four days, they were lifted back to Phu Bai and then trucked to Camp Evans. Phu Bai was south of Hue City, and Camp

Evans was North of Hue City. The trucks are known as "six-bys" because all three axles drive. They were not built for comfort, and the ride was rough. Thus, any trip on six-bys was known as "rough riding."

Ken couldn't help but notice that the front fenders, the floor in the driver's compartment, and the side steps on both sides were all sandbagged to protect against mines.

"Hue City was beautiful, and you could tell the French influence there," Ken says. "We crossed the Perfume River on our way north. We also passed a large Catholic Church right off the highway."

During the Tet Offensive in January/February 1968, the church would be destroyed.

The six-by that Ken's gun team rode had a Black Label beer pallet destined for Camp Evans and the 4th Marines.

"We looked at it for a time and then collectively thought, what the hell," Ken says.

With their KA-BARs and bayonets, they cracked open the pallet and retrieved a couple of cans of very warm beer. This was before pop-tops, so they used their KA-BARs and bayonets to puncture the cans.

"It tasted like crap," Ken says, "but we were so dehydrated, we drank it anyway. After a couple of sips, we were wasted."

When they arrived at Camp Evans there was no place to put the men, so they were placed inside the wire and behind their defensive positions, but not in any of the hardback tents they had. It was so hot that they built hooches with their ponchos for shade.

"And, no, we didn't just lay around in the sun getting tans," Ken says. "We started cleaning our weapons. Cleaning weapons was a constant process. This was particularly true for the M16."

From the beginning, the M16 had a problem with jamming. Over the years, Ken has read all kinds of stories about the cause of the jamming problem, and it was a life-and-death problem. First, the Marines were told they weren't cleaning the rifle properly, then that they had to be careful which way they ran the bore brush so they wouldn't wear out the lands and grooves of the bore (the bore and chamber of the original M16 were not chrome plated).

"The jamming problem was caused by the bean counters in Washington," Ken says. "It was decided that because the government had large quantities of powder in storage for the old M14 on hand, which the M16 replaced, this powder in storage would be used first before the government bought the more expensive powder made for the M16. The problem was that the M16 was not designed to use the same powder as the M14 due to its unique gas operating system. The M14 powder just gummed up the works, causing jams."

In the Hill Fights in April of 1967, up at Khe Sanh, a lot of Marines were found dead with their M16s broken in half, trying to clear the jams. The rifle is made to break in half to open it up so its operator can get to the trigger mechanism and the bolt.

"That single decision by the bean counters in Washington ended up killing a lot of Marines and soldiers," Ken says.

* * *

On June 11, 1967, the battalion came off of Operation Colgate and then, on the very next day, started Operation Choctaw. Each of the four rifle companies were assigned different missions. Delta, was sent north on Highway 1 to establish a roadblock. The After Action Report says they moved by foot, but Ken remembers that they rode by trucks, rough-riding on Highway 1.

On the trip north, they passed numerous villages (villes) that either straddled Highway 1 or sat on either side of the highway. Whenever they rode trucks on Highway 1 (one lane going north and one lane going south), small groups of children would be on the side of the road begging for food or cigarettes. It was no different on this move. More often than not, the children wanted cigarettes, and more often than not, the Marines tossed them cans of C-rats.

It was an excellent opportunity to get rid of the meals they didn't like, such as the ham and lima beans.

"When you opened a can of ham and mothers, you were greeted with a thick layer of fat," Ken says, "followed by pasty white and waxy lima beans, then fatty ham—disgusting."

Ken saw a small child, who could not have been more than 2 years old, smoking a cigarette on the side of the road.

"And this was not the exception," he says. "We saw a lot of young children with lit cigarettes dangling from their mouths."

Photo by William V. Taylor of Charlie Co.

Delta Company reached the roadblock location and dismounted from the trucks to establish the block. The area was flat with light-colored sandy soil. They set up a 360-degree defense, and the platoons rotated each day to man the roadblock. When a platoon was not manning the roadblock, it sent out patrols.

Ken began going on patrols with a squad from 3rd Platoon, led by his friend Frank Holsomback.

Frank was a half-Cajun from Louisiana. They joined the company at Khe Sanh in December 1966 and became very good friends. Wounded in early May, Frank had just returned to the company. He had taken over an under-strength squad and had asked if Ken would go on patrols with them to add an extra rifle to the team. Since guns were doing nothing but manning the roadblock every third day with the 3rd platoon, Ken started pulling patrols with Frank and his squad.

Most patrols lasted four to five hours under hot and humid weather. On the first patrol, they were out for over five hours. A couple of hours into that patrol, they spotted half a dozen NVA moving across a dry rice paddy about 1,000 meters from a slight hill they were moving up and from which they had good fields of observation. Artillery was called in, with a mix of air burst and super quick fuse settings. From their position, they could clearly see the rounds landing right on top of the NVA.

"No more NVA," Ken says. "Just bits and pieces."

They were all out of water four hours into the patrol, even though most of them carried three to four canteens. They came across a couple of old, small rice paddies. The water was clear, but the paddies were crawling with leeches. Ken had never seen so many at one time.

"It was like the bottom of the rice paddy was alive with slithering leeches," he says.

He took out his canteen and tried to fill it. As soon as he placed the canteen in the water, leeches tried to swarm his hand. He made several more attempts, as did the others on patrol, but finally gave up—it was impossible to get water into the canteen without sucking several leeches in through the spout.

* * *

"Pulling duty on the roadblock was interesting," Ken says. "The vehicles coming through were mostly overcrowded buses and a few old French Renault automobiles. We detained a few people and handed them over to the South Vietnamese Police—generally because they had discrepancies in their ID cards. Typically, it was birth dates that didn't match up with age. It didn't help when the ID card indicated a man in his 80s, yet the man in front of us looked like he was in his 40s."

One bright side of the operation was that the Marines could buy large blocks of ice from the ice trucks that occasionally came through while on the roadblock. Otherwise, their days were spent either on long, hot roadblock days or patrols and ambushes.

* * *

On June 21, they moved by six-bys to the 4th Marines at Camp Evans. Upon reaching Camp Evans, they bivouacked inside the wire again and began cleaning weapons. A warning order was passed that they would be moving out by foot after dark to continue Operation Choctaw. They could shave and brush their teeth because they had access to water bulls (a 500-gallon fresh water tank on wheels that could be towed by a truck). Their utilities remained filthy. Water in the field remained a precious commodity for drinking first and foremost. If there was extra, they could brush their teeth and shave. The reality was that most of them were shaving peach fuzz as it was, including Ken.

They wore their utilities until they fell apart or were torn too badly. It was usually the crotch that tore apart first. When they received a resupply of utilities, they could not be picky about sizes. They once received "Small Regular." Ken was "Medium Long." He took the "Small Regular" and wore them, looking like Little Abner with the tops of his boots showing.

The company moved out sometime after dark. Resupplied with

ammo and C-rats, they left the security of the 4th Marines wire, crossed Highway 1, and began what was to be an arduous movement lasting the entire night and into the afternoon of the next day.

They moved in a single file that snaked along, starting and stopping, as the point element of the company navigated their way in the light of a full moon. They were already physically exhausted and dehydrated when they started this movement, but at least the moonlight made navigation and keeping track of the Marine in front easier.

The movement was stop-and-go. When the column stopped, Ken would place the butt stock of his M60 on the ground and lean over, supporting himself by the bipods to get some relief from the load he carried. He was so tired that, at times, he fell asleep standing up. Fortunately, no contact was made during the movement.

"We were operating in the same area we had operated in at the beginning of June and Operation Bear Bite," Ken says. "We continued our movement, and as daylight turned, we began a company-sized sweep through the area. Once again, we were in the Street Without Joy—running into snipers, booby traps, and punji pits. I made a point of staying away from the combat engineers this time."

Late in the afternoon, the company set up a 360-degree defensive perimeter and dug fighting holes for night defense.

The sandy soil made the digging more manageable, but the water table was only a few feet below the surface. As the Marines dug past that point, the hole began to fill with water.

"So, at night," Ken says, "when we stood watch, our boots were in the water, and our feet were wet. And we never took our boots off at night when we were in the field. You never want to be looking for your boots in the middle of a nighttime firefight."

An hour before sunset, the company went to a 100 percent watch—everyone in their fighting holes, with their gear on and weapons ready.

"I got into position with a rifle and looked out over the dry rice paddy in front of our machine gun. It was a full moon with good visibility. You could have read a book in the moonlight. I thought I was looking out over the rice paddy when, in fact, I had fallen asleep and didn't know it! In the next hole over, a friend, Jerry Carerro, saw my head drop to my chest. Not only was I asleep, but somehow, I got turned around and was facing into the lines. Jerry came over and whispered my name. I woke up, startled, looked up, saw the moon, thinking it was a flare, and immediately rolled into the hole, dropping to the bottom and landing on my knees in four inches of water. That scared the hell out of me, and I felt stupid at the same time."

The next day, they continued making the sweep with light contact, and then, on June 23, they moved back to the 4th Marines at Camp Evans.

* * *

On June 25, the Marines started Operation Maryland, their fourth operation for the month.

The company helo lift began at 0530 in the morning by way of the UH-34s, which could lift no more than 5 combat-loaded Marines at a time. This meant that little more than one platoon could be lifted at a time. By the time Ken loaded on the third lift, it was daylight. Their three-man gun team and two riflemen loaded the aircraft. The crew chief, who manned the M60 on the right door of the helicopter, yelled over the sound of the engine.

"Be ready, guys," he said. "On that last lift, we were getting shot at when we landed—small arms!"

The aircraft took off, and Ken double-checked his rifle. Because of all their jams, he'd covered the flash suppressor on his M16 with the wrapping from an empty C-rat accessory pack. A complete accessory pack carried a small box of four cigarettes, a frustratingly small pack of toilet paper, Chiclettes chewing gum, salt, pepper, coffee, creamer, sugar packets, waterproof matches, and a white nylon spoon. A rubber band secured the wrapper. The green towel he usually wore around his neck was wrapped around the receiver and magazine to keep the sand out that usually kicked up when they landed. It was a short and tense flight.

"It was obvious that the pilots wanted to get in and get out as fast as they could because they dropped into the LZ like a rock, Ken says. "And as we dropped in, I could hear the 'pop, pop, pop,' of small arms fire."

Since there were no seats or seat belts, Ken sat on the deck across from the crew chief. After watching the '34 go into the ocean in April, he'd made a point to always position himself so that he could get out quickly if they went into the water.

Two holes suddenly appeared in the aircraft's skin—sunlight lasering over the head of their rifleman. The two rounds exited the left side of the helicopter. Within seconds, they were on the ground, and Ken was exiting as fast as he could move. He could still hear the small arms fire over the sound of the rotors and engine. As the aircraft lifted off, they moved to the edge of the perimeter and located the rest of 3rd Platoon.

They had been the last lift, and as the helicopters took off and pulled away from the LZ, the small arms fire sputtered out. While waiting for the word to move out, Ken pulled his green towel away from his rifle and found that, despite the protection of the towel, sand had gotten into the lower receiver and magazine well. He pulled the magazine and quickly cleaned the rifle with a toothbrush. He wasn't the only one—they had all learned that when you land by helicopter in a sandy area, the odds of rifle jamming rise dramatically.

After forming up, they moved towards their first objective. They proceeded down a sandy footpath through a lightly wooded area containing thin (2-3 inches thick) pine trees, brush, and small planted fields with intersecting footpaths. The area had several villes throughout. They heard a firefight going on in the distance to their front and began to get a lot of stray rounds passing over their heads.

Word was passed that an ARVN unit was in a hard fight.

They halted, moved to the side of the trail, and sat down, using their flak jackets and packs to brace their backs so they could sit up. The sporadic small arms fire continued off in the distance, with occasional rounds flying over their heads. Looking down the trail, Ken could see Marines starting to nod off and go to sleep. He was himself fighting to stay awake after a month of little sleep.

Off to his left, he heard someone yelling. He couldn't make out the words, but it was definitely a Marine yelling. Out of the corner of his eye, he saw movement. Someone was running, and there was more yelling. Because of the number of trees and underbrush, he couldn't tell at first who was running, but then the runner came into view, and Ken could see that he was NVA.

"To this day, I can close my eyes and see this individual as clearly as if he was standing before me," Ken says.

He looked young, 17-18 years old, and he wore an NVA uniform. He was moving fast in a crouched run about 20 meters away from Ken.

Ken rose quickly to a standing position from where he'd been lying against his flak jacket and pack.

"I still don't know how I did that because, not only did I have my flak jacket and pack on, but I had my cartridge belt with magazine pouches, canteens, and 400 rounds of machine gun ammo crisscrossed over my shoulders and chest."

As he stood, Ken brought his rifle up to his right shoulder at the same time—his left hand lightly gripping the front of the magazine well, his right hand wrapping around the pistol grip, left index finger on the trigger, right thumb pushing the selector switch from "Safe" to "Fire." It felt as if everything was happening in slow motion. His eyes were open as he aimed over the top of the rear sight. At this range, looking through the sight was unnecessary—he simply lined up the tip of the front sight blade with the top of the rear sight. Plus, it was easier to track a moving target.

He squeezed off three rounds rapidly, and then his rifle jammed. "Shit, shit, shit!"

His shooting caused everyone to wake up. He cleared the jam, then moved forward to where he saw the NVA soldier run. One round had hit one of the small pine trees, blowing it in half. A fire team came over. Ken told them what happened, and they took off in the direction the NVA had been running.

The body of an NVA soldier was found down one of the side trails, but Ken never went over to see if it was the guy he was shooting at. He just didn't care.

"Over the years, I have thought about this incident numerous times," he says. "Many times lying awake at night replaying the entire sequence repeatedly. I have dreamed about it many, many times. This NVA wasn't the first person I had shot at, but he was the one I had the clearest view of because he was so close. By this time in my tour, I had become hardened to the idea of killing, as I think we all had."

Shortly after this incident, the company began to move forward again and began to encounter ARVN troops walking down the trail with rifles over their shoulders. The ARVN had fired all of their ammo and were calling it a day, which, to the Marines, was disconcerting.

The Marines wondered if the reason they'd heard such a high volume of fire from them was because they just wanted to shoot all of their ammo and get the hell out of Dodge alive. The Marines never trusted the ARVN or the occasional Popular Forces they encountered. Nor did they think much of their ability to fight.

As they continued to move forward through more ARVN, the shooting up front began to die out. They swept through several villes, making no contact, not even snipers, and then set in for the night—Ken's 3rd Platoon digging in along the edge of a very large, dry rice paddy.

Sometime after midnight, several explosions were heard down the line to the right of Ken's position. They went to 100 percent, remaining so for a couple of hours, and slowly, word was passed up the line that there had been a grenade fight between a squad from 3rd Platoon and an NVA infiltrator.

As soon as it was daylight, Ken went down to the squad involved. What had happened was the Marines had heard movement in front of their position. A frag was thrown at them, exploding just short of the line. They threw a frag, which was promptly tossed back at them, exploding again in front of their position. The Marines threw another frag, which was again thrown back. Then, they "cooked off"—pulling the pin, releasing the spoon, letting the fuse burn a couple of seconds before throwing it. As the NVA soldier picked it up to throw it back, it exploded, killing him instantly.

Ken went out with some others to look at the body. The frag had been effective. It had gone off in the NVA's right hand as he had reared it back to throw. It had taken off his right hand and part of his right arm. There was a large hole in his chest with numerous smaller holes. No head remained above the lower jaw.

Ken went back to his gun position. Word had been passed that they would stay where they were and each platoon would send out patrols.

Frank Holsomback's squad of five Marines was tasked with a patrol back through the area they had been in the day before. Frank asked if Ken would mind going, and again, Ken agreed.

The remainder of the operation was uneventful, except for snipers and booby traps that seemed to be everywhere. They moved back to Phu Bai and then to a beach near Hue. The beach was part of the rear area of the 7th Separate Bulk Fuel Battalion. When they arrived, they were shocked at what they saw: steak and hamburger barbecues, ice-cold beer and sodas, Marines swimming in the ocean, and sailing small sailboats. The Marines in Delta Company hadn't seen a shower in 30 days and had been eating out of cans.

"These guys were in swim trunks, drinking beer and eating steaks as if they were on vacation," Ken says. "The reception we received was better than what we had at Phu Bai earlier in the month, though.

They seemed happy to feed us, though our stomachs had shrunk so much we couldn't eat much. At least the beer and soda were cold, though a couple of sips of cold beer pretty much knocked you out, so I stuck with the soda."

Ken would see this dichotomy between themselves, the infantry, or as they called themselves, grunts, and rear echelon Marines (better known to them as REMFs for Rear Echelon Mother Fuckers) several more times during his tour. He always had the impression that they were never entirely welcomed, though tolerated, and at times unwelcomed by those in the rear—maybe even feared.

"You could see it in their eyes," Ken says. "It was as if they were watching wild animals walking amongst them. And, in a sense, I suppose we were. The grunts went where they feared to go—outside the wire that surrounded their camps."

The grunts were generally filthy, with torn uniforms, and armed to the teeth. Most of them carried knives, generally KA-BARs, along with bayonets, frags, and a lot of ammo. They never went anywhere without their weapons, and they typically walked a little hunched over due to the weight of everything they were carrying.

By the end of the month, the battalion began to backload to the USS Okinawa. Ken didn't get back aboard until July 2. Once aboard, they cleaned weapons, traded their filthy and torn uniforms for new ones, and took a shower for the first time in 30 days.

The word was that they would be aboard the ship for at least five days refitting. Ken realized he would be alive to see his 19th birthday on July 4. He also had almost reached the halfway point in his tour but tried not to think about that.

"I had pretty much stopped thinking about home or going home," he says. "I didn't think about yesterday or tomorrow, but only about the moment I was in. We did not talk about it much, but we each always felt that death was near."

Delta's compartment on the Okinawa held the entire company, and as they filed in, Ken claimed a rack on the very bottom of a five-rack tier. Wearing the first pair of clean utilities he'd worn in 30 days, he slid into the rack. For a brief moment, he felt the fresh, cool breeze from a nearby air conditioning outlet and then promptly fell asleep.

Operations Bear Claw, Buffalo and Hickory II

```
Bear Claw: July 2 - 14, 1967

Buffalo: July 2 - 14, 1967

Hickory II: July 14 - 16, 1967
```

Operation Buffalo began on July 2nd, 1967. Alpha and Bravo companies from First Battalion, Ninth Marines (1/9) moved out of the perimeter at Con Thien, moving in a single file east along the Trace and north up Highway 561 towards the DMZ. As they neared a place called "The Market Place," they were arrested by enemy sniper fire and then soon after heavily engaged with elements of the NVA 90th Regiment.

The NVA used flamethrowers in combat for the first time, setting fire to hedgerows along Highway 561. Forced out into the open, the Marines were then exposed to artillery, mortar, and small arms fire, which caused heavy casualties and prevented the two companies from linking up. A single NVA artillery round exploded within the Bravo Company Headquarters and wiped out the entire command group. The company commander, two platoon commanders, the radio operator, the forward observer, and several others were killed. By the end of the day, Bravo Company would be reduced to 26 survivors, and Alpha Company would have only 90 effective Marines remaining. The two rifle companies started out that day with nearly 400 Marines. Bravo Company would suffer the largest single-day loss of Marines killed in action from one company during the Vietnam War. From that day forward, Bravo 1/9, and eventually First Battalion, Ninth Marines, would be known as the "The Walking Dead."

The next morning, a day before Ken's nineteenth birthday, he and the rest of the 1st Battalion, 3rd Marines would be called into the fight.

* * *

Just as soon as Ken had laid down and closed his eyes in the cool, conditioned air of Okinawa, his mother called out as she had done so many mornings before school.

"Ken, wake up!"

He thought he'd gotten away from her when he joined the Marines. And now she was on board the ship and yelling at him.

"Ken, come on, get up," she said. "We gotta saddle up."

"What the hell is she doing on board ship?" he thought.

"Ken!" she said again, "Wake the fuck up!"

Ken opened his eyes to see his squad leader, Bob Gallo, looking down at him. The compartment had all the lights on. As Ken blinked his eyes into focus, he heard a lot of talking and the soft noise of Marines getting their gear ready.

"What time is it?"

"It's a little after midnight," Gallo said.

Ken had been asleep for a couple of hours.

Gallo told him about the situation—that a company from 9th Marines had been overrun by two NVA battalions and that they had to be ready to fly off the ship at daybreak to join 3/9 for combat and to recover the dead from 1/9.

Ken rolled his feet out of the rack to put on his boots. The compartment had been supplied with numerous crates of ammo and C-rats. Marines had opened them up and were beginning to load magazines. They were told to take as much ammo as they could carry. In addition, the riflemen would carry additional gun ammo for the machine guns. The 3rd Platoon guide was already gathering additional belts of gun ammo for his platoon.

Ken pulled his gear off his rack, pulling all 10 magazines out. He grabbed 4 bandoleers of 5.56mm ammo and speed-loaded the magazines. Each bandoleer carried 140 rounds of 5.56mm in 7 pouches in 10-round stripper clips, plus a speed loader. With the speed loader, Ken could load rounds very quickly. He placed the loader on top of the magazine, inserted a 10-round stripper clip, and then pushed down on the rounds in the clip to guide them into the magazine.

After loading magazines, Ken grabbed four fragmentation grenades, a couple of smoke grenades, and four battle-dressing. Two battle dressings would go on his helmet, held in place by a large piece of inner tube cut like a giant rubber band, and two would go in the pockets on his utility jacket. He then grabbed six 100-round belts of machine gun ammo that he would carry. Each belt weighed 7 pounds. Each gun team would carry 1,500 rounds of gun ammo (7.62mm). Canteens were filled.

The Marines were told to take three days worth of C-rats and were issued nine meals, which was impossible because of the small packs they carried—hand-me-downs from World War II. Ken broke the meals down further, taking a can or two from each—all the fruit cans and cans with cookies in particular. He took toilet paper from the accessory packs and tossed the rest. Ken stuffed the C-rat cans in his extra socks and then placed the stuffed socks in his pack, along with rifle cleaning gear and shaving gear. He strapped two ponchos to his pack, sharpened his KA-BAR and bayonet with his wet stone, and then adjusted his pack straps to fit over his flak jacket.

The word was that they would fly out at first light. They were given some more information: Expect NVA artillery. Also, the NVA were using flamethrowers.

Good morning.

The company saddled up and moved to the staging area on the ship's hanger deck, where they laid in their helo sticks and waited—

most of them going to sleep as soon as they learned they wouldn't be loading immediately. It was early afternoon when the word was finally passed to start loading. With all their gear, the Marines had to help each other up. Ken rolled over to his knees, grabbed a piece of the ship's piping, and struggled to stand.

They shuffled to a hatch that exited outside, climbed a ladder (stairs) to the flight deck, and moved in their sticks for loading. A sailor came and led the Marines of Ken's stick their helo. Last to load, Ken sat on the deck of the '34 near the crew chief. The helo revved with power, climbed sideways away from the Okinawa, and circled so the other helos could form up.

The crew chief, a buck sergeant who looked to be in his fifties, took out a canteen and handed it to Ken, yelling in his ear, "Drink!"

Ken shook his head, "no," he didn't need any water.

"Drink it!" the crew chief yelled.

Ken unscrewed the canteen cap, took a swig, and almost choked. It was whiskey. The crew chief grinned and then waved his hand, indicating that Ken should pass it around, which he did. When the canteen returned to Ken, he handed it back to the crew chief.

"Good luck!" the crew chief said.

Ken nodded at him, "Thanks."

As they flew, the '34 passed over some Army 175mm artillery batteries. It struck Ken that the barrels on the 175s were awfully long. Looking out the right-hand door, he could see other '34s returning to the ship from a previous lift. The word passed was that they would land two clicks (two thousand meters) south of the Trace.

The helicopters quickly dropped into the LZ, the Marines jumped off, and the choppers lifted away. They had landed in a large open field surrounded by trees. 3rd Platoon rallied and then moved to its assigned portion of the perimeter. Additional lifts came in, and the Marines continued to wait.

Because of the tree line, nobody could see any terrain features beyond the trees. As the last lift took off, Ken saw the officers getting together with their maps out. They had landed in the wrong LZ, and no one knew where they were.

"Great," Ken thought.

After sitting for some time, Ken observed a '34 flying over them very low. It disappeared over the tree line, and the engine's sound faded. Then, it flew over them again from a different direction. They were flying a "resection" to determine where they were, which, as it turned out, was several clicks south from where they were supposed to be. Orders were passed, and they slowly began to move off the field and onto a dirt road (never a good idea unless you wanted to be ambushed) and began to move north in a staggered column.

* * *

By the time they finally started to move, it was late afternoon. They moved in a staggered column, heading north towards the DMZ, and by their standards, they were moving fast. The terrain on either side of the road was flat, with moderate woods, brush, and the occasional open field. They were moving without flankers out—no fire teams or squads on either side of the column far enough out to protect the column. They were in a hurry, which meant that time was more important than moving tactically. It was hot and humid, and they were loaded down.

"Sweat just poured out of you," Ken says. "Wearing a flak jacket was like wearing a plastic bag in summer while carrying 70+ pounds of gear draped over it."

If Ken had removed his gear, it would have looked like he'd been hosed down with water. Riflemen could wear their flak jackets unzipped and open, but in machine guns, the ammo belts were crisscrossed over their shoulders and chests, so the flak jacket was effectively closed, trapping all body heat.

They may have moved for over an hour, but it was hard to tell—time had no meaning. They began to slow down at some point, and their movement became stop-and-go.

In the distance, Ken heard incoming artillery exploding—sporadic but unmistakable. From their operation in the DMZ in late May, he already knew what it was like to be under incoming artillery. This operation would make May look like child's play, but he didn't realize it at the time.

The staggered column of Marines changed to a single file as they moved into an open area where all of the vegetation was gone—all of it for 600 meters across, from south to north, and from Con Thien in the west to Gio Linh in the east. Ken could see Con Thien off in the distance to his left. To his front (north) was an open field with a tree line, barely visible since they were moving slightly uphill. To his right, as far as he could see, there was no vegetation. The road ended, and there was just a footpath that went north across the field. It was the Trace—part of McNamara's line.

The hot wind kicked up dust as they moved slowly north across. Several mounds of debris had been piled up at various spots throughout the Trace, like small hills. The Marines' movement became herky-jerky (start, stop, start, stop), and when they got about half the way across the Trace, Ken was parallel to one of the mounds when they stopped. Ken looked down, and to the right of his boot was a human torso with its ribs exposed through a tattered shirt—no head, legs, or arms. He could not tell whether the torso belonged to a Marine or NVA; it was in such poor condition. He looked back to the third man in his team, Jerry Carrero, and pointed his rifle to the torso. Carrero looked at it, then looked back at Ken, and they both mouthed the word "Fuck!"

They started moving again, slowly towards the broken tree line on the north side of the Trace. As they moved closer to it, they could see the occasional artillery round explode. It was NVA artillery.

As they approached the north side, Ken observed that all of the standing trees were missing their foliage; they had been denuded by artillery fire. He noticed a knocked-out Ontos to the left of the trail.

The Ontos was a small tracked vehicle with six 106mm recoilless rifles, three on each side, that had apparently run over a large mine. A large crater, several feet across and a couple of feet deep, surrounded the burnt-out craft.

The knocked-out Ontos provided cover for several passing Marines on Operation Buffalo, including Lee Edgemon (Delta, 1st Plt, 2nd Sqd) who provided this photo. "I crawled under it," says Edgemon. "We had to close lines to help Charlie Company. Just after, we were told to fix bayonets."

There was discarded equipment and bloody battle dressings, and to his left, as they approached, Ken saw dead Marines, stacked like cordwood—each layer of bodies covered with ponchos. The blond hair of one Marine protruded from the bottom of the stack in bright contrast against the dirt and the combat green. When the dusty wind subsided, a sickly smell of rotting flesh filled his nose. These were Marines from Bravo Company 1/9. Over the years, Ken would dream about this scene many times, and throughout his life, whenever he encountered the scent of death again, he'd see those tufts of light blond hair blowing in the wind.

A Marine with no helmet, weapon, or gear sat up against a tree not far from him. The Marine's uniform was filthy, his eyes bloodshot and sunken. He was mumbling to himself. All Ken could think of was the painting "Dante's Inferno"—a picture of hell. And now they were in it. He was in hell.

Just then, Ken heard the "pop, pop, pop" of artillery being fired—incoming. He and Jerry Carrero jumped into the crater surrounding the Ontos. This was going to be a hard fight.

* * *

They received about half a dozen rounds of artillery. After the last round, Ken and the team continued to stay put for at least 20 minutes or so. Ken and Carrero remained in the crater, with the destroyed Ontos providing some cover. A Corpsman ambled by, checked Marine bodies on the stack, and scribbled notes—taking names and checking the casualty cards, Ken assumed. He didn't envy the Corpsman's job and was thankful for his willingness to do it.

"No one takes care of Marines better," Ken says. "Nor is there anyone we respect more than our Navy Corpsmen. We thought of them as Marines: they dressed like us, endured the same hazards as we did, ate the same C-rats that we did, or, like us, did not eat when we could not be resupplied. They went on patrol, ambushes, and operations with us. I never saw a Corpsman ever hesitate to go to a Marine who'd been wounded. I was convinced we had the best Corpsmen in the Navy attached to our company."

The company began to move again but didn't get further than a couple hundred feet when Ken heard the "pop, pop, pop" of NVA artillery being fired again. He saw a small, square hole to his right and jumped into it, kneeling into it as far as he could. Jerry Carerro jumped in on top of him. The hole was just big enough to squeeze the two of them in. Ken looked down and saw that the bottom of the hole was crawling with ants.

When the last round exploded, he yelled at Jerry to get off him so he could get out of the hole and get the ants off. Somewhere nearby, there was a desperate cry for a Corpsman.

Late in the afternoon, the company advanced and set up their position for the night. They placed their gun in a small crater, facing north. Riflemen were positioned in fighting holes to the left and right, creating a defensive line.

The terrain was a mix of open fields and thickets, with varying elevations that provided some natural cover. The layout of bushes and clearings created a complex landscape that would influence any potential engagement.

A tank had previously passed through the area when the ground was wet, leaving six-inch deep tracks that were now hardened in the dry earth. About 10 meters to their left front, a grim reminder of recent combat lay across these tracks: a dead NVA soldier. He was on his back, legs slightly bent, one hand reaching up, bloated, with his skin peeling and turning black. He had been shot through the head, the round entering the right side because the left side was completely gone.

Directly in front of them, at the opening in the thicket, was another NVA soldier. He had been split from groin to chest, wholly eviscerated.

All during this time there was sporadic artillery being fired by both the Marines and the NVA, and sporadic small arms fire clacking all around them. It had been a very long, hot day and by now they were low on water, but no resupply was coming. They were told they had to make do with what they had.

Their platoon commander came by, checking each position and talking to them. You would have thought he was on an evening walk back in the neighborhood. He spoke to each of the men. Ken had seen him do this on other operations. He made sure that they all saw him and knew he was as much in this fight as they were. Ken learned a great deal about combat leadership from him and the other officers in the company because they were all like that. They made sure the grunts knew they were there, that they were seen by their Marines, and that they were taking the same risks as the men—they led from the front.

"It was always 'Follow me,'" Ken says. "I have served under many officers, both as enlisted and as an officer, but none were better than the 2nd Lieutenants I had in Vietnam. It helped that three of them were prior Staff NCOs. To them, the privilege was in leading the men, not in holding a rank—a concept often forgotten by some officers I would later serve with in peacetime."

It was to be a long night. The Marines didn't have a good idea of the situation or what was happening. They were told they were to hold their position no matter what. Ken knew they were tied into 3/9 (3rd Bn 9th Marines), but where they were tied in, he didn't know. As darkness fell, they remained at 100 percent watch. The small arms fire had died off, but there were still occasional artillery rounds, NVA and the US, being fired. The Marines were getting artillery support from Cam Lo and from the fire support base at J.J. Carroll. They were told that at J.J. Carroll, they drove the Army self-propelled 175mm howitzers down the road to get them in range. They would fire in support of the Marines that first night, dropping several short rounds inside the Marines' perimeter. Luckily, all the rounds that landed inside their perimeter were duds.

"But it was scary to hear the gunfire behind us," Ken says. "We heard the round coming in and then heard a 'thud' as it impacted. Scary."

There would be no sleep the night of July 3rd. At one point, they thought they would go to a 2/3 watch in the gun team, two of them on a staggered watch with one off, but that lasted less than an hour. On top of that, they hadn't eaten since the evening of July 2nd. Ken retrieved a C-rat can, but it was too dark to tell what it was. He slowly opened it with his John Wayne, making sure he made no noise. It was a fruit cocktail. He passed it around. Ken was not a big fan of fruit cocktails, but that one was the best he had ever tasted.

At some point, it became disconcertingly quiet, except for the occasional mosquito. Then, the silence was broken by the sounds of US artillery rounds being fired over the Marines' heads. In the distance, Ken saw white flashes and what appeared like small white stars flying up and over in arcs. There was a delay, and then he heard the "puff, puff, puff" sound of Willy Pete going off. Willy Pete is white phosphorus. It starts to burn as soon as it hits oxygen and continues to burn until it either burns out or loses its oxygen supply, burning at 5,000 degrees Fahrenheit. Ken could see the white smoke billowing in the distance. Willy Pete is used for marking targets, for creating a smokescreen, or for eliminating troops in the open. When you mark a target, you use one round at a time. There was no need for smoke screens at night, so Ken knew that someone had called in Willy Pete for troops in the open.

* * *

It seemed to Ken like it took forever for the sun to come up.

The word was passed that the company would be moving out after daylight to recover 1/9s dead and kill any NVA they happened to cross while doing so. They still had yet to receive a resupply of water, and Ken only had about half a canteen left out of the four that he was carrying. The day before, temperatures had exceeded 100 degrees, and this day would be no different.

It was July 4th. Ken had survived to see his nineteenth birthday, but as the sun rose, he wasn't sure he was going to see the end of the day. He thought that even if he survived the day, the week was going to be very difficult. They now had three Marine Infantry Battalions (3/9, 1/3, and 2/3) engaged with at least a couple of thousand NVA who had artillery support as the Marines did—a full-scale battle in the DMZ and several ways that Ken could die on his birthday.

As the sun came up, the wind picked up, along with the smell of the dead that were scattered all about—particularly the two dead NVA that were in front of Ken and his gun team. The team quickly cleaned their weapons, not all at once, but staggered, running bore brushes, then patches through the bores, and dusting the weapons down with their paint brushes. Jams were the last thing they needed.

The night before they had linked up 500 rounds of gun ammo. Machine gun ammo came in one hundred round belts, made up of disintegrating black metal links. One could link up a couple of belts or a hundred belts, though they would never link all the ammo together in case they had to get up and move. Now they were broke it back down to hundred-round belts and saddled themselves up for movement.

There was a company of Marines a hundred or so meters in front of Delta Company with a couple of tanks as Delta began to move. They got out of fighting holes, one at a time, and started to move forward. Marines in the hole to Ken's right stood and started moving. When their turn came, Ken and the rest of the gun team got up and moved out.

After moving half a dozen meters or so, Ken heard the "pop, pop, pop" of NVA artillery firing from the north. As they were in the open, on flat ground, the men scrambled to reach the six-inch deep sunken tank tracks. Ken threw himself into one of the tracks, along with several other Marines from the platoon and gun team who were close enough to do so. A dozen or so artillery rounds came down around them, and then another dozen or so.

"The noise was terrific, with the sound of shrapnel flying everywhere," Ken says. "I flattened myself into the ground, turning my head sideways to present a lower profile."

Someone yelled for a Corpsman. When the artillery finally stopped, they got up to move and then were overwhelmed with small arms fire. Rounds were cracking and snapping all around them. The tanks in front of them opened up with their coax 30 cal. machine guns (a coaxial machine gun is one that is mounted to the left side of the tank's main gun. It is bore-sighted to the main gun so that where the gunner points the main gun, he points the coax). The gunners fired very long bursts.

Because of the Marines in front of Ken and 3rd Platoon, he and his team could not fire. U.S. artillery began firing in support. The outgoing small-arms fire built to a crescendo and then petered out. Word was passed that the company was to move back to their original positions and wait for further instructions.

Close air support started working—A-7 Crusaders, F-4 Phantoms, and A-4 Skyhawks were flying in support of the Marines throughout the day. The A-7s were Navy, and they all came in steep dives from high altitudes, pulling out early. The Marine F-4s and A-4s came in low, often dropping below the tree lines before pulling out. There was a constant cacophony of sounds—roaring jet engines, bombs exploding with concussion waves, occasional small arms, and sporadic artillery.

They pulled back to their original positions. It was hot, with a warm wind blowing now, and the Marines were out of water. They dropped back into their holes but kept their gear on. No one knew what was going to happen next. Time had ceased to have any meaning to Ken. Having returned to their morning fighting positions, they broke out C-rats and ate. It was the first full meal Ken had eaten since they had left the Okinawa.

"It was kind of surreal to be sitting on the edge of the hole," Ken says, "sporadic small arms flying about, our outgoing artillery firing, their sporadic incoming artillery, and close air support being run while we opened cans of C-rats and ate as if it was just another day at the office."

At some point, an entourage of reporters came towards Ken's position—three men and one woman. One of the men was extremely overweight, red in the face, and sweating profusely. When they arrived at Ken's gun position, they wanted to know if there were any dead NVA they could photograph. They also wanted to know what was going on.

"Yeah, I can show you two dead NVA," Ken said. "As to what's going on here? What can I say? It looks pretty obvious, don't you think? We're fighting."

Ken led them up to the first dead NVA—the one on his back, with a hand sticking up with fingers frozen in a rigor mortis claw—the one with the side of his head gone. Both the bodies were extremely "ripe" by this time. They were bloated; their skin had turned black and blistered, and each was covered with maggots and a cloud of flies. The smell had gotten so bad that Ken could taste it. By this time in his tour, Ken had seen enough dead Marines and NVA that he'd become hardened, but he reckoned the reporters were going to get sick between the smell and the sight of the bodies.

He then took them forward to where the second dead NVA was located—the one who'd been eviscerated from the groin to his chest. With their hands over their mouths, the reporters averted their eyes from this one. In front of them, Marines were on the move, which drew the reporter's attention.

"Be my guest," Ken said. "But if you head in that direction, you're on your own."

They did, and it was the last that Ken saw of them.

When he got back to the gun, a kid named McKeon came up and asked if Ken would help him bury the two NVA. The Marines called McKeon "Ricky Recon" because he wore the thickest glasses they had ever seen. The smell had gotten to the point where Ricky Recon couldn't eat. He had his e-tool, a small shovel, in his hand, but no one else was willing to help him, so Ken said, "Sure."

Ken grabbed his e-tool and headed to the first NVA, where he and Ricky started shoveling dirt onto the body.

"We need to leave the hand exposed because that's the left-limit marker for our gun," Ken told him.

When they finished with the first, they moved over and covered the second NVA with dirt.

"It did improve the air quality to an extent," Ken says, "but there were enough dead NVA around that we were never completely free of the smell. We finished and went back to our positions."

Off in the distance to their right, a couple of hundred meters away, Ken watched Marines move up a slight hill in the open. At the same time, he observed an A-4 commencing a bombing run. As he watched the A-4, he realized that the pilot was heading for the Marines moving up the hill.

"I remember yelling that the A-4 was heading for the Marines," he says. "I could no longer hear the roar of the jet engine, nor anything else—it was like watching a silent movie. I could hear nothing. At that moment, everything began moving in slow motion. I watched the A-4 release its bomb, the fins opening to retard the bomb's descent so the aircraft could get away without damage when it went off, the bomb slowly descending, impacting on the top of the hill the Marines were moving up. I saw the bomb explode a few meters in front of a Marine and saw the shock wave but did not hear the explosion, nor did I feel the concussion from the exploding bomb. Two days later, we would move up that small hill and find a Marine's foot, still in the Jungle boot. It had been sheared off from shrapnel as cleanly as if done with a scalpel."

It would be another long night. They tried again to do a two-thirds watch (two awake and one asleep), but there was too much going on. Between H&I fire (harassment and interdiction), occasional small arms fire, illumination being fired most of the night, and the occasional dud artillery round landing in their perimeter from one of their fire support bases, they were constantly awake.

* * *

After his birthday on July 4th, Ken would lose track of the days. One day would bleed into the next, and the sun rising and setting would be his only markers of time. He and everyone else were exhausted and filthy. Early in the morning, they received incoming mortar and artillery fire. The recovery of 1/9's dead fell mostly on Ken's battalion.

"More dead Marines were found with what appeared to have superficial wounds, but who had been shot in the head at close range," Ken says. "I didn't think, at the time, that any of us would be taking prisoners if the opportunity presented itself. After seeing what had been done to Bravo 1/9, we were not about to give any quarter."

Ken was wrong, because at some point, and he doesn't remember what day it was, they obtained two NVA prisoners late in the afternoon towards dusk.

"They didn't look very fearsome with their hands bound behind them. Whoever captured them had roughed them up," Ken says. "Having seen all of 1/9's Marines that appeared to have been executed, we had no sympathy for the gooks. Had the word not been passed that those prisoners were to be kept alive, they would have been killed. Would that have been wrong? Probably, but I don't think any of us cared. We would have looked at it as retribution for the Marines they executed. The prisoners were eventually moved back to Battalion. During my entire time in Vietnam, I don't believe I saw us take more than five or six prisoners. They just didn't give up."

* * *

At some point, they had a casualty within the platoon that needed to be taken back to the Trace for a medevac. An expedient litter was put together with a poncho. Four men, including Ken, grabbed corners of the poncho and began moving the wounded Marine back to the Trace. No one had to be asked to grab the poncho to move the wounded Marine; they just jumped to the task as soon as he was in it. They had to stop a couple of times because of a few incoming artillery rounds. They stopped, laid down, let the rounds explode, and then got up and moved again. At the Trace, they dropped off the casualty and then moved back to the platoon.

A line of Marines came through Ken's platoon carrying ponchos containing 1/9's dead—about half a dozen bodies. It was a stop-and-go process because of the sporadic fire. The Marines carrying the first poncho came to a stop and lowered it next to Ken's position. The dead Marine's head was gone, and his body was bloated, as were the bodies of the other dead Marines being carried. As the litter bearers got up to move again, some of them told Ken and his team that they'd been finding dead Marines with jammed M16s, shot through the back of the head, execution style. As they passed, the smell stayed with Ken and his gun team for a long time.

Shortly after that, one of the tanks rumbled past. The vehicle was a grim spectacle, loaded on the front and back with the lifeless bodies of at least a dozen Marines—their limp limbs swaying and trembling with each jarring movement.

The word was passed to form a working party to go to the Trace and pick up water cans, which were brought back to the platoon and used to fill two canteens per man.

"Water never tasted so good as it did then," Ken says. "I had had nothing to eat since July 2nd except the shared fruit cocktail."

The word was then passed that they would remain in their position overnight. The Marines dropped their gear and took advantage of the moment to break out C-rats.

At some point in the operation, towards twilight, Ken saw a SAM missile shoot down one of the American jets. The pilot ejected and landed in the DMZ. It wasn't until years later that Ken learned that he had successfully evaded the NVA and was rescued a couple of days later.

Each day seemed more challenging than the previous day. There were no easy days. At some point in the day, they were told that Delta Company would be moving north and forward of the lines, with a Force Recon Platoon accompanying them.

Again, the day was blazing hot. As they slowly moved forward, Ken could see the ground was littered with bloody battle dressings, busted up gear, including AK-47s, magazines, spent shell casing, shredded packs, canteens, dead NVA and parts of dead NVA, and shrapnel from expended ordinance and artillery.

Delta moved into a position, and the company set into a 360-degree perimeter where someone else had previously started digging fighting holes. They were told to dig in. Ken's hole looked out onto a large open field with a scattered tree line several hundred meters away.

It was about 4:30 in the afternoon. Just as they started to dig in, enlarging the fighting hole to accommodate three men, Ken heard the "pop" sound of an NVA artillery piece firing from the north. The round landed several hundred meters to their front. There was another "pop," and that round landed a hundred meters to their front. The NVA had eyes on them—an F.O. (forward observer) was adjusting their artillery on them.

Someone yelled, "Get in your holes!"

Numerous shells were fired, "pop, pop, pop, pop," followed by the roar of the incoming artillery. Ken's hole could barely fit two people, but all three of them squeezed into it. The artillery landed on the company, and then the NVA began to search and traverse their perimeter with artillery.

"They pounded us," Ken says. "One of our machine gunners, Mike Brugh, was severely wounded in both legs by shrapnel. He would have to endure 50 operations on his legs."

When the artillery finally ceased, the order was given to saddle up. They were moving back to the perimeter. Within minutes of moving back to their original positions, all hell broke loose again. The distinctive "pop, pop, pop, pop" of incoming artillery commenced with rounds roaring in on top of them.

"There was no let-up," Ken says. "In a crouch, I pushed myself against the side of the hole as the rounds would explode with each new volley. The noise was horrific. I got up after one series of incoming rounds to see that one of them had exploded only five feet from our hole."

Ken's team moved the machine gun down into the hole with them so it would not be damaged from the shelling. They had linked up 500 rounds in anticipation of the infantry assault they knew was soon coming. The NVA artillery was again searching and traversing their position. Exploding rounds rolled over them, then moved to a different portion of the perimeter and back again.

Someone yelled for a Corpsman. The platoon commander, who'd been in the next hole to Ken's left and above them, had been standing up in between the volleys of incoming artillery and had been severely wounded. The platoon sergeant, Staff Sergeant Orlando, took his place.

Ken would later learn that a couple of Marines in the company went crazy during the incoming artillery, having to be knocked down and sat on as they tried to jump up and run away. None of the Marines thought anything bad about them.

"Sitting under the incoming artillery and just taking it tested everyone," Ken says. "I was surprised that more didn't crack up."

The word was passed for 3rd Platoon to get ready to move, but to leave their packs. The word was that a portion of the line might be overrun. As Ken and his gun team broke down the ammo, artillery rolled over the company again. When it moved to another portion of the line, the gun team got up and started moving.

"We hadn't gone very far when we heard the artillery being fired again and the rounds coming in on top of us," Ken says. "We were in the open, moving on flat ground—no place to hide and no defilade. The rounds exploded all around the platoon. When the last round exploded, we got up and started moving. Again, we heard the artillery being fired, and a second later, the rounds roared in on top of us, exploding within 3rd Platoon."

Shrapnel "whiffed" and "buzzed" through the air. Ken's squad leader took shrapnel in the hip but continued to move with them.

"When I look back on it, the only way I can describe it is that it was like running through rain and not getting wet," he says. "Those of us that got through it, I don't know how we did it. I thought for sure there was no way we could survive it. If you have seen Band of Brothers, there's an episode during the Battle of the Bulge where they are hit with German artillery. Watch the episode, and if you have a good sound system, turn it all the way up, as high as it will go, and that will give you just a small inkling of how the NVA artillery sounded to us."

Unknown to the Marines then, the NVA had mounted a mass Regimental assault on the Marines of 3/9 and Ken's battalion, 1/3. They fired over 1,500 artillery rounds, with over 1,000 rounds hitting 1/3. The fighting continued until just after 2200 hours (10:00 p.m.).

"At times," Ken says, "the small arms fire sounded like being in the butts at the rifle range during rapid fire, with the crack and clacking of the rounds being fired all around us. At some point, as the fighting died down, 3rd Platoon was moved back to our original position, where we picked up our packs and then moved to a sunken road to reinforce another platoon. We spent a long night at that position."

* * *

When daylight came on the morning of July 8th, Ken noticed that there was no small arms fire or artillery.

"It was a little disconcerting to suddenly not be in the middle of a maelstrom," Ken says. "We'd had small arms fire, incoming artillery, and jet aircraft crossing overhead since crossing the Trace on July 3rd. I was somewhat surprised that I was still alive. When we had run through the artillery the day before, I didn't think we would live to tell that tale."

In the quiet, the priority became cleaning weapons. Ken finally got the opportunity to brush his teeth.

"What a difference it makes on your outlook on life that just brushing your teeth has on you," Ken says. "We all looked like death warmed over."

Other than a quick cat nap here and there, the Marines had little sleep since July 2nd. They were filthy, unshaven, covered in dust, with grimy faces and dark circles under their eyes from lack of sleep. They could see the tension on each other's faces. Five days in almost continuous combat had rung them out.

"We all looked like a bunch of old men," Ken says. "And we moved like them."

Unknown to the Marines, the NVA had disengaged during the night hours and were pulling back north—leaving over 800 NVA dead surrounding them.

A resupply of ammo, water, and C-rats was delivered to the battalion, which wolfed down cold C-rats and waited. The word was finally passed that they were to move south, back across the Trace, and dig in on the south side of the Trace.

As they waited to move out, they sat on the ground, braced against their packs and flak jackets. Ken took off his helmet for the first time in six days. He ran his hand through his hair and felt a gritty wet mix of dirt and sweat. Down the line, others were doing the same. As he watched, he saw many start to nod their heads. Some jerked their heads up as they tried to stay awake, but many others let their heads drop to their chests, fast asleep. Ken struggled to stay awake.

The movement across the Trace was without incident. The Marines fired some outgoing artillery and the NVA fired some sporadic incoming artillery, but nothing like the previous six days.

The Marines moved in a long single file, a little east of where they had come across the Trace, and then immediately began to dig in. With the memory of the NVA artillery fresh in their minds, they dug in earnest and would stay in their new position for several days. Once their holes were dug, they commenced a thorough weapons cleaning. Patrols left through the line every night and headed north across the Trace. Though they were combat patrols, they went without helmets and with blackened faces and returned just before dawn.

Ken's gun team went to a one-third watch and tried to catch up on sleep during the day. Ken was on watch one morning, looking out across the DMZ. It was a bright, sunny day. As he sat on the edge of the fighting hole, he noticed that small rivers of dirt were falling into it from the corners—a slight tremor in the ground.

Ken looked out across the DMZ. From their position, the ground swept down for several thousand meters and then back up for several thousand more. In the distance, he saw a wall of explosions and heard a deep rumbling. He looked up and scanned the sky until he saw three aircraft. B-52s were dropping bombs. If not for the sun glinting off their silver-metallic surface, he may not have seen them; they were so high in altitude.

On another day, while on watch in the hole, he looked east and saw a jet flying low and westward, parallel to the south side of the Trace. As the jet reached Ken's position, it made a sharp right-hand turn northward, moving quickly out of sight. As it went over, the plane was low enough to see markings on the aircraft, but Ken saw none. Within minutes, two F-4 Phantoms came screaming over his position, heading north in chase. Ken's guess was that the jet being pursued was a Mig doing photo reconnaissance.

The Marines ran patrols north and south of the Trace until July 14th.

* * *

On the morning of the 14th, the Marines were told to fill in their holes and prepare to move. They were starting another operation.

There was no talking, bitching, or cussing out the leadership. The Marines pulled their E-tools out and began filling in their holes. They were given about 10 minutes and then told to saddle up.

It was another hot day as they moved south. The tanks were with them, which meant they continued to attract the occasional bit of sniper fire. The extra firepower was nice to have, but the tanks continued to be bullet magnets. Ken and his team stayed as far away from them as possible.

The company moved quick, making no real contact but covering distance. At one point, Ken heard a large volume of small arms fire for about five minutes. Someone was making contact, but at least it wasn't Ken and the men close to him.

By late afternoon, they stopped and dug in. Ken had no idea where they were other than southeast of the Trace. It had been a long, hot day with no water resupply. One can go without food for weeks, but one cannot go without water for more than a few days. They were rationing their water by drinking canteen capfuls—one capful per man. This wasn't the first time they had done this, nor would it be the last. If the Marines didn't have a water source or were not resupplied, they did without. Same with C-rats. No one bitched or complained, it was just part of being a grunt.

"Years later, after the war," Ken says, "I listened to news reports from Operation Iraqi Freedom about some Army troops complaining they weren't getting three MREs a day. It was reported as a big deal, as if it was some sign that things weren't going well. I smiled a bit at that, remembering going a week, on more than one occasion, without a resupply of anything—C-rats or water, which meant we just didn't eat; it wasn't a big deal. But, I guess it is now."

It was a quiet night, or as calm as it got in the DMZ; there were always air strikes, H&I (Harassment and Interdiction) fire by artillery, and flares drifting in the sky giving off a flickering, ghostly light.

One hour before sunrise they went to 100 percent and we were moving within a half hour after daylight. It was another sweep, though not as fast as the day before, and still with the tanks and the occasional shots fired at them.

No contact was made the second day and they dug in again. On July 16th, they started another operation: Operation Kingfisher, continuing their sweeps in and around Cam Lo. It was another two days like the previous two days on Hickory II, but at least in the afternoon of the 16th, they got a resupply. On July 18th, they moved through Cam Lo up to the highway, really just a dirt road, where they found six-bys waiting for them.

"Such a sweet sight," Ken says. "Six-bys stand kind of tall, loading from the tailgate. We were so worn out that we all struggled to climb aboard; we each had to help one another get up. At least we weren't climbing a cargo net to get back aboard the ship. Small mercies."

They rode back to Dong Ha in a convoy. At the front of the convoy was an army Crop Duster, an old M-41 tank chassis mounted with WWII twin 40mm anti-craft guns in an open turret. Another Crop Duster brought up the Tail End Charley position in the convoy. The 40mm could pump out 400 high-explosive rounds a minute in a pinch. It was nice to have along.

At Dong Ha they offloaded the six-bys, loaded onto an LCM (Landing Craft Medium), and then headed out to the Okinawa. There wasn't much talking.

"I think most of us were trying to digest the last couple of weeks and the fact that we were still alive," Ken says.

When they got to the Okinawa, they had a ladder that went from the hanger deck to a platform that the LCM docked against. All they had to do was climb a short ladder from the LCM's well deck to the deck, then step across to the platform on the side of Okinawa and walk up to the hangar deck.

As they reached the top of the ladder and entered the hangar deck, they saw several sailors standing around. On one bulkhead, someone had tallied all of the statistics of Operation Buffalo: Artillery rounds fired by type of gun and from where (JJ Carroll, Cam Lo), number of air sorties flown in support, bombs dropped, and the amount of 20mm fired by the planes, gallons of napalm used, amount of naval gunfire and how much by ships (apparently there were a couple of heavy cruisers in support with 8" naval rifles), number of incoming artillery rounds by type and caliber that landed on the Marines, and number of NVA killed.

Ken wondered who had kept track of all of it. That board might as well have been written in Japanese. His brain was too tired to make sense of it.

"It must have had meaning to someone," he says. "but not to me or any of my friends."

The Marines formed loosely into platoons and began unloading their ammo. The Navy didn't like anyone taking frags down into the troop compartments, so while the Marines disarmed, a large number of sailors watched them. The Marines were filthy, wore dirty, raggedy utilities, were unshaven, and smelled pretty bad. The sailors were wearing dungaree bell bottoms and starched blue short-sleeve shirts.

"I had the feeling they were thinking they were pretty damn glad they weren't Marines," Ken says.

After turning in ammo, the Marines started cleaning their weapons. Cleaning gear had been brought to supplement what they carried. Small conversations broke out as they cleaned the machine guns, rifles, pistols, knives, and bayonets. The Marines mainly spoke about what they had seen and done, trying to make sense of it.

The Marines went to chow after the weapons were cleaned and turned in. They had not had the chance to get cleaned up because of weapons cleaning. The Navy was nice to the Marines, letting them go down to the mess deck as dirty as they were. Ken loaded a metal tray and sat down with the rest of the machine gun section. He started to get up to get something to drink when a couple of sailors came over and stopped him. They asked him and his gun section what they wanted to drink and then fetched the drinks for them—the first time that had ever happened. The sailors also asked if there was anything else they could do for them.

"No," Ken told them, "were good to go."

"So," one of the sailors said, "how rough was it out there?"

A tired and quiet voice whispered out from the group of Marines. "You don't want to know."

* * *

Every year since he returned from Vietnam, Ken has thought about Operation Buffalo, as he has done with the other operations he was on during his tour, but that one, more than any other, except the day his best friend, Frank Holsomback, was killed.

Part of the reason is because the operation started the day before he turned 19. That July 4th, he didn't think he would survive the day, let alone the week.

"Every July 4th since," Ken says, "my thoughts go back to that time—to the ferocity of the violence that I saw and inflicted. I have dreamed about the operation. I have laid awake at night, more times than I'd like to think about, trying to figure out the whole experience, trying to put it in some perspective that I could understand and reconcile. When we came home, no one sat down with us to talk about what we had seen and done. We were ignored, at best. In college, I had an English professor ask the class to write about a significant event in our lives. I wrote about the first four days of Operation Buffalo and received a C-minus for a grade. In the right-hand margin, for several pages, the professor had written, in red ink, how terrible it was for me to write about the experience in that 'unlawful war' and how I should have been ashamed of what I had done."

CODY BURLESON

Operation Beacon Guide

```
Beacon Guide: July 21 - 30, 1967
```

The last SLF operation of July 1967 was Operation Beacon Guide, 18 miles southeast of Hue City along the coast. According to a battalion's intelligence brief, they would be chasing an NVA division.

It was another early day, getting up at 0200, going to chow, heading back to the compartment, drawing weapons, ammo, C-rats, filling canteens, and staging on the hanger deck to wait. On the hangar deck, Ken and the gun team promptly fell asleep until the word was passed to stand up in their sticks and prepare to fly out.

Though the landing in the LZ was uneventful, they still exited the '34s as fast as they could, spreading out about 15 meters and then getting down as the aircraft took off. They then got up, moved towards a tree line, and set in, waiting for the rest of the company to arrive.

It was a typical day in Vietnam—hot and humid, with temperatures above 100 degrees. Their destination was a mountain top on the south side of a bay. On the map, the mountain was over 400 meters high and covered with heavy vegetation. The company had two war dogs with them and their handlers.

They reached the base of the mountain after a couple of hours and commenced climbing up a very steep trail. They were loaded with ammo, flak jackets, water, C-rats, and packs, so it was slow going and arduous. They often had to help each other climb because the terrain was so steep. Ken would pass the machine gun up to a rifleman, who would take it and pass it up to another rifleman further up to hold, then he reached down to take Ken's hand and pull him up to his position. Ken would then turn and do the same thing for the Marine behind him, and so on.

They were further delayed as they came across caves that needed to be searched before proceeding further up the mountain. Part way up, the word was passed that the two war dogs had died of heat exhaustion.

By late afternoon, they reached a saddle on the side of the mountain. The word was passed that they would stay the night in that position and be resupplied. They had run out of water a couple of hours before. On either side of the saddle, a small opening appeared to be wide enough for a '34 to come in and resupply them.

Within a half hour, Ken heard the sound of a radial engine. He moved down the saddle to watch the bird come in. The '34 approached the opening slowly, with its crew chief leaning out the right side hatch and watching the rotor blades and trees as it approached. Ken could see that the bird was carrying water cans. The saddle sloped down steeply on either side of the trail. As the helicopter reached the point where it was hovering directly over the trail, power was applied to the engine, and the aircraft moved forward past the trail, slipping down the side of the mountain. The rotor blades hit some trees, and pieces began to fly everywhere. Ken threw himself on the ground, as did a dozen others watching. The rotor blades disintegrated. Ken heard the crash. The engine ran for a moment, then stopped. The only sound was a ticking coming from the downed '34.

Ken got up with the others and ran towards the downed '34. It was lying on its side, the rotor blades gone, the water cans scattered about the aircraft's interior, the crew chief crawling out through the right hatch, and the pilots trying to get out. Fortunately, there was no fire.

The crew chief had no broken bones but did have a nasty gash across his forehead. The Marines immediately began moving the crew up to the saddle so they could be treated, and to get them away from the ticking aircraft, which now smelled of gasoline. A working party started pulling the water cans out. Ken noticed that a little further down was another '34 that had crashed sometime before they got to the mountain. It, too, was sitting on its side without rotor blades.

After removing the water cans from the downed helicopter, they returned to the saddle. Ken then watched as the rest of the resupply helicopters came in, coming through the opening in the trees the same way as the first helicopter had before it crashed and delivered their resupply. Half a dozen helicopters came in the same way. A few tree branches flew when rotor blades hit them, but it did not stop the aircrews from resupplying the men. Ken was duly impressed with their skill.

* * *

The helicopter resupply brought in water and C-Rats and took out the aircrew from the downed '34. Delta set in for the night around the saddle without digging any fighting holes, as the ground was nothing but rock. It was a long, hard, slow climb to get to that spot, and they were exhausted.

The next morning, 1st Platoon, 2nd Platoon, 60mm Mortars, and the company CP headed back down the mountain, while 3rd Platoon and the machine gun squad continued heading up.

By early afternoon, they had reached the top of the mountain. They were not the first ones to have been there. At some point, artillery had been airlifted to the top and dug in. The trees and brush had been cleared about 30 meters in every direction. The Marines moved in and set up a 360-degree perimeter. Their positions were close to the tree line, four to five meters. The tree line and brush were very thick so that one could see only a few meters into it. The trail they had come up bisected the clearing and continued on the other side, apparently moving down the mountain, but they could not see exactly where it went because of how thick the trees and brush were.

Ken's gun team positioned themselves so that their principal direction of fire was straight down the trail they had come up. The other gun was set on the opposite side with its principal direction of fire down the trail where it crossed over the other side of the mountain.

Once the guns were positioned, the rifleman set in—the ground rocky and difficult to dig. It took them the entire afternoon to get down about 2 feet.

After digging in, they cleaned weapons and then ate C-rats quietly. They were out there by themselves. There was no way the company could reinforce them other than provide fire support from the 60mm mortars, though no fires were registered while they dug in. Registering fires means that the mortar section, or artillery if they had it, would fire a round at a particular grid coordinate or terrain feature on a map and record the map coordinates and the direction in mils or degrees from the mortar to the target. It could be a hilltop, trail junction, road intersection, or other terrain feature. Mortars would then assign a target number to that registration. Marines could call fire on that registration point or adjust fire from it, e.g., "From registration, Alfa X-Ray add 600, left 300." That is all in meters and not feet. It is a quick way to call in mortars or artillery, assuming they had registered fires to work with. Otherwise, they would do it the old-fashioned way with a target-observer line (the compass direction from the observer to the target in mils or degrees), the target location in a 6 or 8-digit grid, a description of the target, whether danger is close or not and requesting a one round will adjust. That all takes time. If you have pre-registered fires, it is easier and faster, and in a firefight, faster is better than slower when calling for supporting arms.

An hour before dark, they went to a 100 percent watch, sitting on the edge of their shallow fighting holes and waiting. The two-man fire team LP (Listening Post) left the lines at dusk. The LP came by Ken's gun position, stopped, kneeled next to the hole, whispered to them how far down the trail they would be, and confirmed that they both knew the challenge and password.

They started with a clear sky that night, with a partial moon.

"Even with that much illumination," Ken says, "when you looked into the tree line, it was like peering into a black ink well. We could not see into it or make out anything, even though we were pretty damn close to it."

It clouded up within a couple of hours, and they had a torrential rain shower that lasted about 15 minutes. They had been ordered not to put up hooches for the night because they could easily be seen. The rain woke those not on watch, so they just lay there and got wet. The rain ended as fast as it started. The word was passed to go to a 100 percent watch sometime after midnight. The LP down the trail in front of their position had radioed back that they were hearing movement.

Shortly after that, the squad saw movement on the trail at the edge of the tree line. The challenge was whispered, and the password came back. It was the LP. They ran up the trail, moving in behind Ken's position. They had been ordered over the radio to move back into the line. They whispered to Ken and the squad that they had heard movement around them.

Shortly thereafter, Ken and the Marines around him began to hear some movement. A rifleman in the hole next to them threw a frag, but it hit a tree and bounced back before it exploded a few meters from his position. A couple of more frags went out and they did the same thing. The word was passed to stop throwing frags.

The squad's grenadier moved down to Ken's position and tried firing several M79 rounds into the tree line. He was too close, and the rounds did not have time to arm before being deflected by the trees. He then decided to use the M79 like a mortar, shooting it up into the air at a high angle.

He fired the first round. It appeared that he was firing almost straight up. Ken waited and waited, finally hearing an explosion that sounded like it was way down the mountainside. The grenadier adjusted the angle even steeper and fired again. There was another long wait before they heard the explosion further down the mountainside. Apparently, that round came close to hitting the company CP because the word was passed to cease firing the M79.

They continued to hear movement around their perimeter for several hours, but no push was made against them. They stayed at 100 percent until daylight. They stayed several days at that position before moving down the mountain. Every night, they had movement but were never attacked. Whether the sounds of movement were NVA or rock apes was never determined. It just made for tense nights.

All in all, minimal contact was made during the operation, which was fine with the Marines, though a lot of rice and some weapons were found. On July 31, they were picked up by '34s and flown back to the Okinawa.

CODY BURLESON

Operations Beacon Gate and Cochise

```
Beacon Gate: August 7 - 11, 1967

  Cochise: August 11 - 27, 1967
```

When the battalion returned to Okinawa on July 31, it was pretty raggedy. In a two-month period, June to the end of July, it had conducted 8 combat operations and spent all but three and a half days in the field. It had been hit by artillery and rockets and engaged in significant combat. Its Marines were wound pretty tightly.

When they disembarked from the helos on the Okinawa, the men didn't run from them; they walked. Ken had been tired before, but after this two-month period, he was physically and emotionally wrung out. They went to the hanger deck to clean weapons and turn in ammo.

During this period, they would lose their company commander, Capt Ed Aldous. Instead of getting an experienced officer from within the battalion or one of their sister companies, they got a fresh captain from the States. He had never been to Vietnam.

The company first met the new CO at the change of command ceremony on the Okinawa a couple of days after returning from the field. Capt Aldous wore faded, unpressed jungle utilities and jungle boots where the leather no longer had any black die on them. The new company commander wore brand new starched jungle utilities and spit-shined jungle boots. He also had gold jump wings above his left breast pocket. He was from Force Recon.

"He gave some speech in which he practically insulted us," Ken says. "Then we were informed there would be a weapons inspection the next day."

The men drew their weapons and cleaned them again, spending the rest of the day working on them.

"I don't know what he expected to find," Ken says.

There had been a lot of bad press about the M16 and jamming problems, all of which was true. However, what was not true was the initial assessment that the jamming was caused by the Marines' dirty and improperly cleaned weapons.

On operations, cleaning weapons was a constant. If the men stopped for 10 minutes, they would alternate running a clean patch through the bore and making sure the M16 was dusted down with a paintbrush. If they stopped for a longer period, they pulled the bolt carrier out and wiped it down, making sure the bolt floated freely within the bolt carrier. With the machine gun, Ken would lift the feed cover, remove the belt, and run a paintbrush and rag over the inside to ensure everything was moving smoothly.

"You had to be careful with lubrication when you were in sandy areas, particularly when you came off a helo," Ken says.

They all had the impression that the new CO believed they weren't maintaining their weapons or gear.

The company was formed on the hanger deck by platoons: Headquarters Platoon, 1st Platoon, 2nd Platoon, 3rd Platoon, and Weapons Platoon. This inspection included not only weapons but also bayonets, magazines, pistols, etc.

The machine gun section had laid out the machine guns on ponchos, broken down into six main groups for easy inspection—each team standing behind its gun. The new CO came through, looked at receivers and feed covers, peered through barrels, and commented here and there. He asked the section leader if he had ever heard of boot polish. At first, we all thought it was a joke, but he was serious.

Didn't he know that looking at the boots was the quickest way to determine who was a grunt and who was not?

"There was no black on their boots," Ken says. "It had all been worn away from being in the field on operations. It was a point of pride for us grunts. It separated us from everyone in the rear who were required to polish their boots."

The inspection was anticlimactic. The new CO complimented the company on how well-maintained all the weapons were.

On August 7, the battalion started Operation Beacon Gate. They were helo-lifted southeast of Hoi An, south of Da Nang. They would spend four days sweeping through small villages, crossing rice paddies (some wet, some not), and running into snipers, booby traps, and punji pits. The battalion had 1 KIA and 12 WIAs. At least in Southern I Corps, there was no incoming artillery. Small mercies.

A cardinal rule in Vietnam was never to take the same route twice in a row. It was beaten into the Marines to always vary their route, try and be unpredictable, and stay off trails as much as possible. Fight smart, not stupid.

The company's new CO apparently thought otherwise, so they moved up and down a trail through several villes, going and coming exactly the same way for three days straight. They were fortunate in that they only ran into snipers and booby traps. But, the new CO was not off to a promising start with the grunts.

* * *

Operation Beacon Gate ended without fanfare on August 10. The battalion was told that they would be starting a new operation the next day, one that would take them beyond the range of naval guns and local artillery support. The operation, Cochise, would be 20 miles inland in the mountains around the Que Son Valley. Initially, they would only have air support: fixed-wing and helo gunships.

The company and battalion were picked up in a large, dry, rice paddy on a hot and humid day by '34s. Humidity and heat had an adverse effect on the lift capability of helos—they could not carry as heavy a load as they would in cooler air. Ken was sitting on the deck of the aircraft right across from the crew chief as they began to take off and move forward. He noticed that they were only about 3 feet off the ground. He looked at the crew chief and yelled over the engine's noise.

"What the hell is going on?"

"We gotta gain airspeed so that we can fly," the crew chief replied.

They used up most of that rice paddy, several hundred meters across, before gaining altitude. In Vietnam, for a grunt, there was always more than one way to die other than being shot or blown up. Helos were very fragile aircraft. Aircrews wore heavy porcelain flak vests that could stop a .50 cal. The Marines just sat on the decks of the aircraft. Some used their helmets as seats, but Ken never saw the point in it; an AK-47 round would go right through the helmet.

This would be the longest flight in a helicopter Ken would take while in country. They flew west, way back into the mountains. They were told that they would be landing in the vicinity of an NVA regimental headquarters. The crew chief informed Ken that they were approaching the LZ, and the previous lift had received some fire.

"When I say he 'informed me,' I mean he had to yell at me so that I could hear him because of the noise inside the aircraft."

As they approached the LZ, Ken could see a river with a bend in it, a road that appeared several meters wide that headed further west up into a valley and into the mountains, smoke from the close air support that had prepped the LZ, and a body on the far side of the river at the bend, clad in black. They crossed the bend in the river and landed in an open area. As soon as they jumped out, the helo lifted off, making a sharp left-hand turn, along with the other helos in the lift.

Ken's stick linked up with the rest of 3rd Platoon and moved off the LZ, moving up a small hill that overlooked the LZ and the bend in the river. All the vegetation on the hill was dead, as was all the vegetation surrounding them. It appeared as if the plants had grown and then collapsed.

The LZ was part of a small valley that the river cut through and was surrounded by hills, mountains, and dead vegetation. What they didn't know at the time was that this area had been sprayed with Agent Orange.

They set up a hasty perimeter and waited for the rest of the company to come in. The mountains in the distance looked rugged with steep sides. Subsequent lifts brought in 4.2" mortars (called "Four Deuces"). They would act as a blocking force for 5th Marines. Contact was made throughout the day.

They were told the road that cut through the valley went all the way to Laos, which, according to their Platoon Commander, was not very far away; it was only several miles up the road. The road had been built by the French. It ran alongside the base of a hill, west through the small valley, and up into the mountains. A squad was pushed out into that valley, establishing an OP (Observation Post).

The company would spend a couple of days there. At one point, the word was passed for Ken's machine gun team to move to the Platoon CP. There was firing going on up the valley where the OP was located. The lieutenant told the gun team that they were to provide covering fire so the squad could withdraw back to the company.

There was no finesse to the operation. They double-timed up the macadam road with a fire team and the lieutenant until they found a spot off the road that overlooked the small valley. Ken set the gun on its bipod, and his A-gunner linked up 500 rounds. The lieutenant got on the hook (radio) and told the squad they were in place and that they should start withdrawing back toward them. Ken and the Marines sent to cover the squad were about 15 meters above the valley. The field appeared to be planted with some kind of small trees.

The lieutenant told Ken that as soon as the squad made it back to his position and was accounted for, he was to start firing ten 12-round bursts, walking "lazy Ws" through the field, which stretched out several hundred meters in front of him.

The fire team with Ken and the gun team, all two of them, had taken up positions, one on each side of the gun team, as they waited. One of the riflemen caught movement in front of them; it was the squad from the outpost. Ken saw them running. He could hear the lieutenant saying something on the radio, but he was concentrating so hard on what was happening in front of him that the words didn't register.

The lieutenant yelled that the squad was coming in. Ken had set the sights on the gun at 300 meters, which would be the far side of the field. Since he was not sighting in on a particular target, he looked through the sights with both eyes open and watched his tracers as he walked the fire through the field in a lazy W pattern. This was strictly suppressing fire unless something popped up.

The squad was at the base of their position, moving up to where they were off the road. The squad leader was at the front, and when he reached the covering Marines, he counted each of his people in, the last being one of his team leaders.

Before the lieutenant could say anything, Ken cut loose, following his tracers and walking the rounds up and down the field in a lazy W. He went through those 500 hundred rounds very quickly. As he was firing, the squad from the outpost double-timed back down the road to the company perimeter while Ken's gun team, the fire team, and the lieutenant stayed to provide covering fire.

When Ken fired the last burst, the lieutenant yelled for them to pack it up and return to the company. The gun was hot.

"I mean goddamn hot," Ken says. "The barrel was 3rd degree burn hot and was smoking from the oil that was on it."

Ken lifted the feed cover and flicked out the last couple of links. His A-gunner, Jerry Carrero, placed a new belt in the feed tray. Ken lowered the feed cover, placed the weapon on safe, stood up, grabbed the gun by the carrying handle above the forearm assembly (there was no way he was placing the gun on his shoulder as he would have been burned), wrapped the belt of ammo around the receiver, and took off running down the road with his team. The fire team brought up the tail end-charlie.

They hightailed it back to the company as fast as they could move. They were definitely running on adrenaline. When they returned to the company, Ken's A-gunner asked him if he had seen the rounds impact in front of the gun, but Ken said no. He was concentrating so much on walking the rounds in a lazy W that he never heard any rounds being fired at them. In fact, he didn't even remember the M60 being loud when he fired it. His brain had shut down all the loud noise. He could hear the gunfire, but it wasn't loud; it was a muffled background noise.

They moved back into their position with the platoon. As the adrenaline began to wear off, they felt exhausted. Weapons were cleaned, 500 rounds of linked 7.62 were pulled from the riflemen (they carried extra ammo for the gun team), and they ate. Word was passed that they would be moving the next day out of the mountains and back towards the coast by foot.

* * *

The next day, Delta Company moved across the river—almost waist-deep. The body that Ken had seen when they had landed a couple of days before still lay where he had seen it, only now it was ripe and smelled pretty bad. They walked right past it—an old woman with grey hair lying face down, with the ground around her stained brown from dried blood. Ken's guess was that she had been killed either by the prepping air strikes or by the Huey gunships. Death had become so commonplace to Ken that seeing her meant nothing. He had turned off all emotions when he saw the dead.

As they moved up the trail into the hills, it began to rain, and it would continue until they came out of the mountains.

"It was pure misery," Ken says. "We were all soaked through to the bone. There was no point in wearing a poncho because you still got wet. My hands were wrinkled from being so wet."

The terrain was so thick with trees and vegetation, mostly single and double canopy, that when they pulled off the trail for the night they could not dig in due to the density of roots. They simply moved into the vegetation a meter or so, sat down, and waited for darkness. Because 3rd Platoon had been tail-end Charlie in the day's movement, they were at the end of the column when they stopped for the night. Ken's gun was placed off the left side of the trail, facing down the trail they had just come up from. An LP consisting of a 2-man fire team moved down the trail 30 or so meters.

Because of the cloud cover and rain, when it became dark, it became pitch black. It rained all night long, and none of the company got any sleep. When it became light enough to see, Ken found a leech attached between his eyebrows.

He had no bug juice, and the soaked C-rat matches, which were supposed to be waterproof, would not light, so the leech could not be burned off. Their squad's Corpsman finally found some alcohol in his Unit-1 bag, and he got it off of him.

"I hated leeches!" Ken says. "Leeches and mosquitos. They were such a pain in the ass."

They moved all the next day in the rain, continuing through the mountains. The movement was slow and arduous; the trail was muddy and slippery, with steep climbs and downhill slopes, but they were slowly moving downhill. When they finally stopped for the night, it was a relief. They were all exhausted. They set in like the night before for another long, wet, sleepless night.

* * *

The next morning, the rain stopped just before daylight. The company saddled up, with 3rd Platoon taking the point in the company's movement. As they left the position they had occupied the night before, they moved further downhill on the trail. To their right, a small, rapidly moving stream ran parallel to the trail— a couple of meters wide and a couple of feet deep. The ground began to flatten out, and then it opened up on the left side of the trail to a large, water-filled rice paddy, the rapidly moving stream on the right, with a tree line to the right of the stream. The rice paddy extended to their left front for a couple hundred meters, ending at a tree line. The clouds were still low, almost to the deck, but were beginning to burn off.

Ken's gun was with the lead squad as they moved out into the open. They hadn't gone very far when automatic weapons opened up on them. When the firing started, Ken could see the squad in front of him moving in a staggered column. The rounds impacted along the trail, through the squad and his gun team, and in the rice paddy. He rolled to the left into the rice paddy and into about 6 inches of water.

He wasn't in the paddy for more than a couple of seconds when the squad he was attached to got up and started running. He yelled for his gun team to follow him as he followed the rifle squad across the small stream to the other side of the tree line, moving parallel to the tree line and forward towards the sound of the automatic weapons fire.

The fire was coming from the tree line that was in front of them and at the end of the rice paddy that paralleled the trail they had been on. They moved into position and started firing as the rest of the platoon passed them on the right, maneuvering to flank the tree line. Ken fired, traversing the tree line left and right with a long burst.

The word was passed to cease fire as the rest of the 3rd Platoon swept the tree line. Ken asked if everyone was OK on his team and got a thumbs-up. The rifle squad leader did the same for his team.

The rifle squad was told by radio to displace themselves and move forward to rejoin the 3rd platoon. The rest of the company followed.

When they rejoined the platoon, they found out that one of 3rd Platoon's riflemen had taken a round through his helmet.

The round had entered a couple of inches below the top, deflected slightly upwards, traveled between the helmet liner and the steel helmet, and exited out the top. When the round hit the rifleman's helmet, it knocked him flat on his ass. Typically, rounds went straight through the helmet. He had been very lucky.

* * *

The company regrouped and moved out about twenty minutes later with 3rd Platoon at point. As the clouds burned off, the heat became oppressive, bearing down on them with suffocating intensity. They had been moving for about an hour before they stopped. Ken took the gun off of his right shoulder, sitting it on the butt stock. As he looked down at the ground and his boots, he noticed something alarming: blood was oozing out of the brass eyelets on his right jungle boot. He also saw that his right trouser leg below the knee was bloody. With a jolt, he realized he had been hit without even knowing it.

Ken set the gun down on its bipod and butt stock and ran his hands down the outside of his right trouser leg, from his right hip to the top of his right boot, looking for the wound. He could feel no tears or holes, but there was a lot of blood. He called the Corpsman to come over as he stood up and began taking off his gear—ammo belts, pack, flak jacket, cartridge belt with canteens, .45 pistol, KA-BAR, frags, smoke grenades, and a thermite grenade.

The Corpsman came over as Ken loosened his belt and dropped his trousers. As Ken let them fall to the ground, he saw a 6" long leech in the folds of his trousers' right leg. It must have come loose from his calf while he was walking. It was obvious that it had gorged itself because it was big and fat. The Corpsman looked at the site where the leech had been attached to his calf and painted it with iodine.

"Leeches produce an anticoagulant," the Corpsman said. "You can expect this to bleed for some time."

He placed a battle dressing on the wound and tied it down. Ken killed the leech.

He pulled up his trousers and used a canteen to rinse down his right trouser leg below the knee, trying to get some of the blood out. Putting on his gear, he got ready to start moving again.

They spent the rest of the day sweeping through the valley and several villes, running into sniper fire and booby traps. They set in late in the afternoon in and around a ville. Their gun was positioned in a water buffalo pen filled with dung. They dug in and spent a long night in shit.

The next morning, Ken thought he had better look at his calf and see how it was doing. Even with the smell of water buffalo dung, he could smell a hint of rotting flesh—his own blood. Pulling up his right trouser leg, he saw that the battle dressing was soaked; the blood had drained into his boot. He carefully pulled the battle dressing off and examined the site. The blood had coagulated, with a thick strand of it running down into his right boot. Next, he unlaced his boot, pulling it off. Turning it upside down, a large glob of smelly, coagulated blood slid out of the boot. It was the consistency of chocolate pudding, and it smelled really bad.

Their Corpsman cleaned the site again and repainted it with iodine, putting a new battle dressing on. Taking out a canteen, Ken poured water into his boot, sloshing it around, then pouring it on the ground. Pulling off his sock, he rinsed that too, with water from his canteen. He realized the sock was a lost cause, so he pulled a pair of socks out of his pack, emptied them of the C-rat cans, and put them on. He tossed the bloody sock and its left foot companion away. Putting his boots back on, he got ready to move out. A request for new jungle utility trousers and new jungle boots was made by their platoon guide to the company Gunny.

The company moved all day, sweeping through villes and rice

paddies. They were sniped at a few times and turned up a few hidden stashes of weapons and rice. Ken's right boot fell apart late that afternoon. The boot's leather was vulcanized to the sole, and that was where the boot came apart. The boots had lasted seven months. He had their Corpsman wrap white adhesive tape around the boot several times so that he could walk in it.

They set in again late in the afternoon and received a helo resupply. No utilities and no boots. Ken was told that Battalion Supply said they were out of his size, 11W, and there were no utilities on the bird. *Great. Who the hell were these idiots in supply?* Not only did his utilities still smell from the blood, but they were now ripped from the crotch to the knees. This was not the first time they had encountered supply problems, nor would it be the last.

Ken would walk on a taped boot for the rest of the operation. The funny thing was when he was on working parties in supply several times between operations, they always seemed to have large quantities of everything.

By the end of the month, they had covered a lot of ground as they moved toward the coast. On their last day in the field, they moved out early, moving on a dirt road in a staggered column. Within a short time, Ken could see that they were approaching a fire support base. Word was passed that helicopters would pick them up and take them to Chu Lai.

They set up near the designated LZ in their sticks and waited. They heard the helos before they saw them: CH-53s. This time, they would be riding in style in choppers with seats, though none of the Marines used seat belts.

* * *

It was a short ride to the airstrip at Chu Lai. The company was moved to hard backs—large, raised wooden structures with canvas tops, like tents, and sides covered in wire mesh so a breeze could blow through. They were staying at the Ritz. They each found spots on the wood floor and dropped their gear—Ken's gun team staying together.

Within minutes of settling in their new hooch, a sergeant walked in. He was wearing a starched soft cover, clean, starched jungle utilities, and shined jungle boots. He had heard that a battalion of grunts were coming out of the field, and he just wanted to see if there was anything he could do for them. He was in Supply. Ken asked if he could get him new jungle boots in size 11W and new jungle utility trousers in size medium-regular or medium-long. The sergeant told Ken he'd be right back.

Ten minutes later, he returned with the new boots and jungle utility trousers. What the hell was wrong with our battalion supply, Ken thought? The sergeant would spend the next hour with them, asking about the operation they had just come off.

"I think we scared the hell out of him," Ken says. "I don't think he'd been around grunts before. When he heard what we regularly did out there, you could see he was glad he wasn't one of us."

Word was passed that they would eat hot chow in a mess hall. It just kept getting better—new boots, jungle utility trousers, and now hot chow. The company formed up (they left a fire watch with each hardback to watch their weapons and gear, who were later relieved so they could eat). The line slowly snaked into the mess hall. As they entered, they all became slacked jawed; there were 2 Red Cross girls (women, though the Marines called them "round-eyes") serving food. These were the first American women they had seen in eight months. They wore light blue dresses with the Red Cross patch on their left shoulder.

It was the first hint of home that any of the grunts had seen or thought of since arriving in Vietnam. It verified that there was another world out there that was safe, where no one shot at you or tried to blow you up, and all they had to do was survive long enough to get back to it.

They all loaded up their trays with food, but their eyes were bigger than their stomachs, which had shrunken over the months of eating C-rats. Three or four bites, and they couldn't eat anymore, tossing out the rest into a GI can. Ken guessed it was the thought that counted, and in this case, it counted for a lot. Their battalion commander didn't have to argue with the base commander to get them fed as he had when they were in Phu Bai. Except for the supply sergeant, the other Marines and sailors stationed there kept their distance from the grunts. This "keeping their distance" by rear echelon troops was something that Ken would experience throughout his time there.

The next day, the company moved back to the ship. It had been a long month.

* * *

The eighteen days they had spent on Operation Cochise resulted in a dramatic change in the company—they began to lose Marines due to rotation. These were the Marines who had joined the Company in July and August 1966 and were now squad leaders, fire team leaders, and solid riflemen. They were the ones everyone looked to because of their experience and were the steadying force during the hard spring and summer operations; now they were leaving the company, and those under them were taking their place without adequate replacements to fill the gap.

Ken was happy the Marines were rotating because they were getting out alive. They had done what Ken was beginning to believe was nearly impossible. They had survived their 13-month tour—a lot worse for wear, but they had survived. There was some trepidation among those who filled their shoes because the life-and-death decisions would now be on their shoulders; they would be making those decisions.

New replacements began to dribble in during August as the old salts (all 19, 20, and a few really old ones at 21) began to leave. Ray

Kelley came by to visit Ken, asking him to write his name, address, and telephone number in a notebook so he could contact him and keep in touch. Ken wrote the information with a pang of envy that Ray was getting out of the hell hole of Vietnam while feeling glad that a good friend had survived and was rotating.

The replacements they received were a mixed bag. Some were just out of basic infantry school, but others were re-treads from other MOS specialties. The battalion was getting corporals and sergeants who had been Remington Raiders (clerk typists), cooks, mechanics, and the like. All had been Marines for 2-4 years but had never been out of the States. In talking to some of them, Ken learned that they received orders notifying them that their MOS was being changed to 0311 (rifleman) or 0331 (machine gunner) and were ordered to report to either ITR at Camp Pendleton, California, or Camp Lejune, North Carolina and then to basic infantry school.

They felt that they had been screwed.

"They were NCOs that none of us would follow or listen to because they had no experience," Ken says.

When they joined the battalion, they were told to keep their mouths shut, watch, listen, and follow the more experienced grunts until they gained some experience. The company had PFCs and Lance Corporals leading fire teams and squads, with Corporals and Sergeants as riflemen.

The thing that irked the experienced grunts the most was that it screwed up their promotions. They had very few billets requiring an NCO because they had been filled by replacements who were NCOs that had been cooks or clerks two months before. The replacements felt screwed because they thought they had skated past Vietnam with their MOS. Now, they were in a combat rifle company. Some complained that this was not what they had signed up for. Ken and the others had no sympathy for them.

* * *

As the company's "old salts" began to rotate out during Operation Cochise, replacements filtered in by helo. They didn't just present a danger to themselves because they lacked experience; they also presented a danger to the new "old salts," who had been in the country for 5 to 9 months.

Late during the operation, the company had received a batch of these "replacements." In 2nd Platoon, Ken had a very good friend named Bill Southern. Bill and Ken joined the company about the same time when the battalion was at Khe Sanh in December 1966. When Ken joined the machine gun section, he went to 2nd Squad Guns, which was attached to 2nd Platoon. Bill was a rifleman with that platoon, and because they were both "new dudes," they became friends.

One afternoon on Operation Cochise, the company had dug in for the night and was set in a 360-degree perimeter. In Vietnam, there was never a "front line"; an attack could come from any direction. A replacement who had joined 2nd Platoon as a rifleman was on watch in a fighting hole down from Bill's position. That replacement heard some noise coming from his right, down the line. It was Bill coming off the watch, and the rifleman that Bill had shared a hole with was going on watch in his place. The replacement pulled a frag and threw it at Bill's position.

Ken, who was on watch, heard the explosion. There was some commotion, and Ken could hear someone calling for a Corpsman. They went to 100 percent as they did not know what had happened, bracing themselves for a potential fight.

Eventually, the word came down the line that a replacement had thrown a frag at another fighting position, and Bill Southern had been seriously wounded. Because it was dark, a medevac would not be coming in until first light.

At first light, Ken moved up to the company CP, where the casualty collection point was, to see how Bill was doing. He found Bill with their company Corpsman. He had taken a piece of shrapnel to the forehead, and his forehead was badly swollen. No battle dressing had been placed on the wound as there was little blood; the entry hole was very small. Bill was out of it mentally, and Ken was not sure he knew that he was there. He only had a few minutes with him before the sound of the medevac helo could be heard coming in. Ken asked the Doc what he thought. He told Ken that it was serious, but he just didn't know if he would survive because he didn't know the extent of the brain injury.

This was an incident of "friendly fire" caused by the stupidity of a replacement. Death was not always at the hands of the NVA; sometimes, the Marines inadvertently killed one another. Inexperienced replacements could be more dangerous than the NVA.

Ken would spend the next thirty-one years thinking that Bill had died on the medevac, only to meet him at a Third Marine Division Association Christmas party near San Diego in 1998. Though Bill's brain still carried the shrapnel, it was apparently fully functional; he had married, had children, and lived a good life.

Operations Beacon Point, Fremont, Ballistic Charge and Shelbyville

```
Beacon Point: September 1 - 5, 1967

  Fremont: September 6 - 9, 1967

Ballistic Charge: September 16 - 21, 1967

Shelbyville: September 22 - 28, 1967
```

In August, the battalion had spent twenty-four days in the field on two combat operations. In September, they would spend 30 days in the field and participate in four combat operations.

Beacon Point took Delta Company back to the Street Without Joy, along the coast between Phu Bai and Hue City—back to the land of booby traps, snipers, and abandoned Catholic churches. After Operation Cochise, they had spent two days on the ship before starting Beacon Point. They had received an influx of replacements during August, some joining them in the field and others when they returned to the ship after Cochise. The company had spent those two days trying to integrate the replacements into the company, platoons and squads.

A few of those wounded from previous operations also returned for duty. It was good to see them and have them rejoin the company. One, Johnny Kelley, a rifleman, had been wounded in early May and was just returning to them at the end of August. Ken spoke to him after they got back aboard the ship, and Johnny expressed that he was nervous about rejoining the company. Johnny kept telling Ken that he didn't want to return to the field. At the time, Ken didn't think much about it, as he could understand his nervousness; Johnny had been wounded once, and he was now going back out into that conflagration that was life for grunts in Vietnam.

"Reveille had been at 0200, with the usual steak and eggs breakfast provided by the Navy," Ken says. "As before, I don't remember eating anything. We drew ammo and C-rats, and we filled canteens. You had to be careful when drawing ammo, particularly explosives like fragmentation grenades. The frags came in a wooden case that contained black cardboard cylinders; the frags were inside the cylinders. You peeled off the sealing tape and slid the frag into your hand."

The first thing Ken did was to tighten the top of the frag. There were two parts to a frag: the body and the fuse, with a pin (a cotter pin with a ring attached to it), a spoon, and a blasting cap. The fuse and all was screwed into the frag body and had a tendency to loosen up. Next, he would bend the end of the cotter pin back around the top of the spoon. Finally, he would place a piece of black electrical tape around the top, including the spoon, so that if the pin worked its way out, the spoon still could not be released.

The operation started on September 1 with a helo lift from the Okinawa. The landing in the LZ was uneventful, and the men formed up and began their sweep. They began to receive sniper fire but continued to push forward through fields and small villes. They came across numerous booby traps, mostly punji pits, some rigged with CHICOM grenades—nothing new there.

* * *

Though the area they were operating in was the Street Without Joy, it was different from where they had operated in the past. Many of the fields they moved through were sunken, or I guess you could say the trails were raised above the fields.

As Delta Company moved through one of the sunken fields, they began to receive sniper fire. The rounds were going way over their heads, so they ignored them. One of the new replacements for 3rd Platoon had thrown himself on the ground when the first sniper round went past them. Ken recognized the rifleman as one he'd met aboard the Okinawa. Ken had caught him standing in front of a mirror in their compartment with his rifle. He'd been making faces in the mirror and growling, and when Ken asked what the hell he was doing, he had said that he was "practicing to go out and kick ass." Ken had only shaken his head at the kid.

Now, the kid appeared to be trying to bury himself into the ground.

Ken told the kid to get up as the platoon kept moving forward.

"We're in a sunken field and in defilade," he said. "Those rounds are going way over our heads."

A fire team leader then came back and grabbed the kid, pushing him forward and cussing him out. The false bravado he had displayed on board the ship had dissolved with the reality of the rounds snapping overhead, even if they were 15 feet above them.

"There was always that reality check for replacements," Ken says. "There was nothing more real than what we did, and it was always a matter of life and death. No in-between. No do-overs. No timeouts. No second chances. We lived at death's doorstep, always banging on the door to get in."

Ken's gun squad had a couple of replacements, too. A kid in his team had also thrown himself on the deck. Before they started the operation, Ken had told him to do exactly as he did. Ken told him to get up and that he could only get down if he got down.

"Do as I do," he said.

Late in the afternoon, the company set in, digging into a raised trail that overlooked a field covered in large, circular mounds—a Vietnamese graveyard. As Ken's gun team dug down several feet, an e-tool full of sandy dirt was tossed out, and they noticed it had black hair in it.

Shit!

The sickly smell of rotting flesh suddenly filled the air around them. There was a body buried a little further down. They stopped digging. They shoveled about a half foot of soil back into the hole, and the smell dissipated.

* * *

Because Ken had a new replacement, or what they called a "new dude" in the team, Ken stood his own watch and then stood watch with the new dude. He would do this with the new dudes for the first several weeks or until he was sure they were competent enough to stand a watch by themselves without killing one of the Marines. Ken was not going to have a replacement in his team kill someone because he heard a noise—the memory of what had happened to Bill Southern was still very fresh in his mind, as was the memory of how scared he'd been on his first watch up at Khe Sanh when he first got in country in December '66.

They had gone through the first three watches without incident, and now Jerry Carrero, Ken's A-gunner, was on watch. Ken slept behind the hole until Jerry whispered his name, urging Ken not to sit up.

"Someone's firing at us," Jerry said.

Ken's brain kicked into gear, and he half rolled and half slid himself into the hole. He heard the "crack" of the weapon being fired. The impact thuds from the rounds hit their parapet, and a splash of sand and dirt propelled over them.

Whoever was shooting at them continued to do so. All of the enemy rounds impacted into their parapet. Ken told Jerry to give him his rifle. Laying against the hole, he edged himself just around the right corner of the parapet so he could look out over the field in front of them. He heard the "crack," and another round impacted the parapet, but he saw no muzzle flash. AK-47s didn't have a flash suppressor.

He took the rifle, put the selector to "auto," and eased himself around the parapet, with the rifle flat on the ground to present as low a silhouette as he could. He looked over the top of the rear sight and squeezed off two bursts.

They received no more fire the rest of the night. Whether Ken scared the shooter off or hit him, he had no idea, but the shooting stopped.

The next morning they moved out early into another hot and humid day of snipers and booby traps. The company eventually moved into a position where they would spend two days.

They dug into a tree line that overlooked several fields planted with some kind of crop. Between the fields and their positions was a small berm, about a meter or so high, covered in scrub brush. A trail went through the center of it. The berm was about 25-30 meters from Ken's position. The berm was high enough so that the team could not see what was beyond it when they were in their fighting holes unless someone walked right up to the berm. During those two days, they would make sporadic contact, see NVA moving between tree lines a couple hundred meters away, and receive some incoming fire. On the morning of the fourth day of the operation, the word was passed that they would be moving out, past the berm, and sweep the villes on the far side of the tree line.

The movement order was 2nd Platoon, 3rd (the platoon Ken's guns were attached to), Headquarters, Mortars, and 1st Platoon.

As 2nd Platoon moved out, they were no more than twenty meters from 3rd Platoon's position; Ken could see that Johnny Kelley was walking point, moving along a trail that bisected the berm. Johnny moved up the berm, and as he reached the top of the berm and started down the other side, there was a sudden flash, the black/brownish grey of smoke, and the crack of an explosion, all simultaneously. Johnny disappeared in that explosion.

One of the 2nd Platoon's Corpsmen ran up and went over the

other side of the berm and the platoon moved up and over, also deploying to the other side. The word was passed to 3rd Platoon that they would get up, push through 2nd Platoon, and take the lead in the movement. Once they passed the berm, they would move into a fire team, squad, and platoon wedge.

The rifle squad that Ken's gun team moved with went right over the top of the berm where Johnny had gone. Ken could see what had happened as they moved up the berm single file and passed the Corpsman and Johnny. The Corpsman had wrapped battle dressing around Johnny's stomach and was doing compressions on his chest, then mouth to mouth. Johnny was lying on his back, his legs bent under him, flak jacket open, covered in blood and the grey residue of the blast, as was his face and hair. His eyes were open and glassy.

Another Corpsman from 2nd Platoon had moved up and was working with the first Corpsman.

Johnny had tripped, what they called a "Bouncing Betty." A booby trap that shot a small warhead up about groin to waist high, which then exploded. This Bouncing Betty had exploded just below Johnny's flak jacket, with the force of the blast and shrapnel hitting him under the open jacket. It was a mess. All the work by the Corpsmen was for naught. Johnny died on that berm.

Over the years, Ken would lay awake at night thinking about what happened to Johnny, replaying the conversation he had with him when he rejoined the company just before the operation; Johnny's fear that he was going to be killed, Ken watching him move out over the berm, the explosion, and then walking past him, seeing the Corpsman compressing his chest and breathing into his mouth.

There were several times during Ken's tour in Vietnam when he thought he was going to die, but the feeling would always pass, and Ken would move on. Once Johnny returned, he'd always felt he was going to die, and yet, even still, he went out and did his job.

"I saw more true courage in my time in Vietnam than I have ever seen since I came home," Ken says. "It wasn't the courage of doing heroic actions; it was the courage of doing your job day in and day out, knowing that each day could be your last."

* * *

After moving past Johnnie Kelley, 3rd Platoon pushed past 2nd Platoon and moved out in a large platoon wedge through a large open field and toward a tree line. Word was passed quietly through the platoon to watch out for mines and more booby traps.

Ken looked back at their new replacement, who was about five meters behind him as they moved. With each step, the replacement tamped his foot on the ground around him.

"What are you doing?"

"Looking for mines," the replacement said.

Ken shook his head.

"Get the fuck away from me," he said. "As far away from me as you can. Or I will shoot you myself."

They finished sweeping the area and ran into a few more booby traps and snipers.

The next day, the company moved to Camp Evans on foot.

* * *

At Camp Evans, the company stayed inside the wire and cleaned weapons—there was no hot chow, only C-rats.

On the morning of September 6, they climbed aboard Six-bys and convoyed up Highway 1 to a point south of Quang Tri. The trucks pulled off to the side of the road, and the Marines jumped from the tailgates.

The battalion was to operate as a blocking force for 4th Marines, moving west across Highway 1 and into an area that was a free-fire zone. They encountered a few booby traps, snipers, and incoming mortar fire.

On September 9, the battalion backloaded onto the Okinawa and headed down to an area southwest of Dai Loc, south of Da Nang, in the 1st Marine Division's tactical area of operation.

Returning to the Okinawa, they went through the familiar routine of turning in ammo and cleaning weapons. Once the weapons had been cleaned and turned in, the men got cleaned up. When they first returned, there were always a few sailors hanging around the compartment, trying to find out if the Marines had any souvenirs.

"I don't know what they thought we were doing out there," Ken says, "but looking for souvenirs was at the bottom of the list."

* * *

On the 16th, reveille went at 0200, with chow at 0230. The Marines drew weapons, ammo, C-rats, filled canteens, and then went through the now familiar routine of loading onto the aircraft.

When they landed in the LZ, they began to take sniper fire. They pushed out to the perimeter of the LZ as additional lifts came in with the rest of the company. The sniper fire came to an end. It had been more of a nuisance than anything else, but it did keep the men on their toes.

The company moved out and began a sweep through their area of responsibility. All four rifle companies were on the move with different objectives. Sporadic fire could be heard all around them. At one point, Ken's platoon came to a berm that ran for 100 meters or so. Across from the berm was a field, then a tree line. They pulled up to the berm, stopping as another platoon approached them.

Just as the other platoon arrived, they began to take fire. Ken had already set the gun up on its bipods. No one was firing back. Several rounds cracked right past his head. He cut loose with several long bursts, traversing the tree line across from him. The firing from the tree line ceased. No one had fired except Ken. His A-gunner told him several rounds had impacted near Ken while he was firing, but

Ken hadn't noticed.

The word was passed to get up and move toward the tree line. Both guns were left at the berm to provide fire support if the platoons were hit going across the open ground. A fire team was left to protect the guns. The platoons moved across the field without incident, and once across, the gun teams picked up and moved across the field, rejoining 3rd Platoon.

* * *

As they swept into the ville, platoons broke down into squads, which broke down to fire teams that searched each hooch. Since the area was a free-fire zone, there were not supposed to be any civilians present, but there were.

"Every free-fire zone we ever went into had civilians in them," Ken says.

Someone had torched the grass roof of a water buffalo's pen. The pen was below ground with a thatched roof over it. Ken could hear the water buffalo making all kinds of racket—snorting and thrashing in terror under the flames. Ken was about 10 meters from the pen when the huge water buffalo burst out—charging in Ken's direction, angling rightward as it approached him. Ken snapped the gun off his right shoulder, tucked it under his arm, and fired. The first round was a tracer. It hit the buffalo right behind the left shoulder and low. Ken pulled the gun to the right and let it climb, watching the rounds strike across the side of the buffalo from below the left shoulder, across its midsection, to just below its backbone, above its left hip. He ceased firing as the buffalo turned around and ran away from him and the rest of the platoon. Then, the buffalo disappeared somewhere beyond the ville.

The new company commander was nearby and came over, wanting to know who fired at the water buffalo. He sounded pissed. Ken said he had done the shooting. He said, "OK," and left it at that.

"To this day, I have no idea why he sounded pissed or why his answer was simply 'OK,' and then he left," Ken says. "I had just stopped a very large water bull from rampaging through our platoon and possibly injuring me or some of the Marines. Why would he be pissed at me for doing that?"

There would be several running gunfights as they swept through the villes in the area (supposedly a free-fire zone). Delta Company eventually moved to an area where they established a company-size perimeter. The ground was flat, with dry rice paddies and tree lines between the paddies and villes. Ken's gun was dug in behind the dike of a dry paddy that overlooked a large water-filled paddy. There was a sparse tree line at the edge of the paddy where they dug in.

The next morning, Ken's machine gun squad went on patrol with a rifle squad. The day was overcast, and they started receiving sporadic rain showers. A couple of hours into the patrol, they spotted an NVA squad approximately 700 meters away and took them under fire. The Marines chased them for a while, engaging in a running gunfight, but lost them. The other gun in their machine gun squad had a malfunction. The gunner on that team was a friend of Ken's who had originally been in Rockets (Marine rifle companies used to carry a 3.5" rocket launcher, also known as a "bazooka," which was of Korean War vintage). They removed the "Rockets" when the company started receiving LAAWs - Light Anti-Armor Weapons. A one-shot, throw-away mini "bazooka."

When the gun malfunctioned, he tried firing it a couple of times, working frantically with nothing happening. Then, unbeknownst to Ken, the gunner had failed to clear and lock the weapon as he should have.

Word was received over the radio to move back to the company. They moved to the CP for a debrief as they entered the company lines. The company CP was always a collection of cats and dogs: FOs (Forward Observers for artillery, 81mm mortars, and their radio operators), the company's own 60mm mortars (Delta had three), and their crews, combat engineers, a FAC (Forward Air Controller)- their FAC was not an officer, but enlisted, which doesn't occur today) and his radio operator, radio operators, and runners for the company commander and XO (executive officer), the company gunny, the company Corpsman, and others. In other words, a lot of people milling around.

As they entered the CP area, Ken observed two of their combat engineers talking to each other. They were about 10 meters or so from him. The other gunner in their machine gun squad had started cussing out his gun as soon as they came into the company lines (when on patrol, they did not talk unless they had to, and when they did, they whispered until they got into a firefight - then everyone yelled because of the noise). He had a temper, and he was pissed about the malfunction. Ken had been walking with his team behind him, watching him. He stopped and then threw the gun down on the ground. The bipods were out, so the gun landed on the bipods and the butt stock. Ken heard the gun go off. It was pointed at the two engineers. When it went off, one of the engineers had extended his arm while talking to the other engineer.

The round passed through the engineer's forearm. He looked at his forearm in stunned silence. Dark red blood began to pour out of his forearm a couple of inches from the elbow. It was like someone had turned on a faucet. The engineer grabbed his forearm with his other hand and dropped to his knees as the blood seeped through his fingers.

All hell broke loose with people yelling and running around. The engineer was fortunate; it was a clean hole, missing both of the bones in his forearm.

There would be an investigation after they came off the operation. The Marine who accidentally shot the engineer would spend only two days in the brig before starting the next operation—the battalion was short of men.

It rained for the rest of the operation. The dry rice paddy that they had dug into filled with a couple of inches of water, and they were miserably wet for a couple of days.

* * *

The battalion finished Operation Ballistic Charge on September 21 and commenced Operation Shelbyville, on September 22 with a short helicopter lift to LZ Hawk. They were under operational control of 1st Marines.

The area was another free-fire zone.

Upon landing, the battalion immediately came under sniper fire. Each of the companies pushed off in different directions. Ken's company, Delta, would have a series of running gunfights that first day. In addition to small arms fire, they ran into punji pits and some booby traps, suffering casualties along the way.

The terrain was flat: sandy farm fields, with some kind of crop growing, sugar cane fields, rice paddies, and tree lines between the villes. Delta Company was receiving sporadic fire from their flanks, so each platoon pushed out a squad to each flank as the company moved towards its objective. Ken's gun was placed on the right flank, while their other gun was placed on the left. Putting the guns on the flanks was not something they often did, but with the problems of the M16s jamming, they would find themselves out there to provide reliable firepower.

At some point in the morning, as they moved through a ville that had been hit by several air strikes, the Marines captured three shirtless NVA soldiers. The air was heavy with the smell of burned napalm, smoke, and small fires. One NVA had been shot through the right side of his chest, with an exit wound on the lower right side of his back. The other two had not been wounded.

Someone found a 2x4 that was about 6 feet long. The wounded NVA was put on the 2x4 and carried by his two compatriots to be evacuated at an LZ. While carrying him, they dropped the wounded

NVA half a dozen times. Each time, the wounded NVA would roll off the 2x4 and land on the ground with an "oomph." Blood squirted out of the entry wound when he landed, and he groaned. The two other NVA would place him back on the 2x4 and start carrying him again, only to drop the wounded NVA a short time later.

No aid was given to this wounded NVA. After Operation Buffalo, and seeing the dead Marines that had been executed by the NVA, shot through the head at close range, and after all the Marines they had lost, no Marine would consider helping, nor was anyone ordered to do so. The wounded NVA died before they got him to the LZ.

This would be the last time Ken would see prisoners during his tour.

Late in the afternoon, the company dug in an area with numerous small fields growing crops of some kind, including sugar cane. To their right flank, there was a small river, tree lines, and numerous hooches throughout the area. The soil was sandy, which meant easy digging.

Ken and his gun team dug in and set up a hooch behind the hole. To their front, some 10 meters, was a sugar cane field. It stood only about a meter high but was thick. Just before dark, a two-man LP moved to their position and told them they would be moving into the sugar cane. After confirming the password and counter-sign, they moved out into the field.

Clouds rolled in late that afternoon. As it started to get dark, the clouds lowered, and it began to drizzle, then a light rain. The clouds were right on the deck. Visibility was limited, but there was light from a full moon above the clouds. A couple of hours into their watches, they began to receive sporadic small-arms fire around the company perimeter.

The company went to a 100 percent alert—everyone in their fighting holes, gear on and ready for an attack.

Within minutes, Ken heard an airplane circling above—Puff had arrived. The aircrew pushed an illumination flare out. There was a "pop," followed by a "woof, woof, woof" as the empty flare canister tumbled end over end toward the ground, then a "thud" as it hit the ground within the company perimeter. The illumination flare ignited, and because of the cloud cover down to the ground, its light was eerie, giving off shadows that made it difficult to distinguish anything as it floated downward under its parachute.

"It was a scene from a Basil Rathbone Sherlock Holmes movie," Ken says. "It was eerie."

The LP that was in front of the gun team was pulled in. They were nervous, letting Ken and his team know they had heard a lot of movement around their position. It would be another all-nighter. The company would stay at 100 percent until daylight. The night would be interspersed with small arms fire, Puff, the flares, and the empty canisters landing within the perimeter, some of them dangerously close to the Marines.

The next morning, the clouds burned off. The Marines cleaned weapons but remained in place. Late in the afternoon, word was passed that Ken's gun team and the squad it was attached to were going on patrol. They would be moving back over the ground the company had covered the day before.

They headed out that afternoon, moving down the same trail the company had used to arrive at their current position. The point fire team consisted of two Marines, a rifleman, and the team leader, who carried an M79. The squad leader was next, followed by Ken and his gun team and the last two fire teams.

They had been moving for a short period when the point man cut loose with a burst with his M16, followed by the thump of the M79 firing and the explosion of its round going off. The point man had shot at an NVA soldier but missed. The team leader's M79 high explosive round had hit a tree branch above the NVA's head and exploded, knocking him down. He immediately got up and started running back down the trail away from them. He had been carrying a Thompson sub-machine gun, which he had dropped when the M79 round exploded over his head. The Thompson had blood all over it. They began to chase him, following the blood trail.

As they chased him, they found his bloody green poncho, some web gear, and more blood. They knew they were probably heading into an ambush but kept pushing forward. The squad leader had Ken start firing down the trail and to its flanks, trying to trip the ambush before they got into the kill zone.

Ken had fired over 400 rounds when the gun jammed. He cleared it, reloaded it, and attempted to fire again. The bolt seemed to go home, but the bolt would not lock, so the gun would not fire. He would later determine that a burr on the operating rod where the bolt attached prevented the bolt from closing, locking, and firing the round. Now, he had 23 pounds of scorching steel to carry. He pulled his .45 cal pistol, and they continued to chase the wounded NVA.

They came out of a tree line to an open field that had some kind of crop growing that was a couple of feet high. About 100 meters across the field was another tree line. They moved left paralleling the field until they reached a trail. A ditch ran parallel to the trail as it headed to the tree line on the other side of the field.

The entire squad, all six of them, plus Ken's three-man gun team, were on the trail, moving towards the tree line, when all hell broke loose with automatic weapons fire. They were on a trail, in the open, and in the kill zone. By all rights, they should have all been killed or wounded when the firing started. The only thing that saved them was a three-foot deep ditch on their right that ran parallel to the trail. They all rolled into it and into about six inches of water.

Every M16 was jammed, and Ken's gun malfunctioned. The only weapons functioning were the team leader's M79 and Ken's 45 pistol. The team leader with the M79 started firing. Ken jumped up, fired his 45, emptied the magazine, and then got down. As he changed magazines on his 45, he watched the impact of the incoming AK rounds along the top of the ditch. He jumped up and fired another magazine. He dropped down again, holstered his 45, and pulled two frags, one in each hand. They were getting some movement to their right. Ken pulled the pin on one frag. While still in the ditch, he popped the spoon to cook off a couple of seconds on the frag in his left hand, stood up, and threw it as hard as he could in the direction he heard the movement. He dropped down again and shifted the other frag to his left hand. When the first frag exploded, he popped the spoon on the second frag, cooked it off, jumped up, and threw it. As he was doing this, the team leader with the M79 kept a steady stream of 40mm grenades going into the tree line.

The incoming small arms fire became sporadic. Ken had his A-gunner toss him two of his frags, which he also threw. The squad leader radioed to bring the company's 60mm mortars to bear. The team leader with the M79 continued to lay down fire with it. Ken fired one more magazine with his 45.

All the M16s were still down. While Ken and the team leader had been firing, the squad leader had the company's 60mm mortars dropping a dozen rounds on the tree line.

The squad leader announced that they would be moving back towards the company as soon as they linked up with the platoon that had been sent out to reinforce them.

Firing had stopped. The squad leader told them to move back to the tree line behind them. Ken could see Marines on either side of the trail that entered the tree line. As they approached the tree line, he moved down the ditch and then out of it.

Operations Bastion Hill and Medina

```
Bastion Hill: October 10 - 20, 1967

Medina: October 11 - 20, 1967
```

The Battalion Landing Team returned to work on October 10th with a helicopter assault south of the City of Quang Tri. They would operate as a blocking force for First Marines assaulting the Hai Lang National Forest by helicopter.

The flight and landing in the LZ were uneventful. Upon landing, Ken's stick moved away from the helos and got down as the helos lifted off for the return trip to the Okinawa. Once the helos had lifted off, they stood up and moved to link up with the rest of 3rd Platoon. The Marines pushed out to establish a perimeter, waiting for additional lifts to bring in the rest of the company.

The area they were in, west of Highway 1, was flat with rice paddies full of water and leeches. The Marines crossed the paddies on narrow dikes.

"You could always tell a replacement by how many times they slipped off the dike and fell into the rice paddy," Ken says. "I had long ago learned how to walk a rice paddy dike and stay dry."

They slowly moved, ran into a few booby traps, and then in the early afternoon, they set in for the night. When they set in, they were in low, rolling terrain, with scattered scrub brush about half a meter to a meter and a half high.

Since the ground was too hard to dig their typical gun position,

Ken decided that he and his A-gunner would dig a two-man prone position for the gun instead. Their ammo humpers dug their own prone positions near the hole. All watches would be in the two-man prone position with the gun.

After a couple of hours of relentless digging, they had only reached a depth of about 12 inches. It was like digging in concrete. Ken went over to some of the riflemen's holes and found they weren't doing any better, so he decided to stop digging any further because they wouldn't get significantly deeper before dark.

Instead of continuing to dig, they carefully cleared fields of fire. When Ken laid down in the prone position behind the gun, he could only see a few meters to his front and flanks, so good fields of fire were necessary. The rifleman also attempted to clear their fields of fire. Ken, his gun team, and the riflemen began to discuss their concerns about their positions. The ground was flat and hard, and the brush obscured too much, too far out. They were too indefensible.

Because it had become dusk, they ate cold C-rats. As Ken worked through the watch schedule, sporadic small-arms fire was heard around their position. Later, at about 0400, he was woken up by an ammo humper to hear a large volume of small arms fire coming from his left. He rolled in behind the gun and rose to a kneeling position to see over the brush. Off to his left was a hill about 700 meters away where the battalion's Charlie Company was positioned.

Red and green tracers were flying everywhere. Ken saw some flashes from grenades and, two seconds later, heard the sound of their explosions. Charlie Company was in a desperate fight. He would later learn that the NVA had broken through the company's perimeter all the way up to the company CP, wounding the company commander and killing the company XO. Charlie Company's former CO, Captain Reczek, led a counterattack to retake the company CP and push the NVA out of the lines. That night, seven Charlie

Company Marines were killed and seventeen wounded.[1]

Though Delta Company had some sporadic small-arms fire during the night, it was otherwise quiet where they were. Ken stayed up for about ten minutes, then told his ammo humper to wake him if the NVA came over to their company, or no later than 0500, when they would all go to 100 percent. The fight was over 700 meters away, about half a mile. Ken thought there was no point in getting excited until they got closer.

Each platoon sent out patrols on the morning of the 11th, but no contact was made.

On October 12th, Frank Holsomback, Ken's closest friend in Vietnam, would be killed in action. They had both arrived in the country at about the same time, joining the company at Khe Sanh the previous December. Frank was from Louisiana, part Cajun, and Ken had grown up in Los Angeles' San Fernando Valley.

Frank was shot through the thigh. Unknown to the Corpsman, the round severed the femoral artery. The Corpsman, who was new (just out of Field Med School and with no prior combat experience), didn't check for the exit wound or for pulsating bleeding, which is a clear sign that an artery is involved, nor did he apply a tourniquet. Frank simply bled out.

"Of all the deaths I saw," Ken says, "of all the friends I saw killed, Frank's death was the hardest for me to handle because we were such close friends. I grieve his death to this day."

They both had two months left in country, a light at the end of a very dark tunnel, and it was a wound that Frank should not have died from.

"Today, he wouldn't," Ken says. "Corpsmen receive better training and would have worked on gunshot wounds before deploying by spending several weeks at a county hospital emergency room. That,

---

1   In his best-selling memoir, On Full Automatic: Surviving 13 Months in Vietnam, author William V. Taylor fought with Charlie Co. when their lines were broken. He describes the event in vivid and dramatic detail in his book.

and the development of coagulants to stop the bleeding, have pretty much prevented bleeding out."

Ken's wife, Audrey, will tell you that from about April to December, Ken is at times moody, short-tempered, and difficult (some would tell you that he's always difficult). The combat operations started in earnest in late April 1967, as did the killing and dying, but October is always a difficult month for Ken because of Frank's death.

"Time does not heal all wounds," Ken says. "When I was going to school, working, drilling with the Marine reserves, and very busy, my experiences in Vietnam were muted by being so busy, but they did not disappear. They were always in the background like having a TV on, with the sound turned down a bit. During the downtimes, however, particularly at night, it was as if the volume had been turned up all the way. I have re-lived that experience and the deaths of my friends more times than I like to think about."

What has made it worse is the way he was treated when he came home. The comments he received from those who were never there, whether from Marine officers who avoided Vietnam (he had his loyalty questioned because he was a Vietnam combat veteran), college professors (he had his college grades lowered because professors didn't like what he wrote or said about his experience), friends, colleagues, or strangers. Many of the comments he heard over the years were vicious in nature. Some comments were innocent but still cut him deeply.

"It seemed to me as if everyone in the country decided to rid themselves of the collective guilt over Vietnam by blaming the Vietnam veteran for what happened," Ken says. "My friends and I didn't run the war; we just fought it. We weren't the ones who decided to go to war, but we bore the brunt of the American public's dissatisfaction with it. By the time I got out of the Marines, at 20 years of age, I still wasn't even old enough to vote."

Frank's death put Ken in a very dark place, and yet he would not be the last friend killed in action. Between October 10th and early

December 1967, eight Marines from his company would be killed, one an accidental homicide, all friends.

On October 15th, 1967, Patrick Doyle was an accidental homicide. Ken had seen two prior unintentional shootings, one by a machine gunner in the company and another when an M16 fired while Marines were changing watch at night. The round took the Marine's jaw off. The Corpsman wrapped his jaw in a water-soaked battle dressing, placed the jaw on the Marine's chest, and sent it out with him on the medevac. It would eventually be used, with a bit of bone from the Marine's hip, to reconstruct his jaw. Everything they did was dangerous, even changing their hole watch.

On October 28th, 1967, Teddy Hisaw was killed in action.

On November 11th, 1967, Michael Yartymyk, Dennis O'Dell and William Davidson would be killed in action. Michael Yartymyk was in the company's 60mm mortar section and was liked by everyone.

In Early December 1967, Donald Riggs and Damon Billingslea would be killed in action on Ken's last patrol. Billingslea would leave behind a wife and a very young child.

Ken was medevaced during the operation. Back in July, during Operation Buffalo, he had developed a small open wound on his right leg, just above the top of his jungle boot. Ken had no idea how it happened: It could have been a small piece of shrapnel from the incoming artillery or a dozen different things. He hadn't noticed it until they crossed back over the Trace. A platoon Corpsman had cleaned it, painted it with iodine, and placed a small bandage.

From July to October, Ken would have the Corpsman and, when possible, the battalion surgeon look at it. Each would paint it with iodine and put a dressing on it, but the hole would not heal, and it grew larger as time passed.

When he returned from a patrol on Medina, Ken noticed that the bottom of the right leg of his utility trousers was bloody.[1] He

---

1   When the Marines were in the field, most did not "blouse" their utili-

pulled the trouser leg up to look at the wound above the boot and saw that it was black, dark purple, and red—slowly oozing blood and swollen. The battalion surgeon looked at it, determining that Ken had blood poisoning.

Back on the ship, a surgeon thoroughly and painfully cleaned out the open wound, first with hydrogen peroxide and cotton swabs, then alcohol and cotton swabs. Ken would receive penicillin shots until it healed. The ship's surgeon told him that if the wound and infection did not appear to be getting better within three days, they would have to take his right leg off above the knee; they could not risk having the infection move further up his leg.

It healed, and Ken went back to war.

---

ty trousers. That is: they did not tuck them into their boots or roll the bottom of their trousers in an elastic band so it would blouse at the top of the boot.

November - December

In late November 1967, the battalion moved by trucks from Dong Ha, the 3rd Marine Division's forward combat headquarters, to Cam Lo. Cam Lo was south of the DMZ and was a fire support base. Mostly 105 and 155 self-propelled artillery.

Ken was, by this time, a short-timer with less than a few weeks left in country. He was due to go home on December 20. Up until that time, he had given no thought to going home. There had been several times when he thought that he would not survive a particular day, let alone a week. Death was always around the Marines, just at the edge of their existence. Ken simply pushed it out of his mind. They had a saying: Only new guys and short-timers were ever killed in action. New guys, because they did not know what they were doing, and short-timers, because they became overly cautious and made mistakes. Ken did not want to make mistakes or become overly cautious, so he kept the thought of going home out of his mind and always focused on the job at hand.

The ride out to Cam Lo on the six-bys was uneventful, but as they neared the base, they were assaulted with the smell of decaying flesh. Outside the base's defensive wire was a minefield that went all the way around Cam Lo. Within that minefield were the rotting remains of water buffalo that had wandered into it and were killed by the exploding mines.

Delta Company and the battalion moved through the fire support base on the road north to Con Thien. For over a hundred meters, all the vegetation on either side of the road had been cleared.

"Typically, moving down a road is a very bad idea," Ken says.

"You are just asking to be ambushed; there is never any cover or concealment."

They were apparently in a hurry (also never a good idea) and needed to be at Con Thien before nightfall. They also had no flankers to the edge of the cleared vegetation.

By the time they reached Con Thien, it was twilight. They moved off the road and simply dug in where they were. Again, generally, this is not a good way of doing things. There was no effort to create an organized defense. They simply stopped in place and started digging. Machine guns are the backbone of a company's defensive plan. They are the only weapons capable of sustained, heavy fire. This was even more important because of the jamming problems with the M16.

When it stopped for the night, the general SOP (Standard Operating Procedure) for a rifle company was to go into a 360-degree perimeter and dig in, i.e., dig fighting positions (they do not call them foxholes). Because they had stopped at twilight, they simply dug one-man prone positions (the length of your body and about 10-12 inches deep) as there was no time to dig more than that. The ground was hard red clay and difficult to dig in. Except along the coast, which was sandy soil, the ground in the DMZ, from Con Thien to Gio Linh, was hard clay.

The riflemen stood a two-man watch. It was two hours on and two hours off until the company went to 100 percent watch an hour before daylight. In machine guns, they typically stood a three-man watch.

Either way, they were always physically exhausted from lack of sleep, lack of a decent diet, and constant physical labor. Ken would come off watch, lay down behind their fighting position, close his eyes, and then, without any sense of the passage of time, hear his name whispered to wake him up to go on watch again. While on watch, time slowed down and dragged by, but not with sleep.

Ken has no memories of ever dreaming when on a combat operation.

"You never shook anyone to wake them up," he says, "unless you wanted a rifle, pistol, or a KA-BAR in your face. I always slept with my .45 on my chest in my right hand, loaded, with a round in the chamber and the weapon on safe. And I always had my KA-BAR close at hand."

For years afterward, Ken would wake up three times a night, like clockwork, coinciding with a schedule for the watch in Vietnam.

The DMZ was different than any other place in Vietnam. At night, there was a constant cacophony of noises: "H" and "I" fires (harass and interdict) from the artillery bases (Cam Lo, JJ Carol, and the like), aircraft flying and making night strikes on suspect NVA positions, flares, occasional small arms fire, tracers flying in the distance (green and occasionally white tracers were the bad guys), and just all around craziness. There were no quiet nights.

The next morning, they moved out, heading east and staying south of the Trace. As the company moved east, they went into the area they had been through in July on Operation Buffalo. Between July and November, there had been a B-52 strike. They moved through where the bombs had landed. It was total destruction. Bomb crater after bomb crater after bomb crater. The devastation was over 100 meters wide and over half a mile long. Ken had seen B-52 strikes from a distance, a very long distance. It was always a wall of explosions and the ground shaking.

This was the first time he had walked through the aftermath. There was not a single tree standing.

As they moved slowly through the devastation, Ken spotted a green NVA pith helmet at the bottom of one of the craters. It looked in pristine condition, which means it was meant to be seen, indicating a potential booby trap. A Marine in front of Ken must have spotted it at about the same time, and he ran to the bottom of the crater to pick it up. Ken began to yell at him to leave it alone when the Marine went down to pick it up. Ken instinctively turned away and braced himself for the explosion, but nothing happened.

"He was one lucky son-of-a-bitch," Ken says. "Booby traps and mines were a constant threat."

That afternoon, as they continued their sweep east, it began to rain and continued to rain, and would rain, on and off, until Ken rotated.

"Very miserable conditions," he says.

They were headed to a place called Alpha 3, which was on the south side of the Trace, between Con Thien and Gio Lin, though slightly closer to Gio Lin than Con Thien.

When they reached it, a company occupied the position from 1/4 (First Battalion, Fourth Marines; "one four"). It was a couple of small, barren, low hills that sat on the south side of the Trace. They were immediately greeted by a dozen or so incoming NVA artillery rounds. Alpha 3 would continue to receive incoming NVA artillery, as many as 50 or more rounds a day, until Ken left by medevac.

That first week there, it rained mostly at night and drizzled all day, so the Marines were never really dry. Time was spent digging in, improving their defensive position, and bailing water out of fighting holes. There was only a single strand of concertina wire around Alpha 3. The ground was red clay and hard.

When they arrived at Alpha 3, they were happy to see a platoon of Marine M-48 tanks. In between the two gun positions was a draw where one of the gun tanks had been backed up and camouflaged. Ken's gun squad borrowed a couple of picks and shovels, real picks and shovels—not the small e-tools they carried. They were making real progress when an engineer appeared on a green Caterpillar dozer. They had watched him move from position to position down the line, digging holes.

Ken and his team tried to waive him off, but he ignored them. He dug a hole behind the fighting hole they were digging and then poured the dirt he'd excavated into the hole they'd been digging. Their hole was destroyed, and they spent a couple of days digging in the rain, trying to rebuild it.

The incoming artillery was sporadic and constant. The Marines always received an early morning volley of fifteen or so rounds, then sporadic shelling throughout the rest of the day.

The Marines always kept one ear pointing north to hear the "pop, pop, pop" of NVA artillery being fired. The guns firing could be heard just a second or more before the incoming rounds landed.

"Movies do not do justice to what it is like to be under artillery fire, small arms fire, or what combat is really like," Ken says. "Part of the problem is that you don't have any of the smells of a firefight, the smell of the dead, or the smell of fear. If you did, I suppose people would stop going to the movies. Watching a war movie has no impact on me because they don't replicate the sounds of the explosions, the actual explosions, or the sound of the shrapnel accurately. It looks make-believe. That, and the actors do many things the Marines just wouldn't do in real life."

"You hear the artillery firing first a 'pop, pop, pop,' followed by the rounds screaming in," he continues. "It sounds like a low-flying jet going over your head, and then the deafening crack of the explosions and the sound of flying shrapnel. Smaller pieces make a buzzing noise, like angry metal bees, while larger chunks produce a rhythmic 'whump-whump-whump' as they tumble through the air. The sound is deafening at times. It's menacing and physical in its intensity. Even now, just thinking about it makes my heart race."

* * *

During the second week at Alpha 3, Ken's platoon was tasked with a patrol that took them outside the wire and southeast of the Trace. As a rule, they never went out in the DMZ with less than a platoon, and even that was too small of a unit. The Platoon Commander was a twenty-year-old second lieutenant who Ken felt had no business being in a rifle company.

"He should not have been in command of anything, actually," he says.

A Marine officer always comes into a unit with a presumption of authority and competence. But, it is a rebuttable presumption. At the beginning of 1967, the officers they had were all rock-solid, good combat leaders who led from the front. It was always "do as I do and follow me." If it was dangerous, they did it first. But, by December 1967, they had either rotated home or were on the Battalion staff. What the battalion received in their place was less than stellar.

When Ken was in boot camp, about a dozen recruits were pulled out of training and ordered to report to the company Quonset hut. They were met by their series commander, a captain who informed them that they had all scored high on the intelligence test. Because of that, they could apply for OCS, Officer Candidate School, and be commissioned 2nd Lieutenants. The only kicker was that they had to be 20 years old on the date of commissioning.

Ken was barely 18 years old and had no desire to wait two years to turn 20 so that he could be commissioned.

The point is that in the summer of 1966, the Marine Corps was going through infantry 2nd Lieutenants like water pouring through your hand. They were pulling Staff NCOs and commissioning them to help fill the gaps and slow down the hemorrhaging. This hemorrhaging of infantry 2nd Lieutenants would continue throughout the Vietnam war.

Their 3rd Platoon Commander at A-3 was the result of this commissioning program. There may have been a lot of good 2nd Lieutenants commissioned through the program, but Ken was sure this one was not one of them.

We had moved several clicks, and the platoon was moving in single file on a trail—up, down, and around small hills, sparsely covered in low-lying scrub brush. The terrain was conducive to opening up from a single file to squad and fire team wedges and moving off the trail. Staying on a trail was something one never wanted to do if it could be avoided. It was not always avoidable, though. Because they were on a trail, the Marines were moving in a slightly staggered column, about 7-10 meters between each.

"We had crossed several rice paddies by bounding fire teams across to the far side," Ken says. "They would secure it before the rest of the platoon moved across. Meanwhile, machine guns held the near side of the paddy to provide fire support if the Marines were hit moving across the paddies."

The lead fire team was Don Riggs, who was on point, and Damon Billingslea, the team leader. Billingslea was also carrying the M79. Both had joined the company in August 1967. Billingslea was married and had a child less than a year old. They were followed by the squad leader, another fire team of two Marines, Ken and his machine gun team, the rest of the platoon, and its second gun.

The platoon moved slowly up another small hill along a trail that skirted a large bomb crater on its left. They moved along the right side of the hill, just below the military crest, before heading up over the top.

As the platoon reached the crest of the hill, a claymore mine was detonated. Riggs, who absorbed a huge chunk of the blast, was killed instantly.

"It literally shredded him," Ken says. "Claymores are loaded with a double-ought buck. Those are large steel balls. And a lot of them."

Billingslea, who was behind Riggs, was severely wounded, and the squad leader took a couple of buck shots, and others in the platoon received minor wounds.

"I can still hear the crack of that explosion and see Riggs and Billingslea disappear from view," Ken says.

The Marines instantly moved off the trail, pushing out into defensive positions. There was no incoming small arms fire. Two platoon Corpsmen moved forward immediately, one stopping where Billingslea lay on the ground and the other to Riggs. The Corpsman only spent a few seconds with Riggs, who was obviously dead, before moving to help the other Corpsman working on Billingslea.

The lieutenant began running around, yelling at no one in particular, apparently trying to put everyone in a defensive position. It was clear to Ken that he was in a panic. The Marines had already put themselves in a defensive position immediately after the claymore went off. Since they were receiving no small arms fire, it was not an ambush in the general sense of the word.

The lieutenant tried to call in a medevac. He finally got comm after about 20 minutes with a CH-34 helicopter that was flying several thousand feet above them, but the helo would not come in until they popped a smoke grenade. All the platoon had was red smoke, and no helicopter jockey would ever land when they saw red smoke because it indicated bad guys.

By the time the lieutenant convinced the '34 to land, Billingslea had died.

On the Virtual Wall, Riggs is listed as KIA on December 4, 1967, and Billingslea as KIA on December 5, 1967.

"Which is incorrect," Ken assures me. "They both died on the 4th."

The Marines carried the bodies of Riggs and Billingslea in ponchos to the helo—each poncho leaking blood. Then, their platoon moved back to Alpha 3 after the helo lifted off. It had been a very unpleasant morning.

Riggs and Billingslea were well-liked. They had come from another MOS, and each already had a couple of years in the Marines before joining Delta 1/3 in August. In September, Ken had given up a promotion to corporal so that Billingslea could have it. It was for actions when they had been ambushed, all the M16s had jammed, and the M60 had malfunctioned. Ken figured he could use the extra money for his family since he'd been married with a child less than a year old.

Later that same afternoon, after returning to Alpha 3, Ken went down to the other gun position to fetch a pick they had borrowed from the tank in the draw. The pick made digging much easier in the clay. Riggs and Billingslea had already been compartmentalized in their minds, as is necessary for grunts to do—their focus now back on the work at hand.

When Ken arrived at the position, he jumped in the hole and started talking to his other gun team, two of which were standing outside of the hole. At that moment they heard the "pop, pop, pop" of NVA artillery firing and the roar of incoming. The two Marines outside the hole immediately jumped in and one landed on Ken's right ankle, snapping it.

Ken heard the snap, saw a flash of red, and felt tremendous pain. He was at the bottom of the fighting hole with two Marines on top of him and unable to move until they got off.

Initially, he could not stand on his right foot; the pain was so bad. One of the platoon's Corpsmen helped him hobble up to the platoon CP, where it was decided that the Corpsman should take Ken up to BAS (Battalion Aid Station), located in a bunker near the top of the hill. It was at least a hundred meters or more from the platoon CP to the aid station, all across open ground.

The Corpsman and Ken slowly made their way up the hill, stopping several times and getting down due to more incoming artillery. They finally found the bunker with "BAS" handwritten on a C-ration box and went in.

Inside, it was lit with an actual electric light bulb. Ken was shocked by that, as he did not think there was any electricity up there except that produced by batteries.

The senior battalion Corpsman was a Chief Petty Officer (CPO) who appeared old but was probably in his mid-30s. The Battalion Surgeon was a commander (silver oak leafs—the same pay grade as a Lieutenant Colonel) who appeared to be even older, probably in his 40s. The reality was that Ken was 19, and everyone appeared to him to be much older than he was.

They helped him up on a makeshift examining table fashioned from a couple of crates under plywood. The battalion surgeon told his platoon Corpsman to cut Ken's right boot off.

"No!" Ken insisted. "I will take the boot off myself."

Because of the weather and the NVA artillery fire, resupply flights were sporadic, and it was too hard to get a replacement boot up there. Ken unlaced his right boot and had the Corpsman ease it off his foot.

"It hurt like a son of a bitch!" he says.

His foot swelled up like a watermelon as soon as the boot and sock came off. The skin had already turned several shades of dark purple, black, and blue. The surgeon and Chief Corpsman then set about poking and prodding and talking about metatarsal this and metatarsal that.

After about five minutes of hemming and hawing with the Chief Corpsman, the battalion surgeon announced that the foot was broken and would need to be x-rayed and set, which they could not do. So they filled out a medevac card, priority "routine," and sent Ken and his platoon Corpsman on their way back to the platoon CP.

By now, a light rain had started. Ken was still in a lot of pain, and the sporadic incoming artillery fire did not improve his disposition. He was in pain, and the damn NVA artillery just would not let him quietly hobble back to his gun position without being disturbed. Every time the rounds came in, he and the Corpsman had to flop down on the ground as the rounds exploded around them, then get up and start hobbling again. It was painful to get down and painful to get up. The Doc offered Ken a shot of morphine for the pain, but Ken declined and told him to save it for someone who was really hurt badly.

The next time he heard the "pop, pop, pop" of incoming artillery, the Corpsman got down, but Ken was just too pissed off to get down again. He just stood there while the rounds exploded around the hill, listening to the shrapnel buzzing and woofing by. He did that twice until he returned to his gun position.

"It was stupid on my part," he says, "but there comes a time when you just don't care anymore, and I had hit that point. I had seen two friends killed earlier that day, and I just did not give a shit."

Because Ken was being medevaced, he gave away his KA-BAR,

extra socks, pack, canteens, and everything he owned.

"Actually, everything that had been issued to me," he says, "I left to my gun squad. I was supposed to leave the field in three days to start rotating home."

It took three days for a helicopter to arrive to pick him up. Each morning, he would hobble up to the battalion LZ, which was near the top of Alpha 3, and to one side of the hill where it was flat and wait for a helicopter to arrive.

Since 1/3 had gotten to Alpha 3, there had been sporadic helicopter supply drops, mostly of lumber and engineering stakes used to build bunkers and string barbed wire. Ken found two large stacks of lumber and wedged himself between them. The LZ was exposed, and there were no fighting holes to get into when there was incoming.

A few helicopters came in that first day, but they did not land. They were CH-53s, the new heavy-lift helicopters that the Marines had acquired. Ken had ridden in one several months before. But these birds did not land. They all had a sling load underneath the helicopter. They came in high, dropping very fast to within about ten feet of the ground, cut their load, and climbed almost straight up a couple of thousand feet before leveling off and flying away.

Within seconds of dropping their load they had 20 to 30 rounds of incoming artillery landing again around the LZ.

This process repeated three times over the next three days as Ken waited, wedged between the cover of the lumber. On the third day, there was low overcast and light rain. He had been joined by a friend, a Marine named Gonzales, who came to Vietnam with Ken in December 1966. Gonzales was also rotating. Of the fifteen Marines Ken had come over with (they had all gone to boot camp, ITR, or infantry school together) and that had joined 1/3, they were the last two out. Everyone else had been either killed or wounded.

Ken was looking off to the southeast when he picked up a UH-34 flying very low to the deck. It was slightly obscured by the low clouds and light rain, but it appeared to be heading their way. Gonzales and

Hicks moved down to the LZ, and within minutes, the '34 landed, dropping off a 106mm recoilless rifle and taking on two Marines who were heading home.

Ken sat across from the crew chief as they lifted off, slipping right and heading out again towards the southeast a few feet off the ground. As he sat on the deck of the '34, the crew chief came over, looked at his medevac tag, and said something into his mic.

They slowly began to gain altitude, and within a short period of time, they crossed the coast and headed to the USS Okinawa. As they touched down, sailors in red vests with big white crosses on them ran over and eased Ken on to a stretcher. He kept telling them he could walk, but they would not listen.

He was carried to a lift and taken to sickbay. He was wearing wet, muddy jungle utilities and wet, muddy boots and had not shaved in more than a week. A Corpsman tried to cut off his right boot, but he stopped him and told him he would take it off himself, which he did. He also had to take off his other boot.

They stripped off his utilities, gave him a surgical gown, and sent him for X-rays. After the x-ray, they set him aside on the gurney, upon which he promptly fell asleep from exhaustion.

A Navy doctor woke Ken by calling his name.

"He told me after waking me up that he knew better than to touch us or shake a grunt awake," Ken says. "He had learned that lesson the hard way."

The Doc was a commander, appearing to be in his late forties. He was an orthopedic surgeon and was going to put a cast on Ken's right foot. He told Ken that he was going to receive a Purple Heart. Ken told him that was OK, but he did not want it. He had two friends killed three days before, and he did not think a snapped ankle amounted to anything in contrast.

Two days later, they were flown to Da Nang by helicopter and processed to go home. Their sea bags were inspected for contraband. Ken had taken the camouflaged cover off his helmet and stuffed it in the right cargo pocket of his utilities. That came home with Ken.

The next morning, they boarded a C-130 for a five-hour flight to Okinawa. The plane was jump configured, meaning all the rotating passengers sat across each other with their sea bags between their legs.

As the plane took off, everyone on board cheered loudly. Within the next half hour, the passengers all fell asleep. When Ken woke up, he was numb from the waist down from sitting in a cramped position.

They landed at Kadena Air Force Base and were trucked down to Camp Hansen. Over the next few days, there was additional processing, new uniforms, stripes, dress shoes, skivvies (they didn't wear skivvies in the field), chevrons to be sewn on, ribbons and badges added, haircuts (Ken finally shaved) and inspections to make sure they looked like Marines.

On the second day he was at Hansen, Ken cut the cast off his right foot and wrapped it in an Ace bandage. He would not go home with a cast on.

On December 21, he boarded a Boeing 707 at Kadena Air Force base late in the afternoon towards dusk for his flight home. It was a dependents flight, which was made up of wives and children of military personnel heading home for the holidays.

Ken was seated between a sailor and an airman on the right side of the aircraft. As the plane took off and started to climb, a stewardess announced over the intercom that they would be served three meals and that the flight would take twelve hours. Ken woke up as the aircraft made a right-hand turn over the Bay area and headed down the Central Valley. He had slept twelve hours, missed all three meals, and had no sense of the passage of time. It felt like he had just closed his eyes and opened them again to see the Golden Gate Bridge below them.

"The sailor, sitting to my left, said that they hadn't woken me for the meals because the sailor and airman 'were afraid of me,'" Ken says. "Oh well."

They landed at Norton Air Force Base in San Bernardino on December 20 late in the afternoon (they had crossed the international date line coming home). Ken caught a bus ride to LAX, where he then called his dad to pick him up. While he waited, he got a little taste of the animosity that many, particularly those of his own age group, had against those serving in the military—Marines in particular, it seemed.

It had been about ten days since he had been medevaced. He still found it hard to believe that he was still alive, that he was actually home. It was strangely quiet as he waited. He felt naked without his machine gun. Christmas music was playing softly in the background, and a decorated tree with lights stood in the waiting area.

"It was surreal," Ken says, "and somewhat overwhelming."

His Dad picked him up and drove him to their home in Tarzana. His family had put a big sign up that said, "Welcome Home." When he entered the house, his dog came running up barking—a Cockapoo named Fifi. He had gotten her from the pound when he was twelve, and she was 6 months old. Fifi smelled his leg and began to run around the house yelping, finally stopping right up against his leg—her entire rear end still swinging with her tail. She did not leave him the rest of the night.

When he went to bed that evening, Fifi jumped into the bed and pushed herself against him. When Ken's dad stepped in to check on them, Fifi growled at him as if to say, "Leave him alone. He is mine."

Ken slept another twelve hours—24 hours of sleep over two days.

Adjusting to home was not easy. The next day, his mother wanted him to go Christmas shopping with her. They went to a department store, where he lasted about three seconds before bolting to get back outside.

"I just could not take being around all those people," he says. "I had friends still up at Alpha 3, and these people were clueless about the sacrifices they were making."

He had become a stranger in a strange land. It was home, but it wasn't, and it has never really been since he returned. There had been no parades, no one thanking him for his service (it took thirty-two years for someone to actually do that), and no one buying his lunch or dinner. At best, he was ignored; at worst, he was the subject of nasty comments.

Even in the Marine Reserves, he experienced hostility, generally from officers who had never served in Vietnam. It was as if, because he was a Vietnam veteran, he was damaged goods, never to be trusted.

A day has not gone by since he came home, and he has not thought of that place and his time there.

"When I think of 'Hell,' I think of Vietnam," he says. "I also think of the friends I lost, of what they might have accomplished if they had lived to see old age, and what we lost as a nation with their deaths."

Pink Hearts

Momma cranked the car window down with one hand and spun the steering wheel frantically with the other.

I was fourteen years old and hadn't hit puberty yet, so the g-force of the turn slid my tiny body clear across the backseat. Fresh air was now blowing out the sour stench of acidic bile from my sister's stomach—a mop-water musk from the afternoon rain now softening the taste of vinegar that had been invading my throat. I sat up and stabled myself in the corner of the backseat, and with both arms rigid, I watched little pink hearts dripping slowly out of vomit on the upholstery from the roof of the car and onto my sister's head. She leaned drunkenly, thunked against the passenger window, and then slid forward, leaving a trail of dark, wet hair in her pink vomit on the glass.

"Dammit, Dawn!" Momma yelled, her head turning from the road to my sister and back. She reached over and pushed my sister's limp body up against the seat—brushed some hair behind my sister's ear to get a better look at her face, which was pale, and her lips, which were blue.

"What were you thinking, dammit? What the hell were you thinking?"

The little pink hearts in my sister's wet hair looked like candy to me. Sort of like the kind we passed around in class on Valentine's Day. You know, the kind with little messages printed on them like HUG ME, LOVE YOU, XOXO, and BE MINE. But one look at Momma's eyes in the rearview mirror assured me it was no box of candy that my sister had swallowed.

"Where are we going, Momma? To the hospital?"

"Yes, to the emergency room! We've got to get her stomach pumped!"

Momma was a Licensed Vocational Nurse, she knew what to do.

Dawn was sixteen years old, and she survived it, but I didn't know why she had done it.

I learned later that it was because she'd been desperately heartbroken by some boy. A few months passed, she got back together with him, and then I learned also that he'd been a man, at least four years older than she.

I had opened the door to her bedroom to find her lying on her back with her bare legs in the air—some man I'd never seen squeezing his fingers into the back of her thighs—his pelvis slapping against her.

Dawn looked at me, and then, seeing the surprise in my sister's eyes, the man stopped long enough to turn his head from her to me. He smiled a kind of smile that somehow conveyed a very clear statement without words. I'm sure if my sister had seen what I saw on that man's face, she would've recoiled and covered herself in shame.

"Look at me, gettin' some," his face said—his devilish eyes, indifferent and beaming with pride. "Gettin' some from your whore-bitch sister!"

I closed the door and stood frozen in the familiar darkness of the little cubby hall between our rooms. I contemplated the nature of the darkness on the other side, my heart beating harder than any demon from the horror movies had ever made it do. What was on the other side of that door was from another realm that I did not yet understand, and it scared me good and lasting.

I understand now, though, of course—not just that he was a worthless pedophile bastard thug, but how he wormed his way into my sister's veins in the first place.

Looking back now, I can see how the combination of our father's absence and the lack of our stepfather's regard had put a crack in my sister's fragile heart. It was fractured first by the absence of our father, I know, because it had been all that she had talked about whenever she was broken—an endless longing for the estranged and mysterious man—a faith-like love for him, no matter what...and a faith-like belief that if he only knew her, he would love her back.

Pieces of her own heart had been mixed up with all those little pink hearts dripping from the upholstery—speed pills, or whatever they were. That day had pushed a fissure open that kept growing from then on out. I watched over time as the weight of a thousand little things built up on her, like used-up chewing gum stuck on a tree by young boys waiting in line for a ride at a theme park. She carried the weight of all that glop on her bones, and it eventually brought her to her knees.

Years later, in the hospital, I rubbed lotion into the cracked and calloused skin on the bottom of her feet. At some point years before, her feet started swelling, so she'd given up on wearing shoes.

"If something happens to me, will you look out for my boy?" she asked.

Her boy's true father was a secret that, for some reason, she kept to herself and even from me. I casually shook my head with a "pfft" and said, "Sure. Whatever." But then, on my way out the door of the hospital room that evening, she stopped me.

"No, wait!" she said. "I'm serious. I really need you to promise. I want you to look out for my son. You."

I paused at the door before exiting into the hall and considering just how probable it was that I would have to live up to the promise if I made it. But at that moment, I couldn't play it forward far. I couldn't imagine the implications for my wife, much less that she might inherit this child while grieving for the death of her own mother. I couldn't imagine how the child himself would feel, grieving for the death of his mother while being thrust unwittingly into a world so radically different from his own—how utterly lost he would feel. And neither could Dawn, but she said it anyway as if it was the most natural and perfectly obvious thing for me to do.

"Promise," she said.

I hit the light switch by the door, and all left was the soft glow of a night light on her face. She looked like the sister I once knew long ago—that same wonder-filled innocence that had been on her face before all the boys, the abortions, and the drugs—that same old yearning look in her eyes when she told me time and time again, "I'm going to find our real dad. Wherever he is, I'm going to find him."

I thought about all those little pink hearts and the time she tried to kill herself with them, and I almost asked her why. Why did you do that? What happened? But I stopped myself because, in truth, I knew. I knew in the way that only her brother could know and that no words could explain because I had that same crack in my heart too.

"I promise," I said.

I had already sold our house and moved my family from Dallas to Fort Worth to care for her son by the time I received her ashes in a black plastic box. I put some of the ashes in necklace vials for her two daughters, one for her son, and then some in the palm of my hand. Before I poured her ashes back into the cheap plastic bag within the box and brushed the residue slowly and carefully from my fingers, I held my fingers pressed tight into my palm. I felt the fulness of that little bit of matter there—the gravity of a whole world in my clenched hand.

Dust in the wind. She loved that song.

When I read the verdict on the coroner's report, it made sense to me. It was her heart, most probably; the coroner had written in a sort of medical way. It gave out early.

Of course, it did.

What had been left of it, anyway. Broken a hundred times, battered, bruised, and swollen large and yet still then given freely away—a lot of it to me, and a lot of it to our "real" father who, by God, she finally found, and who, as she had always wished, really did love her back.

PTSD

> *"PTSD is a normal reaction to an abnormal situation."*
> —Ray Kelley, quoting his counselor from the U.S. Dept. of Veterans Affairs

SIX YEARS AFTER I first visited my father in Florida, he went to see a therapist at the VA hospital. It had been almost thirty years since his return from Vietnam. It would be the first time he spoke about the war with anyone who hadn't been there. A fellow veteran had convinced him that it wasn't too late to seek help and pleaded with my father to trust that it would be good for him. Skeptical and unsure, Alan agreed to go.

His therapy sessions were not something I would hear about until many years after they began. Alan and I would not stay in touch as a father and son would, but we grew closer, very slowly, over years. I had kids in high school by the time he told me that he'd gotten therapy.

"I didn't know what was wrong with me," he admitted. "I'd been home from the war for more than ten years before they even had an official name for what I've got."

He'd not been aware that many of the thoughts, feelings, and behaviors that were affecting his life were often symptoms of a mental health condition caused by the trauma of combat. If the psychologists were just coming to understand it, how could he have known? All he knew was that after coming home from Vietnam, he felt lost.

For example, after returning to the United States, he could not bring himself to return to his house for several months. I can only imagine how his parents must have felt to learn that their son ambled about for several months before coming home to see them. Why? He told me he had difficulty explaining it to them, and I suspect that's because he didn't know the reasons. Maybe he knew they would no longer recognize him as the young man they had raised. For them, he'd been gone for a little more than a year, but for him, it had seemed like a whole lifetime.

Being in the Vietnam War was similar to moving at a high speed relative to those "at rest" back home because over there, in thirteen months, a Marine had more unique and extreme experiences than many will have in a lifetime. Young men who'd never left their home states before boot camp were suddenly exposed to a foreign land with a different climate and with different plants, animals, and people. They were exposed to strange new languages, cultures, beliefs, and superstitions. Many were not yet in their twenties but were given the responsibility to operate complex and lethal machinery and to make quick decisions in high-pressure situations that would determine the fate of human beings. The gravity of situations was gargantuan and of that sort, often plentiful. Even if you were to live well into your nineties, you still might not witness as much death as a Marine could witness in a single battle, much less an entire tour. And even then, the death you will have seen would be mostly within the manicured lawns of peaceful cemeteries.

What do you say to the parents you knew a lifetime ago? Where do you pick it up? Where was it even, where you left off? I imagine that it was not one, but many things that played a role in the fact that Alan avoided his parents for so long after the war. It was so many things combined, perhaps, that he just needed time to catch his breath before he could speak to them at all.

I am reminded of the time I almost dislocated my shoulder in a snow skiing accident. It was one of those "hold my beer" moments after which nothing good can happen. After slamming into the ground with what felt like the force of a car, I sat up and thrust my hand into the air like a traffic cop to fend off the concerned friends and family who were rushing to my aid. At that moment, I didn't need or even want them coming into my space. I just wanted air in my lungs and time for the concussion to subside.

Even several months were not enough for the impact of war to subside for my father, however. Indeed, when he finally went home to his parents, his mother struggled to relate to him.

"She said that she didn't recognize me as her son anymore," he told me while rubbing his finger on the wood of the table. "She said I wasn't the same person."

As for his own father, he had little to say other than, "The man would have been jailed today for what he put me and my brother through." Thinking about how I had felt about my step-father, Bill, I have to wonder if Alan was afraid to face his father after the war because of the violence he knew he had become capable of. His therapy, years later, would bring him to understand that because of a very harsh and brutal childhood, he probably had PTSD even before he went to Vietnam.

PTSD, or post-traumatic stress disorder, was the term used to describe the condition that my father has, although it would not be used with him by a psychiatrist until twenty-eight years after his tour. The condition had not been formally recognized and named until five years after the Vietnam War was over. It first appeared in the American Psychiatric Association's manual of mental disorders in 1980.

War-born psychological trauma was certainly not unique to the Vietnam War. Still, it was the Vietnam War that put it center-stage in the field of psychology and elicited the need for it to be formalized as a diagnosable condition. At the risk of oversimplifying it, PTSD can be described as a disorder caused by exposure to traumatic or stressful events. Its symptoms cannot be put simply, but they often involve the disturbance of sleep, constant vivid recall of an experience or experiences, and dulled responses to others and the outside world. PTSD can be caused by a variety of traumatic or stressful situations, not all necessarily related to combat, but war zones are surely its most fertile ground.

The Vietnam War has been so particularly fertile in this regard that PTSD has been stereotypically associated with its veterans. As I write this, I am painfully aware that I may be asserting this stereotype to the dismay of veterans who'd rather be regarded for their bravery than for their scars. I believe, however, that it is important ground to cover for a variety of reasons.

Mainly, it shows that the cost of our veterans' sacrifice extends long beyond their war. Though the degree may vary for each, war leaves a psychological debt that is never fully paid. Even those who've escaped the harsher symptoms of PTSD must still carry the burden of their memory, and while there are surely also good memories of those youthful days spent with comrades, let's face it, the principle of the occasion itself is a hellish thing.

What's more, I think it also shows how war can affect relationships in addition to the veterans themselves. When PTSD is involved, war is like a stone thrown in water—its waves echoing over time through the fabric of a family. That is mainly why I included mine in this story—to show that the war also affected my mother, my sister, and me, albeit indirectly.

"So, this is what PTSD does to a person," my father wrote to me. "You sabotage relationships."

"Every meaningful relationship I ever had, I have sabotaged. Good people that I can say truly loved me—I just walked away from them. And I couldn't put any of this together until I was diagnosed, put in an inpatient therapy group for six weeks, then five or six years of therapy (not to mention the countless medications)." By the time my father came to understand and get a grip on his condition, he'd been married more times than Elizabeth Taylor, no joke.

"Self-medicating" is what he called his boozing—terminology that he probably learned in therapy. It's what some people would call alcoholism, but my father always suspected that alcoholism wasn't really the case for him.

"When I would go to work offshore or just be doing something, projects or something, I did not want to drink," he said. "But, to socialize or to get myself out of the dumps, that's what I did. And when I found out many years later (after or during therapy), I didn't need the alcohol anymore. The meds did what they were supposed to do, and then drinking was just a social thing. I only did it then when friends got together."

My father never mentioned anything about narcotics except to say that, despite another stereotype and some factual reports that came out of Vietnam, his battalion was rarely, if ever, involved with drugs during the war.

"Maybe some guys 'in the rear with the gear' were doing that stuff, but we sure as hell weren't," he said.

No other veteran from his battalion ever contradicted that assertion. They explained that there was hardly any time or occasion to relax and get high. They were almost always moving, or as they would have said in the field, they were "Oscar Mike," which is radio code for "on the move." I was assured it would have been foolish to risk not having a clear head at almost any moment. Besides, they were so often exhausted and hungry that to then put some kind of drug in their body would have been psychological suicide. It was a bad enough trip sober.

"The most I ever had was a couple of warm beers," Alan told me, "and after humping through the bush, just those pretty much kicked my ass."

One drug the men could not avoid, however, was adrenaline—the "fight-or-flight" hormone released by their own bodies in response to stressful and dangerous situations. Those situations were so common for the Marines that when they returned home from Vietnam, many found themselves discombobulated by the sudden safety. Comfort had become strangely uncomfortable.

Back home, my father would do just about anything for an adrenaline rush. He described himself as "a junkie for it"—acknowledging that his obsessive dependency was as dirty and dangerous as any hardcore drug. In Texas, adrenaline dealers were available almost every weekend for anyone willing to strap themselves to a bucking bull. So, in trade for his "fix," Alan entertained the rodeo crowds for what has been called the most dangerous eight seconds in sports.

While in the rodeo circuit, on a strange twist of fate, Alan befriended a calf-roping speed junkie who was also a world-famous hairdresser. Strange, I say, not because I can't imagine a hair-dressing cowboy, but because he somehow convinced my father, a redneck veteran bull-riding Marine, to enroll in his beauty school. Alan did well with the training, and for a while, he and the calf roper traveled to all the hair shows they could find with a nearby rodeo.

Alan actually became skilled at hair styling and was recruited by several big-name salons, but because of the lack of adrenaline offered in those shops, he found it difficult to stay focused. What's more, the weekend rodeo often left him with a broken hand or with his arm in a sling, so he was often too banged up for beauty work.

This is the life my father remembered as he sat with his therapist for the first time, and she walked him through her diagnostic criteria. With each new question, he became increasingly aware that his peculiar quality of life and particular combination of behaviors and outcomes were not unique.

"It was as if she knew my whole life story," he said. "And she was telling it back to me right then and there."

Did he seek out thrilling and potentially dangerous situations such as driving well above the speed limit, intentionally picking fights with people, or engaging in high-risk sports and activities? In other words, did he engage in risky or destructive behavior?

Yes.

Self-medication? Substance abuse?

Check.

Anxiety or seemingly excessive irritability around others?
Check.
Difficulty maintaining lasting and meaningful relationships.
Check.
Feeling isolated and or purposely self-isolating?
Check.
Heightened startle reaction?
Check.
Unwanted and upsetting memories? Nightmares? Flashbacks?

From out of some dark recurring nightmare, Alan would often scream out for Don Minton, who he'd been close to and who had been killed in the May 4th ambush on Delta Company. Naturally, he grew close to all the men in his squad, but Don was someone he'd found a rare kinship with, even outside his squad. Since the two had both come from the piny woods of East Texas, they had related like brothers, and their shared stories gave them each a comforting sense of home in one another. When he lost Don, it was as if he'd lost a brother, and in the years that followed the war, he lost him over and over again.

"Your mom would always ask me who Don was because of the nightmares about that ambush," he told me.

Momma would sit up with him in bed and console him. She would beg for him to tell her what was wrong and what had happened, but it was as if he'd woken to the nearby blast of incoming artillery, and hers was just another muffled voice in the chaos of the aftermath ringing in his ears.

"It was like I could hear her, but nothing would register," he said. "I just couldn't say anything. I mean, I would literally shut down, and the only way I could come back would be if I went to sleep, woke up, and started a new day."

Over time, the nightmares subsided, or perhaps it's better to say, they became less intense—less real. But that which is forged in fire is made firm and made to last. There was far more hardwired deep within Alan's brain than what made itself manifest through his memories and dreams. As much as he tried to ignore the signs and pretend otherwise, the war was still with him. It remained a part of him.

Like ghosts slowly creaking open doors to reveal murderous rooms, flickering lights to make their presence known, and lingering in hollow pockets of frigid air, spirits of the Vietnam War haunted him. From that place now far away and from that time now gone, they still moved things within him, and subtly through him—they moved things in his world. He was haunted for more than thirty years, and I suppose he will always remain haunted to some degree, but when he started therapy, and his PTSD was diagnosed, it was finally a turning point.

His therapist had been like a priest who knew his demon's name, and his therapy had been like an exorcism that had finally freed his soul. He spoke of his therapy with respect and with reverence, but also with a sincere sorrow that it had come so late.

"If they would have had help for me then," he told me, "I would still be with your mother."

Photo by Bruce Axelrod

ACKNOWLEDGEMENTS

In the years spent working on this book, I've received so much help from others that I sometimes feel guilty for putting my name alone on the cover as the author. It is most especially the veterans from the First Battalion, Third Marines, who I must credit for this work. They not only bestowed their sacred trust in me but also spent precious time helping me to understand my father's experience of the war in Vietnam. Hours were spent telling their stories and guiding me to capture them faithfully, or at least acceptably, not only for my understanding but so that we all might never forget their service and the lives sacrificed by their Marine brothers.

This being my first book, I often felt too low for the honor those men truly deserve. I felt like I bit off more than I could chew or more than I should have—that their story belonged to someone with much bigger literary britches than mine. Nevertheless, the veteran Marines of my father's unit went out of their way to help me complete this work. As such, this story really belongs to them, their families, and the proud lore of their Marine Corps; I have been but a grateful scribe.

Let me acknowledge those "co-authors" first—those veteran Marines who help us remember what the scarlet stripes on their trousers represent and what the red on our American flag means.

Delta Company's Major Kenneth (Ken) Hicks (USMC ret.) spent many hours with me, not just telling of his own experiences but carefully reviewing the work in progress and gently encouraging me with corrections and revisions. Ken's sharp memory served as a backbone; this book could not have been written without it. I must also acknowledge Ken's wife, Audrey Hicks, who not only graciously hosted me in her home but allowed me to steel her husband through several days of web meetings.

Delta Company's Raymond (Ray) Kelley dared to share his stories and heart and went out of his way to introduce me to other veterans and their family members. He helped me find contact information and resources that made great contributions to this work and the web pages accompanying this book. Without Ray's ongoing encouragement, I would never have gotten it done. Ray's wife, Rose Kelley, deserves kudos for being a helpful assistant to Ray, putting up with my texts and coordinating connections.

Similarly, Don Bumgarner of Charlie Company was always a welcoming host in the "bunker" at Marine Corps reunions. He paid special attention to ensuring that I met the right people, heard certain stories, and received access to the wealth of reference materials and resources he had been a steward of. Together with Charlie Company's Ron Asher, for example, Don compiled a very thorough history of 1/3 in Vietnam which was of great value to this book. Don is also the creator and faithful maintainer of a website for 1/3 at https://onethreemarines.com.

Delta Company's Alan Burleson, my father, was the catalyst for all of this, of course—the one who opened the first doors and the one who took me to several Third Marine Division Association reunions over the years as well as to various memorials, Marine Corps birthdays, and events. If it had not been for the respect his Marine brothers held for him, I would have never been allowed into their brotherhood.

Donald F. Teal, Lieutenant, Medical Corps, US Navy Medical Officer In Charge of Casualty Care, deserves huge credit for the courage to share the pages of his journal which, as far as I can tell, were originally for his own mental processing and not for publishing. The courage to share his emotion-fueled pages gives us insight into a side of war we rarely see and lets us know of the anguish felt behind the front lines by medical caretakers and receivers of the dead.

Charlie Company's William V. Taylor graciously and bravely allowed me to participate with him as he completed his best-selling war memoir, On Full Automatic: Surviving 13 Months in Vietnam. He not only took me deep into the heart of his war experience but also helped me improve my writing and taught me about the editing and self-publishing process.

Before anyone had any reason to have faith in me, Delta Company's Jesse Hittson was gracious enough to be my launchpad, granting my first interview. That positive start gave me the courage to pursue more interviews and carry on with the work.

In addition to those already mentioned, there were several more who have been instrumental in this work—Marine veterans and Marine family members, writing coaches, editors, and encouraging friends:

- Alexandra O'Connell
- Antonio Ramos, 3rd Shore Party Btn. supporting 1/3
- Bobby Golden
- Bruce Irgens
- Bruce Lane Axelrod, 1/3 Marine Combat Photographer (Feb 21, 1946 - Oct 30, 2023)
- Carl Huddleson
- Charlie (Ski) Sliwkoski, D Co., 3rds Plt.

- Curtis (Curt) Bruce, B Co. and D Co.
- Daniel Cavazos, brother of Cpl. Martin Cavazos of D Co., 3rd Plt., 3rd Squad (Aug 25, 1944 - May 4, 1967)
- Dennis Mannion, nephew of Dennis J. Mannion of D Co., 3rd Plt., 3rd Squad (Mar 8, 1948 - May 4, 1967)
- Ed Kalwara, C Co.
- Gary Wells, C Co.
- George Nelson
- Jack Nelson (son-in-law of Gunnery Sergeant Gilbert A. Gesualdi)
- James (Jim) Arthur Cook, D Co., 2nd Plt, 1st Sqd. (May 13, 1944 - Dec 31, 2018)
- Jerry Reczek, Colonel, C Co., USMC (Ret.)
- Jerry C. Shirley, Lt Col, B Co., USMC (Ret.)
- Jerry Willis, C Co.
- Jesse D. Hittson, D Co.
- Jim (James) Haight, D Co.
- Jimmie (Jim) Shipp, D Co.
- John (Jack, "Doc") DePope, Corpsman, D Co.
- John A McAuley Jr.
- John Villegas
- Ken Bouchard, A Co.
- Kenneth (Ken) Burkitt, C Co.
- Kevin P. Brooks, C Co. (Apr 13, 1944 - Apr 3, 2020)
- Kirsten Jensen and My Word Publishing
- Lee Edgemon, D Co, 1st Plt., 2nd Sqd
- Lester Gary Culp, D Co. 3rd Plt., 1st Sqd (May 14, 1946 - Jul 16, 2024)
- Lynn (Andy) Andrew, D Co., 1st Plt., 2nd Sqd
- Margret Berkheiser
- Mark Kennedy, A Co.
- Michael P. Walsh, Marine
- Michael Wynn, B Co.

- Mike Brugh, Marine
- Nancy Spear
- Oscar De La Garza Jr, Cos D and H&S
- Patti Tsai-Steiner
- Raymond (Ray, "Machine Gun") Kelley, D Co., Weapons Plt.
- Roger Bacon, C Co.
- Richard ("Doc") Kuschel, A Co., Corpsman
- Ron Schneider, the LHS Corporation, and the Old Lecompte High School and Museum
- Ronald Stroud, B Co., 3rd Plt., 2nd Sqd
- Sandy Pannett, sister of Frank Nolan Holsomback and contributor of materials to the Le Compte museum in Louisiana
- Stanley (Stan, "Doc") Hall, D Co., Corpsman
- Steve Berkheiser, D Co.
- Steve Bozeman, Aerial Gunner (UH-34 Door Gunner), HMM-361
- Thomas (Tom) A Nollman, D Co., 3rd Plt.
- Thomas (Tom) G. Jalbert, D Co, 3rd Plt., 1st Sqd.
- Tom Harrison, C Co., Weapons, 2nd Plt.
- Capt. Winfield ("Skipper") A. Spear, USMC (Ret.)

Regarding the craft of writing, I wish to express deep affection for my lifelong friend and fellow writer, Shawn Stewart. Shawn has always been a kindred spirit, sharing the love for stories and the craft of telling them. Without him always with me in spirit, I think the loneliness of this craft and the mind-drill that it can be would've driven me nuts. Shawn, my dear friend, you probably don't know it, but you've given me a million examples and reasons to believe that stories matter.

My wife, Karlisa Burleson, deserves credit for giving up many weekends that she had wished to spend with me and for having to put up with the anguished mind of a wannabe writer.

And finally, dear reader, *thank you*.

CONNECT WITH THE AUTHOR

Contact the Author at

codyburleson.com

The website named above also features additional photos and information about the events, places, and people in this book.

Spread the Word and Leave a Review

If you enjoyed this book, please share your thoughts on social media and post an honest review on Amazon or Goodreads. Your support helps others discover it and would mean the world to me.

Printed in Great Britain
by Amazon